BRITISH POLITICAL PARTIES

CONTEMPORARY POLITICAL STUDIES SERIES

Series Editor: John Benyon, *Director, Centre for the Study of Public Order, University of Leicester*

A series which provides authoritative yet concise introductory accounts of key topics in contemporary political studies.

Other titles in the series include:

Pressure Groups, Politics and Democracy in Britain, 2nd edition
WYN GRANT, *University of Warwick*

UK Political Parties since 1945
Edited by ANTHONY SELDON, *Institute of Contemporary British History*

Politics and Policy Making in Northern Ireland
MICHAEL CONNOLLY, *University of Ulster*

Local Government and Politics in Britain
JOHN KINGDOM, *Sheffield Hallam University*

British Political Ideologies
ROBERT LEACH, *Leeds Metropolitan University*

British Government: The Central Executive Territory
PETER MADGWICK, *Professor Emeritus, Oxford Brookes University*

Race and Politics in Britain
SHAMIT SAGGAR, *Queen Mary and Westfield College, University of London*

Selecting the Party Leader
MALCOLM PUNNETT, *University of Strathclyde*

Does Parliament Matter?
PHILIP NORTON, *University of Hull*

The President of the United States
DAVID MERVIN, *University of Warwick*

The Politics of Economic Policy
WYN GRANT, *University of Warwick*

Introduction to International Politics
DEREK HEATER, *formerly of Brighton University* and
G.R. BERRIDGE, *University of Leicester*

Elections and Voting Behaviour in Britain, 2nd edition
DAVID DENVER, *Lancaster University*

The Law and Politics of the British Constitution of the United Kingdom
PETER MADGWICK and DIANA WOODHOUSE, *Oxford Brookes University*

BRITISH POLITICAL PARTIES

JUSTIN FISHER

PRENTICE HALL
HARVESTER WHEATSHEAF

LONDON   NEW YORK   TORONTO   SYDNEY   TOKYO   SINGAPORE
MADRID   MEXICO CITY   MUNICH

First published 1996 by
Prentice Hall Europe
Campus 400, Maylands Avenue
Hemel Hempstead
Hertfordshire, HP2 7EZ
A division of
Simon & Schuster International Group

Typeset in 10/12pt Times
by Dorwyn Ltd, Rowlands Castle, Hants

Printed and bound in Great Britain by
T.J. Press (Padstow) Ltd, Padstow, Cornwall

Library of Congress Cataloging-in-Publication Data

Fisher, Justin.
    British political parties/Justin Fisher.
      p. cm.—(Contemporary political studies)
    Includes bibliographical references and index.
    ISBN 0–13–353806–0 (pbk. : alk. paper)
    1. Political parties—Great Britain.   I. Title.
    II. Series.
JN1 121.F573   1996
324.241—dc20   96–1544
                                        CIP

British Library Cataloguing in Publication Data

A catalogue record for this book is available from
the British Library

ISBN   0–13–353806–0

---

2   3   4   5   00 99 98 97

CONTENTS

Preface   ix

**1 THE DEVELOPMENT OF BRITISH POLITICAL PARTIES
   AND THE BRITISH PARTY SYSTEM**   1
   Introduction   1
   The modern British political party   2
   The development of the British party system   8
   Factors influencing the development of the party system   15
   Conclusions   17

2 THE ROLE OF POLITICAL PARTIES IN BRITAIN TODAY   19
   Introduction   19
   Electoral choice   19
   Representation   20
   Policy making   23
   Recruitment and the selection of parliamentary candidates   24
   Political education and communication   25
   Political participation   26
   Are British parties in decline?   27
   Conclusions   32

3 THE CONSERVATIVE PARTY   33
   Introduction   33
   Organisation and internal elections   33
   The election of the leader   38
   The selection of parliamentary candidates   45

The social background of Conservative MPs and candidates   45
Funding   48
Ideology   51
Measuring ideological change   55
Groupings and factions   57
Recent history   61
Conclusions   63

4   THE LABOUR PARTY   64
Introduction   64
Organisation and internal elections   65
The role of the trade unions   67
The election of the leader   71
The selection of parliamentary candidates   73
Sponsorship of candidates and MPs   74
The social background of Labour MPs and candidates   76
Funding   78
Ideology   80
Measuring ideological change   86
Groupings and factions   87
Recent history   90
Conclusions   92

5   THE LIBERAL DEMOCRATS   94
Introduction   94
Organisation and internal elections   95
The election of the leader   99
The selection of parliamentary candidates   99
The social background of Liberal Democrat MPs and candidates   100
Funding   102
Ideology   104
Measuring ideological change   111
Groupings and factions   113
Recent history   114
Conclusions   115

6   THE 'OTHERS' IN THE BRITISH PARTY SYSTEM   116
Introduction   116
Nationalist parties in Britain   117
The Scottish National Party   118

Plaid Cymru   124
The parties of Northern Ireland   130
Conclusions   137

7   THE PARTY MEMBERS   139
Introduction   139
The role of party members   140
Who are the party members?   142
The views of party members on political issues   147
The views of party members on their own parties   152
Party activism   154
Conclusions   156

8   VOTING AND ELECTIONS   158
Introduction   158
Trends in election results   159
Studies of voting behaviour   162
Evidence from the 1992 General Election   179
Conclusions   193

9   CONCLUSION   194
Parties and their functions   194
British political parties and the future   199

Appendices   204

References and Bibliography   206

Index   217

PREFACE

Political parties are an established feature of British democracy. They are also an essential one and play a role in many aspects of political life. However, studying parties can be a difficult process. Some parties are more widely studied than others. Inevitably, there is relatively little academic work on the Liberal Democrats given their comparative youth. Yet the Labour Party has generated an enormous literature, whilst its elder rival the Conservative Party, has not been studied to anything like the same extent, though in the past few years this imbalance has been partially redressed. Moreover, some essential aspects of political parties have been examined more closely than others. Party finance is one area that has attracted comparatively little work, whilst party members were virtually ignored before the beginning of this decade.

My aim in this book is to bring together the main features of the political parties and examine them in a way which allows for both study of one party, comparisons with others and analysis of the strengths and weaknesses of political parties in Britain. In a book of this type, one cannot develop great detail on every topic. However, I hope that I have covered most of the principal considerations as well as providing a pointer to the wider literature.

The preparation of this book has left me indebted to many people. Firstly, I am grateful to Avebury Publishing Ltd, Faber & Faber Ltd, Macmillan Press Ltd, Oxford University Press, American Enterprise Institute Press, Patrick Seyd and Pippa Norris for permission to reproduce material. Secondly, I am grateful to the

ESRC Data Archive at the University of Essex for supplying data from the *British Election Survey 1992*. Thirdly, I am indebted to the following for their advice and help: David Broughton, David Denver, Bob Self and Paul Webb. Their advice has been sound and always constructive, though I alone am responsible for any errors of interpretation. Fourthly, I am grateful to Clare Grist, Ruth Pratten and Ian MacQuarrie at Prentice Hall for their drive, calm efficiency and patience. Finally, there are many personal debts and acknowledgements: to Jackie, a woman who is always loving and supportive, my step-daughter Anja, our child-minder Beryl and my colleagues in the Department of Politics & Modern History at London Guildhall University who have provided such a convivial atmosphere in which to work.

The course of writing this book has been a very happy one. I have watched our son, Lewis, learn to walk, begin to talk and love his favourite football team – Brentford. I have also had the pleasure (but not the pain!) of the birth of our daughter, Edie – also a Brentford fan. To them, I dedicate this book.

Justin Fisher
London, 1996

I

THE DEVELOPMENT OF BRITISH POLITICAL PARTIES AND THE BRITISH PARTY SYSTEM

Introduction

Political parties in Britain are relatively recent phenomena. While their position at the core of today's political scene is undeniable, development in their current form has been comparatively recent. There are various reasons for this, but the expansion of the franchise in 1867 which increased the electorate by around one million to 2 230 000 (Pinto-Duschinsky, 1981:24), a third of the adult male population, coupled with a greater element of competition within British elections in the last century would certainly help to account for the growth. It is quite remarkable that in the four General Elections prior to the reform act of 1867, between 43 per cent and 60 per cent of seats were uncontested. By 1880 the figure was only 17 per cent (Pinto-Duschinsky, 1981:19–24). One effect of this was that electoral success became less assured, and men of independent means became less willing to stand for election where the outcome was not predetermined. Moreover, the passing of the Corrupt and Illegal Practices (Prevention) Act 1883 limited the scope further for local political corruption, since not only did it outlaw bribery, it also placed limits upon local campaign spending altogether.

The modern British political party

Opinion is divided about when parties actually began to take their current form. Ingle, for example, takes us back as far as the four-teenth century to illustrate early stirrings of party activity between supporters of the king and those of the barons. If such early refer-ences are excessive, Ingle points out that by the seventeenth cen-tury, historians refer to the existence of parties with regularity (Ingle, 1987:3). Certainly, the seventeenth and eighteenth cen-turies saw distinct groupings develop within Parliament, whereby divisions were discernible and regular. These groupings even had names, the Tories and the Whigs. However, these were not yet political parties in the conventional sense that we understand today. There was no notion of party discipline in the House of Commons in the form of whips; no party manifestos and no extra-parliamentary organisations. Political parties, such as they were, existed within the confines of Westminster.

Because of the absence of such factors so fundamental to today's political parties, it was not until the mid- to late nineteenth century that we can trace the development of the modern political party. Ingle's argument is not perverse, however. While the modern political party may have been born in a later period from that which he identified, the parties did owe some debt to the formative period of groupings within the House. However, we can highlight definite trends to illustrate the development of the recognisable modern party.

First, the rapid growth of the franchise resulting from the 1867 and 1884 Representation of the People's Acts meant that the elect-orate in the 1885 General Election stood at 5 708 000 in contrast with a figure of 1 364 000 in 1866 (Pugh, 1982:6). The result in terms of party development was that the work of ensuring party suppor-ters were registered and able to vote could no longer be conducted on a part-time voluntary basis. As a result, parties began to employ professional agents. Secondly, parties began to organise member-ship on a large scale outside Parliament. Parties nurtured the spon-sored club in an attempt to appeal to the growing band of urban voters. Such clubs provided entertainment through drinking, read-ing and lecture facilities. Finally, as a partial outgrowth of local clubs there began to be the formation of party organisations based upon parliamentary constituencies. This trend was started by Lib-erals, but the Conservatives soon caught up and by the mid-1880s few candidates stood for Parliament without the benefit of an agent, constituency association and network of party clubs (Pugh, 1982:15–17).

The second important aspect of the development of the modern political party was the growth of parliamentary discipline. Traditionally, membership of the House of Commons was regarded as almost a leisure activity, yet while many saw membership as unpaid service to the community, it was also apparent that membership could bring material gain. As an MP, with little party discipline there were many opportunities for personal enrichment through voting in a particular way. As late as the 1860s, it was commonplace for party whips to be ignored by members and for defeats to be inflicted upon governments (Pinto-Duschinsky, 1981:29–30). However, party discipline became much tighter in the 1880s, largely as a result of the growth of government business and Gladstone's move towards ending debates with a majority vote (Pugh, 1982:18). Party cohesion became especially necessary through the clear divide on Irish Home Rule in 1886. The result was twofold. First, and most obviously, party discipline increased and this became even more imperative with the second development, organised opposition in the Commons. In short, the growth of party cohesion meant that cross-bench support became a rarity rather than the norm. Table 1.1 illustrates the growth of cohesion by measuring the percentage of members voting with their party in all divisions and in those where the government of the day invoked whips.

Table 1.1　**The growth of party cohesion in the House of Commons.**

Year	All divisions (%)		Whip divisions (%)	
	Liberals	Conservatives	Liberals	Conservatives
1860	59.8	57.3	58.9	63.0
1871	71.7	76.2	75.5	74.0
1881	82.0	82.9	83.2	87.9
1894	86.9	94.1	89.8	97.9
1899	84.3	94.2	82.5	97.7
1906	93.2	89.8	96.8	91.0
1908	95.0	88.4	94.9	88.3

Note: Whip divisions are those where the Government used whips.
Source: Beer (1982:257).

The third development which contributed to the growth of the modern party was the manifesto. The first manifesto is generally accredited to Peel who published the Tamworth manifesto in 1834, setting out key proposals for the Conservative government in the next parliament (Topf, 1994:150). Although this was in fact published after Peel's government had been elected, it nevertheless established the basis of national party programmes. The practice was not, however, adopted again until Gladstone delivered a similar address in 1874. Moreover, it was not until the 1880s that the practice of issuing a party manifesto became established (Bulmer-Thomas, 1965:81–83). With the development of mass parties, the manifesto (now published before elections) became an authoritative statement of policy intent and ideological belief.

Two final factors should be mentioned which, in their own way, may be said to have influenced the development of political parties into their current recognisable form. First, the emergence of national campaigns. Prior to 1880, party leaders generally refrained from speaking in constituencies other than their own since that was regarded as interference in the community's affairs (Pugh, 1982:2). This changed, however, with Gladstone's tour of selected cities in 1880. The seeds of national political campaigning as opposed to the concentration on local campaigning had been born. This process logically evolved, making campaigning an increasingly national affair, and was cemented by the second factor, legislation within the 1918 Representation of the People Act, which introduced the holding of a General Election on a single day. Prior to 1918, general elections had been held over periods ranging from 2 to 4 weeks, but the unifying election date inevitably gave campaigning a greater national character.

Such, then, were the foundations of the modern British political party. Let us then examine in more detail how the major parties developed into their recognisable form.

The development of the Liberal Party

Given their current semi-minor status it may seem perverse to examine the Liberal Party first. However, there are sound reasons for this, not least that it was the Liberals that first began to display real signs of effective extra-parliamentary organisation and of course, as we have seen, it was the Liberal, Gladstone, who partially prompted the growth of party cohesion in Parliament.

The parliamentary party, while having its roots in the Whig groupings, really only evolved with the defection of Tory free traders following the death of Peel in 1850. The extra-parliamentary party, however, did not develop until the 1870s. It grew from a variety of very active single-issue pressure groups. Although on the face of it these groups may have seemed disparate, campaigning upon issues such as temperance and education, most groups were united by religious Nonconformity. In short, the members of the pressure groups that went on to form the Liberal Party were 'outsiders'. Although often successful as artisans or tradesmen, they did not enjoy social prestige and through these factors and religious ones, frequently suffered forms of discrimination. They were also, more often than not, political radicals who wanted to reform the British political landscape to be more responsive to talent. They were meritocrats. While the roots and aims of the early Liberal Party were evidently diverse, they did nevertheless come together under the Liberal umbrella after the realisation that many shared goals could not be achieved at anything other than parliamentary level. Gladstone's image of puritan incorruptibility was also an aid to radical unity since he appeared alien to the existing norms of politics (Pugh, 1982:26).

Unity was not immediate, however. Perhaps inevitably, single-issue campaigning continued, often running counter to the ideas of the Liberals. These were the actions of so-called 'faddists'. The election defeat in 1874, however, persuaded many that co-operation under a party banner was likely to be more productive than single-issue campaigning. Thus in 1877, the National Liberal Federation (NLF) was formed as the central institutional body for the growing number of Liberal constituency based parties. The NLF played three very important roles. First, it provided a national focus for Liberals; secondly, it provided representation, through the development of political programmes, for radicals from all walks of life. Finally, it provided a means by which the ideas of 'faddists' could be absorbed into a more general party programme.

A final indicator of the clear development of the modern Liberal Party that should be noted was the increasing dependence upon centrally held party funds to finance elections. The Reform Act

Table 1.2   **The growth of Liberal candidate dependence on central Liberal Party funds.**

General Election	% of candidates' expenses provided by central funds
1880	4.0
1906	27.0
1910	24.8
1910	35.7
1923	39.8

Source: Pinto-Duschinsky (1981:49).

1867, the Ballot Act 1872 and the Corrupt and Illegal Practices (Prevention) Act 1883 were all partially responsible, since they combined to put the costs of elections beyond the means of many prospective candidates; first by increasing the number of electors to bribe, secondly by making the vote secret and so, decreasingly, the reliability of the transaction and thirdly by outlawing it altogether (Pinto-Duschinsky, 1981: 24–6). Table 1.2 illustrates how Liberal candidates became increasingly dependent upon central Liberal funds.

By the 1880s the modern Liberal Party was in place. There was increasing party discipline within and outside Parliament; the variety of single-issue pressure groups that formed an integral part of the party had come together to aggregate their interests. The 'faddists' had come to the conclusion that the most effective way to achieve broad liberal goals was to act as one party rather than disparate groups. The party organisation was also in place. The NLF had been set up to organise and represent the growing party on the ground and the central party organisation was becoming increasingly significant in the lives of Liberal candidates.

The development of the Conservative Party

The development of the Conservative Party outside Parliament was largely a response to external factors. First, as we have seen, there was the growth of the electorate, which necessitated a more committed organisation 'on the ground'. Secondly, however, it was a response to the Conservative Party's continuing electoral defeats and the growth of Liberal registration activities. The Conservatives formed the National Union of Conservative and Constitutional Associations (NUCCA) in 1867 as a means of harnessing the support they already enjoyed through the working man's Conservative clubs that were already in existence. Disraeli then went on to form Conservative Central Office in 1870 as a means of stimulating new constituency activity and compiling lists of prospective parliamentary candidates. A further reason may have been that he was apprehensive of an organ of the party under popular control (Pugh, 1982:46). Certainly, the initial roles of Conservative Central Office appeared to duplicate those undertaken by NUCCA and inevitably caused friction, a characteristic that remains in the party today. Moreover, the role of NUCCA was one of support, not one of debate. Again, this role continues.

While, by the 1880s, the National Union had become the principal vehicle for constituency organisation, associations were often small in membership. The party was aided considerably by a volunteer group called the Primrose League. Founded in 1883 it sought to promote certain Tory principles, including the religion and the merits of colonialism. Its membership was remarkable, particularly when one considers the figures for party membership today. In 1886 it stood at 237 000 and by 1891 it had risen to 1 000 000 (Pugh, 1982:50). The League offered cheap forms of entertainment and organised both in town and country, thus involving all social groups. Not only did it help the party through volunteer activities at election time, it provided a means of generating support between elections, principally through the entertainments which were considered to be more fruitful in recruiting supporters than simple political meetings. Again, there are strong parallels with the Conservative Party today. Whiteley, Seyd and Richardson (1994) in their survey of Conservative Party members found that 8 per cent of Conservatives had become party members through a Conservative club and 23 per cent through social contacts. Moreover, 11 per cent claimed social reasons as the most important reason for joining the party and in the previous 5 years, 53 per cent had not even attended a party meeting (Whiteley *et al.*, 1994:74–96).

The final major contribution of the Primrose League was that it involved women in the political process long before they had the vote. Women were admitted as members early on and were often very active, laying the foundations for the Conservatives' superiority at constituency level. Indeed, it remains the case today: the Conservatives have the highest proportion of women members of any of the main parties.

Like the Liberals, then, the Conservatives had become a modern party by the 1880s. Party discipline in Parliament had grown and the extra-parliamentary party was established, if often small in number at the constituency level. This was more than compensated for, however, by the Primrose League which played a pivotal role in spreading the Conservative word. Many parallels can be drawn with the contemporary Conservative Party. Membership of the party is a vague concept and frequently entails embarking upon social activities which recruit supporters. Thus the Primrose League in many ways acted as a blueprint for modern Conservatives. Moreover, its ability to involve women should not be understated.

The development of the British party system

By 1900, the party system was based upon three principal cleavages: class, religion and imperialism. Class manifested itself as a cleavage in two ways; first through the support for the Liberals by elements of the trade union movement, notably the miners. As early as 1874 the miners were to set a future pattern by providing financial support to candidates, and two Liberal candidates were elected to the House of Commons. One had been sponsored by the Northumberland section of the Miner's National Association, while the other was funded by the Labour Representation League, a group whose explicit function was to return working men to Parliament.

Secondly, the class cleavage also developed through the growth of the petty bourgeoisie. Victorian Britain had seen the growth of artisans and small businessmen, yet their position in the class structure was still one of the 'outsider'. The Liberals offered a home for these aspiring capitalists which the Conservative Party did not; itself preferring to centre its appeal on those groups content with the existing social hierarchy, although it was not immune from seeking party funds from wealthy businessmen in return for political honours (Pinto-Duschinsky, 1981:31–44). However, a significant minority of the working class did vote Conservative, particularly in rural areas (Pugh, 1982:82) and among those with a deferential view of society. Moreover, issues such as imperialism also divided the working class, although that division was reflected more in concerns with material well-being rather than any particular commitment to the Empire.

Religion was the second principal cleavage. While Anglicans and, to an extent, Catholics, voted Conservative, Nonconformists tended to support the Liberals. Nonconformists had experienced discrimination and prejudice, and the Liberal Party had provided a vehicle for campaigning against such injustice. The third principal cleavage on which the party system was based was that of imperialism, and policy towards Ireland in particular. Although the Irish question dated back several hundred years, it was Gladstone's proposals for Irish Home Rule in 1886 which made a significant impact on the party system. Home Rule divided the Liberal Party, creating a group of Liberal Unionists, and marked the Liberals very differently from the Conservatives, who also favoured maintenance of the Union. Indeed, it was argued that in the 1880s, the 'Irish Question' became almost an 'article of faith' for Liberals (Pugh, 1982:35). Not only that, the Irish question divided the country. Those in regions closest to Ireland, both geographically and strategically, were drawn in varying numbers to unionism. The question of Ireland also divided the working class. Many urban areas witnessed a working class revolt against the Liberals as a result of Irish Home Rule, fearing and rejecting widespread Irish immigration.

Change in the party system – the development of the Labour party

The Labour Representation Committee (LRC) was established after the disappointing attempts of trade unions to penetrate effectively the established party system. There were isolated successes, such as in 1874, but by the 1880s the trade union political movement had divided into two groups: those who favoured working with the Liberals, and those who desired the formation of a new party, independent of the Tories and the Liberals. Thus, in 1900 the Labour Representation Committee (LRC) was set up by the Trades Union Congress, along with the Social Democratic Federation (SDF), the Independent Labour Party (ILP) and the Fabian Society, the trade unions having 94 per cent of the affiliated membership. The LRC became the Labour Party in 1906 and electoral pacts with the Liberals in that year resulted in a limited electoral breakthrough. Prior to 1906 only two LRC candidates had been elected in the 1900 General Election and a further three in by-elections (Ingle, 1987:97). Also significant was the decision of the miners' union to join with the new party in 1909. Before that, the Miners' Federation had sided with the Liberals. This not only gave the Labour Party an increased base upon which to rally support, but also signified that the party was now the main political representative of labour. In the two subsequent elections of 1910, Labour returned 40 MPs in the first and 42 in the second. The prevalent party system in Britain was to remain, however, until the 1920s.

The replacement of the Liberals by Labour as the main political opposition to the Conservatives was rapid and was a result of a variety of factors. Of key importance were the Representation of the People Act 1918, which extended male suffrage; the split in 1916 of the Liberal Party over Asquith's leadership which lasted until 1923, the loss of the Liberal *cause célèbre*, Ireland, and the increasing importance of class as a social cleavage. With Labour in the ascendancy, the Liberals were well beaten in the 1924 election. Although the Liberal decline varied from region to region it was clear that by the mid-1920s, Britain's essentially two-party system had changed composition and class had become established as the principal cleavage.[1]

The period of the new-two party system was, however, short-lived. Economic collapse in the late 1920s resulted in the formation of the National Government in 1931, which governed Britain until the end of the Second World War. Although formally a coalition which included former Labour leader, Ramsay MacDonald, the National Government was nevertheless dominated by the Conservatives. It was only after the war that party politics really resumed.

The post-war party system

The British party system during the post-war period until the 1970s was strongly bipartisan in character. The Liberal Party was

---

[1] It should be noted that whilst the number of seats won by parties indicated a two-party system, the Liberals still achieved 23.4 per cent of the vote in the 1929 General Election, though only 59 Liberal MPs were elected (Butler and Butler, 1994:215).

reduced to such small representation in the immediate post-war elections that serious consideration was given to a merger with the Conservatives. In the event, this did not occur and the Liberals continued as a small rump in the House of Commons for much of the 1950s. From the late 1950s onwards there were some spectacular by-election successes and fuelled by these performances, an increasing number of Liberal candidates were fielded. By and large, however, political life was dominated by the Conservatives and Labour, whose combined share of the General Election vote never dipped below 87.5 per cent (see Appendix I).

However, the party system was in many ways very different from the pre-war period. Whereas the Conservatives had clearly dominated political life since the Great War, there was now a strong alternative government in the form of the Labour Party. Labour's increased strength can be largely attributed to the war-time experience. First, the practicalities of war had meant that policies such as planning and state ownership seemed far more acceptable. Secondly, the war had generated a feeling not only of national unity in the face of a clear enemy, but had also generated a desire not to return to the far more divided society and the severe unemployment of the 1930s. Thirdly, the co-operation with Stalin's Soviet Union had led to greater sympathy with the left in general and finally, senior Labour politicians, such as Clement Attlee and Ernest Bevin, had shown themselves to be very capable statesmen as part of the wartime Cabinet. There was, in short, a sea change in British politics and citizens' expectations of government and this was clearly illustrated by the Beveridge Report in 1942, which promised widespread welfare reforms once the peace was won.

In 1945, then, Labour were well placed to capitalise upon the new mood, although many still believed that the Conservatives, led by wartime leader Winston Churchill, would win the election. The result was a landslide majority for Labour. In fact, it was the first majority Labour had enjoyed. Whereas prior to the war Britain had had a two-party system dominated by one party, it now had a genuine two-party system. There were then a number of key features characterising this party system until the 1970s. First, elections produced majority rule. During the period 1945–1970, all general elections produced an outright governing majority allowing one party to rule without the need for coalition partnerships.

Majorities did vary in size, however, and the small majorities achieved in 1950 and 1964 prompted further elections shortly after the original ones. The outcomes here were different. When Labour called a General Election in 1951, despite achieving one of the highest shares of the vote of any post-war party (48.8 per cent) it lost power to the Conservatives, largely it seems because of boundary changes that had just come into place. In 1966, however, Labour extended its majority (see Appendix I).

Secondly, while there were majorities, there was a degree of alternation in government. During the period 1945–1970 the Conservatives and Labour both won four elections. Moreover, the Conservatives were in power for 13 years and Labour 12 years. These figures require clarification, however. Despite the apparent equality in governing, there was not genuine alternation. The Conservatives enjoyed a 13-year spell in power during the years 1951–64, while Labour's spells in government occurred on either side of this period (see Appendix I).

This period, then, was characterised by two-party government with a degree of alternation. However, the reasonably lengthy periods in office enjoyed by both parties also contributed to an element of stability in public policy. Essentially, what emerged during this period was a broad consensus on economic and welfare policy. In economic terms there was broad consensus in three areas. First, economic policy was Keynesian in approach. Secondly, there was general agreement on the relative size of the public and private sectors. The 1945–51 Labour government embarked upon a policy of widespread nationalisation of utilities such as the mines and the railways. Once nationalised, future governments largely maintained this level of state ownership. In terms of welfare and social policy, there was also consensus. The 1945–51 Labour government introduced widespread state health provision, as well as further enhancing the welfare state in general. Sensing the popularity of these policies, the Conservatives did not oppose them by the 1950s and largely maintained them. Moreover, they themselves campaigned upon the need for government activity in the economy, pledging in 1951 an extensive programme of house-building. This broad consensus in major areas of government policy prompted many to refer to 'Butskellism', a reference to the perceived similarities in policy espoused by the Conservative Chancellor of the Exchequer, R.A.B. Butler and the Labour leader, Hugh Gaitskell. With such apparent consensus in policy, it is unsurprising that the party system during this period was stable and somewhat impenetrable. While the system was ripe for change before the war, afterwards it became increasingly frozen.

Nevertheless, while it is clear that this period cemented the Conservative/Labour hold on the party system, there was an element of resistance which came to fruition in the 1970s and beyond. First the Liberals, while electorally weak, emerged in the second half of this period with some remarkable by-election victories. Secondly, Britain witnessed the first stirrings of successful nationalist electoral activity in Scotland and Wales. Thirdly, groups in the Labour Party, such as Militant, became stronger in the 1960s, especially as disillusionment with the Wilson government grew.

In the 1970s a number of issues combined to suggest that the party system might be changing. There were a number of relevant concerns. First of all, certain economic conditions affected all governments. Until the 1970s Britain had enjoyed relative and stable prosperity. This changed rapidly during the early 1970s. First, the collapse of the Bretton Woods agreement heralded free exchange rates, thus exposing Britain to potential economic uncertainty.[2] Secondly, the oil shocks of 1973 caused huge problems in economic and industrial policies. The price of oil doubled virtually overnight causing huge economic problems. For the first time since the early 1950s British citizens were issued with ration books, in this case for petrol. By 1976, Britain was in economic crisis and was forced to apply for a loan from the International Monetary Fund (IMF). The result was a shift in economic policy away from Keynesianism and the basis of a new economic consensus, enthusiastically prosecuted by the subsequent Thatcher government.

Coupled with these crippling economic circumstances, Britain also had problems with industrial relations. This problem had had its roots in the 1960s. Harold Wilson's Labour government had become increasingly impatient with unofficial 'wildcat' strikes. As a response, it had attempted measures to curb the activities of trade unions, but these measures failed to become law after

[2] Bretton Woods was an international agreement reached in 1944 which sought to aid post-war economic recovery by seeking to maintain stable and predictable currency exchange rates. It collapsed in 1971 when the central currency of the agreement, the US dollar, could not maintain its international value (Robbins, 1994:214, 301).

sustained opposition from the trade unions and elements of the Labour Party itself. Edward Heath's new Conservative government also attempted to deal with the 'problem', introducing the Industrial Relations Act in 1971. The act was far-reaching but proved to be unworkable in the face of trade union non-compliance. Trade unions continued to exert their industrial muscle through strikes in the coal industry. These resulted in national power cuts and the introduction of a 3-day working week across industry. In the end, Heath decided to go to the country in February 1974, asking 'Who Governs? The government or the trade unions?' Britain, it was argued, had become ungovernable.

The February 1974 General Election provided a new scenario for the post-war British party system. First, there was a minority Labour government. Secondly, there was a surge in Liberal Party support. The Liberals achieved 19.3 per cent of the vote; a post-war high and a considerable leap from the 7.5 per cent achieved in 1970. As a result of this the Conservatives and Labour only managed to score 75 per cent of the popular vote, a considerable fall from the levels achieved at previous elections. Labour called a further General Election in the October of that year, managing to achieve a slim majority. Nevertheless, the two main parties could only increase their share of the vote overall by 0.1 per cent and while the Liberals slipped back a little, gains were made by the nationalist parties.

While Labour achieved a majority, a series of by-election defeats saw it with an overall minority by 1977. A pact was struck with the Liberals, and Labour was able to continue in office. Theoretically this could have prompted a coalition, yet the reality was that Labour dominated the relationship. No Liberals were brought into the Cabinet and no concessions were made to Liberal policy demands. In the end the pact collapsed, leaving the Labour government exposed to a vote of no confidence in the House of Commons. A successful vote was taken in 1979 and an election subsequently called.

During this period of Labour government the issue of industrial relations had partially subsided. Labour was successful in incorporating the trade unions into economic decision-making in return for wage restraint and industrial calm. The Social Contract, struck between government and trade union leaders, helped plant the seeds of an impressive economic recovery, aided by some deft manoeuvres by Chancellor Denis Healey. However, by late 1978 the Social Contract was crumbling and went into full-scale collapse in the winter of 1978–9 after Premier Callaghan pushed the compliance of the trade unionists too far. The so-called 'Winter of Discontent' heralded large-scale public sector strikes, which created the emotive visions of uncollected rubbish and the dead unburied. Britain's volatile industrial relations 'problem' was again at the top of the political agenda. Since 1979, Britain has had a Conservative government and it is against this backdrop that the book provides its main focus.

Factors influencing the development of the party system

There are a variety of factors which have influenced the development of the British party system and continue, in some cases, to have an effect today. First, we should examine the franchise.

The franchise

Full male suffrage together with women aged 30 years and over came about in 1918. This extension of the suffrage to include all of the male working class coincided with developing class politics. This was a contributory factor in the electoral decline of the Liberal Party. While the extension of the franchise to include all adult women in 1928 does not appear to have affected the party system, the reduction of the age of majority, from 21 to 18 years in 1969, may be said to have had some impact. First, unadjusted turnout figures suggest a significant drop in the general elections that followed this move. Secondly, the rise in centre party vote may be explained to a small degree by an influx of younger voters (Heath *et al.*, 1991:220).

The electoral system

Perhaps the strongest contextual influence upon the party system, however, is the electoral system. For national elections, Britain uses a Single Member Simple Plurality (SMSP) (often known as first-past-the-post) electoral system (Crewe, 1993). This system has certain biases. First, in terms of seats, it tends to over-reward the single most popular party. Secondly, it tends to discriminate against parties with widely distributed electoral support. Thus, while it ensures the representation of strong regional parties such as Plaid Cymru and the Scottish National Party, the Liberal Democrats suffer in terms of proportionality, largely because they have few concentrations of support (see Appendix I). Perhaps the clearest example of this problem was the result of the 1983 General Election. The Liberal Democrats' predecessors, the SDP/Liberal Alliance, polled 25.4 per cent of the vote, just behind Labour who polled 27.6 per cent; yet Labour received 32.2 per cent of the seats in the House of Commons and the SDP/Liberal Alliance only 3.5 per cent. Few electoral systems produce total proportionality, but this was a clear example of the disparity that could occur. Of course, proportionality is not a normative concept. Many would argue that despite these disparities, the electoral system does at least aid 'stable government'. This is not an issue for debate here. Suffice to say that the first-past-the-post electoral system is a key factor in the maintenance of the British party system because it militates against the breakthrough of a third party, not only in terms of electoral geography but also in terms of tactical voting, since third party supporters may vote for another party in order to prevent the election of a particular candidate in a certain constituency. Indeed, a survey simulation of the 1992 General Election using a variety of electoral systems indicated that both the Alternative Member System and the Single Transferable Vote would have given the Liberal Democrats the equivalent of over 100 seats (Dunleavy, Margretts and Weir, 1992). In short, although there has been a revival of centre party fortunes since the 1970s, in national terms Britain cannot be said to be a three-party system; it is more accurate to say that there is a two-and-a-half-party system. This is especially true if we examine the changing distribution of contest types. Most constituencies, regardless of location, are broadly two-party contests. There are very few constituencies where the electoral race can genuinely be seen as a three-party affair (Johnston, Pattie and Fieldhouse, 1994:261).

The class cleavage

A cleavage in this context is a division within society. This may be reflected in a number of ways, but is commonly associated with social characteristics of the population. Thus a country may be divided in terms of religion, race or class, for example. It does not necessarily mean that various cleavages within society are logically opposed to each other, simply that we can identify particular groups which have apparently common practices, norms and beliefs. The British party system has long reflected the so-called class cleavage in British society, and while there are obvious signs of cross-class voting, the core support for the Conservative and Labour Parties remain in the middle and working classes, respectively. The Liberals and their successors, however, have not enjoyed this 'natural constituency', although the support of Liberal Democrats today is largely middle class in its make-up.

Party finance

Party finance further reinforces this cleavage between capital and labour. Although the Conservative and Labour Parties do not generate all their funds from companies and trade unions, this institutional form of income still does constitute a significant proportion. The Liberals, by contrast, have seldom enjoyed such patronage and have been dependent largely upon the efforts of their membership.

Conclusions

Modern British political parties really became established from the 1880s onwards. The combination of parliamentary discipline, extra-parliamentary organisation and the increasing importance of the central party ensured that parties developed into those that we know today. While there were clearly party groupings prior to this time which certainly influenced the modern party's development, the move from loose groupings of largely independent men in Parliament to more rigid structures which included large numbers of citizens was critical. Subsequently, Britain has seen three and possibly four phases of the party system. The first, between the 1880s and 1920s, was largely Conservative and Liberal in character. The second, from the mid-1920s to the end of the Second World War, could be described as Conservative, Labour and National Government. Since the war we may observe a third phase, largely comprising Conservative and Labour Parties; yet we arguably divide that into two phases with the division being the 1970s. Prior to the 1970s, the party system was evidently a two-party affair. Since then, however, the growing strength of the Liberals, their successors and the Nationalists has meant that it might be more accurate to describe the situation as a two-and-a-half-party system. On the other hand, despite the surges in support for these smaller parties, the Conservative and Labour grip upon Parliament, at least, remains very strong.

The second point to make is that external factors have clearly been influential in shaping the British party system. Social cleavages, the electoral system and the growth of the franchise had evidently been important. The replacement of the Liberals by Labour and their inability to regain their former position have all been influenced by these factors. Moreover, changing social circumstances have meant that all parties have needed to adjust in order to survive. Parties, then, are an important aspect of British political life. In the next chapter we examine the role of political parties and consider whether they remain at the heart of British politics or whether they are ineffective and unimportant.

2

THE ROLE OF POLITICAL PARTIES IN BRITAIN TODAY

Introduction

Political parties have become fundamental to the operation of parliamentary democracy in Britain. Indeed, over 100 years ago Disraeli argued: '. . . without party, parliamentary government is impossible' (Hansard Society, 1981:9). Since the time of Disraeli their position at the core of political life has, through a period of evolution, become increasingly entrenched. Parties, then, are here to stay; yet political parties are not simply elements of the political scenery. They perform, or claim to perform, a variety of functions which indicates why they continue to be so important. In order, therefore, to understand the importance of parties and their role in British political life, we should consider to what extent parties are fulfilling these functions.

Electoral choice

Political parties purport to offer the electorate a choice, principally through the presentation of alternative political programmes. Some versions of democratic theory require electors to aggregate policy preferences. That is to say, electors evaluate each party's programme and vote accordingly. This viewpoint advocates a focus on the positive forward-looking choice of ·the· policy preferred by society at large (Harrop and Miller, 1987: 248). However, some argue that the electoral choices, between the major parties at least, are more rhetorical than actual. Certainly, not all policy commitments are partisan or in opposition to those advanced by other parties. For example, one survey of party manifestos revealed that 57 per cent of the manifesto pledges were non-partisan (Rose, quoted in Ingle, 1987:194). Moreover, there are situations when all parties offer very similar platforms on major issues. The 1992 General Election was one such occurrence, when all three main political parties pledged support for the Maastricht Treaty relating to Britain's position within the European Community (EC). In this case, the voter who wished to vote for one of the main three parties was offered little or no electoral choice on this issue. Of course, there is nothing to stop an element of consensus in parties' proposed programmes. Indeed, many would welcome it, but there are some who argue that the electorate is presented with little or no real electoral choice.

Nevertheless, parties do offer a choice for voters in that they may vote for this party or that. Indeed elections, in a sense, force voters to make a choice. Moreover, given that many studies of electoral behaviour seem to indicate strong factors of reward or punishment by voters for government competence (particularly in the field of the economy) and rather weaker factors of electoral choice being made on the basis of policy choice, this level of electoral choice should not be underestimated. Additionally, it is quite in keeping with other democratic theories which focus upon negative rather than positive choices; on retrospective rather than prospective judgements. What is important here is the rejection of unpopular governments and since elections can threaten incumbent governments with dismissal, there is a greater prospect for governments acting responsibly (Harrop and Miller, 1987:248).

Representation

Political parties offer a voice to the main segments of opinion and interests within the country. They offer a ladder between the citizen and the state and translate or articulate demands into policies. Political parties often attempt to represent the interests of particular groups, sometimes at the expense of others; but it would be misleading to assume that parties in Britain would overtly represent one group while ignoring the wishes of another. In order to win power, parties must appeal to larger groups than their 'natural constituency', assuming of course that the natural constituency is likely to vote for them at all. For example, if the vast majority of the working class in Britain had always voted Labour, it would never have been out of office. Evidently they have not, thus illustrating that parties must seek to represent many groups to have any realistic chance of winning elections. Of course, the main political parties claim that they seek to favour no one and represent everyone. They claim that they are setting ideological goals in order to establish the best way to run the country. In this sense, parties could be said to be offering representation of major strands of opinion. Thus the parties also play an integrating role, bringing together various groups in society and reconciling conflicting interests in an effort to follow their particular ideas. That said, the electorate do not always perceive things in the same way as the parties. When asked in the *British Election Survey* of 1992 whether each main party sought to represent all social classes or just one, the results were as shown in Table 2.1. Evidently, the Liberal Democrats were the only major party to be seen by the electorate at least as fundamentally 'classless'. Moreover, if the misgivings over electoral choice described above are true, then one may question the validity of the view that parties are offering representation of different strands of thought.

In some ways parties may also be seen as agents by which representation can be compromised. Parties, for example, differ from interest groups primarily in the fact that they aggregate interests. Parties must convert the multitude of pressures from both the electorate and party elites and prioritise these demands. Without

Table 2.1 **Views upon parties' representation of social classes.**

Percentage saying	All classes	Just one class
Conservative	39	55
Labour	35	54
Liberal Democrat	65	10

Source: *British Election Survey 1992.*

this aggregation there would be political chaos. In doing so demands can be given low priority, either through political expediency or through a desire to address what are conceived to be more pressing concerns. In this sense, therefore, representation is compromised by the process of party agenda setting. Given these conditions, single issue groups can flourish should groups consider that their concerns are not receiving sufficient attention or support from political parties.

Secondly, we should examine various aspects of representation which itself has many meanings. For example, we may consider whether parties and elections should provide resemblance, the reproduction of the party or Parliament as the social construction of the nation. If that is the case, then parties and Parliament should reflect the proportions of men and women in the population, the proportion of people from various ethnic backgrounds and so on. Clearly, as later chapters will show, neither Parliament nor the candidates for it provide representation in this way.

This form of representation has often been resisted on the grounds that there were fears that candidate characteristics could threaten the strength of the party vote. However, a study by Pippa Norris and Joni Lovenduski found that there was little evidence to support this theory. Basing their analysis upon the results of the 1992 General Election, they found that for both Labour and Conservatives the sex of the candidate had no effect upon the election result. Moreover, where Labour fielded candidates from ethnic minorities they performed as well and often better than white candidates, especially when they were incumbents. However, there were some negative effects. Ethnic minority candidates fielded by the Conservative Party did worse than average. Overall, Norris and Lovenduski (1995) concluded that candidate effects on the vote were modest, but could be very significant in some marginal seats (Norris and Lovenduski, 1995:233–6).

Even if we accept that representation by parties in government need not necessarily reflect our social make-up, we may still observe elements of compromise in representation. If we examine three models of representation this becomes more clear (Harrop and Miller, 1987:246–7). First, we can adopt the constituency service model of representation. Under this premise, representatives' primary role is to advance the interests of their local constituents.

This would provide representation for that particular electorate. However, it is far more common to observe two different models which may be said to potentially compromise representation. First, there is the trustee model which stresses the independent judgement of the legislator, once elected. Representatives in this model are entrusted with supporting or opposing policies as they judge best, which may run counter to the interests of those whom he or she represents. Secondly, and more familiarly, there is the party model. Here the representative is a supporter primarily of the party, elected on the party manifesto and therefore bound to obey its broad programme, regardless of the interests of his or her electors. Again, representation is compromised. On the other hand, this may be seen in another way as providing representation, since it can be argued that electors vote for the party programme first and the representative second. Thus in this instance the representative is providing representation for those at least that voted for his or her party.

Policy making

Political parties have some role in the formulation of policy. We should stress certain reservations here because as later chapters will show, there is some gap between what parties claim they do and the actuality of the situation. Thus formally, the Labour Party conference can determine party policy. However, empirical evidence seems to suggest that party leaderships act with much more independence than the constitutional position would suggest. Moreover, there are numerous other external constraints on policy making and implementation. These include factors such as external economic conditions which can limit the scope for policy implementation. Nevertheless, parties do play some role in policy initiation. The original ideas for policies will often emerge from parties, although not necessarily from popular forums such as conferences, but from internal policy committees. In that sense, if policy making is broken down into various stages then parties do play a role. Analysis shows, however, that the policy making process may not be so ordered (Ham and Hill, 1994) Overall, parties may be said to have some role in policymaking, but that role should not be overstated.

Recruitment and the selection of parliamentary candidates

Political parties recruit the vast majority of parliamentary candidates. In effect they sanction candidature; but if this sounds a little harsh, one could interpret it as being the main pathway for the selection of the country's MPs. Moreover, with internal policies such as quotas and in the case of the Labour Party, the one time compulsory inclusion of women on candidate short-lists, political parties can help influence the composition of Parliament. Within Parliament, parties invoke strict discipline on members, principally through the system of whips. This helps ensure that both government and opposition is both strong and (relatively) predictable. Of course, even the strongest party discipline cannot force members to vote in a particular way and rebellion from within the ranks of MPs is not uncommon.

Nevertheless, those that do get elected commonly owe their position to an extent to the political party that selects and supports them. Some might argue that a good candidate owes less to the party. However, Norris and Lovenduski found that there was only modest and inconsistent evidence to support this notion. Examining each election from 1955 they found no regular pattern to illustrate any benefits from incumbency. The variations in electoral support that did occur were caused by swings in government popularity and regional trends. Thus, MPs tend to suffer when their governments are unpopular and vice versa. In 1992, for example, Labour challengers performed better than Labour MPs since most challengers were in the South of England, where Labour increased its vote overall more than in its traditional strongholds.

Regarding the length of parliamentary service of a candidate, Norris and Lovenduski found that there was little or no relationship with electoral performance. Only Conservatives appeared to benefit and Liberal Democrats did worse the longer they were in office. Finally, they found that only Labour MPs appear to benefit from the amount of constituency service they provide, gaining up to a 1.2 per cent in their vote share. For Conservative MPs, the electoral consequences did not seem to hinge upon whether they were active or not (Norris and Lovenduski, 1994:226–36).

Other evidence also supports the notion that the party is important regarding the electoral prospects of a candidate. In virtually all recent cases where an incumbent has been deselected by his or her party or resigned membership, the candidate has lost the seat to the candidate from their former party. Thus in 1992 Sid Bidwell, who had been a long-serving Labour MP for the constituency of Ealing Southall, was deselected by his local party. Bidwell stood in the election as an Independent but lost to the official Labour candidate. Similar instances occurred for former Labour MPs in Coventry and Liverpool and for the Conservative MP, John Browne, in Winchester. Only Dick Taverne, who stood against the official Labour candidate as Democratic Labour in Lincoln at the February 1974 election has been successful in recent years and even then, he lost his seat in the October election of that year.

The role of parties becomes even more crucial for leaders. The Prime Minister, in practice, owes his or her position to the party that has selected him or her to be leader. This was graphically illustrated when Mrs Thatcher was replaced as Prime Minister by John Major after Major had assumed the leadership of the Conservative Party. Technically this is not strictly necessary. For example, when John Major precipitated the Conservative leadership election in 1995, he did so initially by resigning as leader of the Conservative Party, yet remained as Prime Minister. Thus for the period between his resignation and subsequent re-election there was no leader of the governing party, yet that party still provided the Prime Minister. Similarly, Mrs Thatcher could have remained in office despite her resignation as leader. Political circumstances dictated, however, that this would not occur.

Political education and communication

Parties attempt to educate the public politically by seeking to explain and promote their policies. Of course, as the goal of the mainstream political parties is to win as many votes as possible, this process may necessarily be less educational and more promotional, by attempting to selectively emphasise their strengths and their opponents' weaknesses. Nevertheless, the parties help set the political agenda for discussion and provide strands of opinion on issues (however selective) for discussion. Parties can also educate voters at elections. For example, they can encourage voters to at least develop basic knowledge about the parties' policies and can educate voters as to which areas of debate are most crucial. This may be a purely subjective judgement made by parties based upon their own interests. The amount of learning, moreover, varies enormously. Nevertheless, competitive elections force people to examine the alternatives. Without an election it is easy to blame a government for a problem. An election forces us to consider whether that problem would be resolved by another party. This is especially important since mainstream parties tend to deflate expectations. Election campaigns can also therefore be an important means of educating voters as to the limits to which parties can act effectively whilst in government (Harrop and Miller, 1987:266).

Political participation

Parties potentially facilitate political participation. They recruit members who in turn can participate in party activities. The extent of participation varies considerably among members, but the parties do at least provide the potential for participation. Studies have tended to indicate that in most areas, party members tend to participate more politically than non-party members. However, party membership in Britain is low. Currently, membership of the Conservative Party stands at between 560000–750000,[1] Labour at 350000 and the Liberal Democrats at 103000. Moreover, studies illustrate that the reasons for joining parties are disparate and include non-political social reasons (Seyd and Whiteley, 1992; Whiteley, Seyd and Richardson, 1994). However, party membership can prove to be a demotivating factor for participation. Parry, Moyser and Day (1992) found that while party membership did tend to lead to higher levels of political participation than among the wider population, members of the Conservative Party were less likely than the general public to approve of or take part in direct action activities. Membership was therefore a de-mobilising agent in this form of political participation (Parry *et al.*, 1992).

---

[1] There is a certain discrepancy in membership figures for the Conservative Party. The figure released from Conservative Central Office is 750000, the figure estimated by Whiteley *et al.*, 1994 and Webb, 1992a. However, Whiteley *et al.* calculated that the Conservative Party is losing on average 64000 members per year. On that basis, given that the estimate of 750000 was calculated in 1992, at the time of writing (1995) this would suggest a membership figure of 558000.

Parties also provide participation opportunities for non-members. They provide candidates for elections, of course, which gives non-members someone to vote for. Moreover, parties provide a focus for partisan identification, of which low levels tend to be associated with low turnout at elections (Crewe, Fox and Alt, 1992:24–7). Parties also initiate or take part in campaigns, such as protests against government policies, which provide further opportunities for political participation by non-members. Indeed, parties can distort the trends of socioeconomic determinants of political participation (Rush, 1992). As a general observation, higher income and educational attainment tends to be associated with higher levels of participation. However, where strong union movements exist that are closely allied with a party, the trend is for increased levels of manual or working class participation. Indeed, in class stratified societies, a working class party may substitute for education and status as a facilitator of political participation and sense of political competence among workers (Rush, 1992).

Are British parties in decline?

Thus, political parties have a number of functions. In short, they bridge the gap not only between the citizen and the state, but between groups within society. In theory, they provide a route for the articulation and incorporation of demands from the bottom to the top. That is, they provide the avenue to pursue interests. However, many argue that in fact the input of the grass roots is far more limited and, in fact, the parties provide little articulation for the ordinary citizen. Moreover, some have argued that political parties are in decline and that they are no longer performing their functions adequately. This is a question that the British political scientist, Paul Webb, has attempted to address (Webb, 1995a).

Webb has taken a number of indicators which may be said to measure party strength, both internally as organisations and externally in terms of anti-party sentiment. As far as party organisation is concerned he does find some evidence for the party decline thesis. First, while low in comparison with other countries, the income of British parties has remained relatively stable. This, however, does not take into account the rising costs of politics. Thus, while parties may be earning as much in real terms, the cost of political life is becoming more expensive. Secondly, while in general the number of party staff at national level have increased slightly, they have fallen dramatically at local level during the last 20 years. Finally there has been a general decline in party membership, although the Labour Party, at least, appears to be reversing this process.

However, if we examine whether parties have declined in the public eye, there are a number of indicators which suggest that British political parties are in fact quite strong. An indication of this is the level of partisan identification. As the term suggests, this is a measure of how many people identify with a party. It is rather like measuring support for a football team, in as much as many more people will identify with a side than will necessarily go and see them play. So, with partisan identification, we measure whether people are supporters of a party separately from whether they actually vote for them. (We will look at this idea in more detail later on.) A further aspect of partisan identification is that it can vary in strength. That is to say, one can be a strong supporter or a weak supporter, for example.

Webb rightly points out that the strength of partisan identification has declined. In the 1950s and 1960s partisan identification appeared to be relatively stable in terms of strength. However, in the 1970s it appeared as though voters' partisan anchorages were becoming less secure and that Britain was experiencing class and partisan dealignment. The 1970s saw, first, a decline in the strength of partisan identification. Voters were (and still do) classifying themselves as partisan, but the intensity had declined. Thus, while in 1964 93 per cent classified themselves as partisan, in 1992 the figure was 89 per cent. In terms of strong partisans, however, the figure fell from 43 per cent to 19 per cent. Nevertheless, interpretation of these figures differ.

Although partisan identification has declined in intensity, there has been no growth in overall voter volatility (the total amount of voter movement) to match the decline in strength of partisanship. Moreover, the 'homing tendency' of partisan identification has survived and continued to yield an important influence on individual voting behaviour (Heath, Jowell and Curtice, 1992). That is to say, voters have continued to return to vote for the parties that they normally do, even if they have gone through a period of voting for other parties. Further, although the intensity of partisan identification has declined, the proportion of the electorate that has some partisan identification has not declined to any significant degree. Thus, voters have not abandoned political parties; they simply are not quite as attached to them as they once were.

Webb also points out that the decline in partisan strength has been accompanied by a growth in voter hesitancy, electors being undecided about voting decisions much closer to an actual poll. This, he argues, may be seen as part of a more general pattern of party decline in terms of loyalty. However, on the other hand it may be viewed as an indicator of a more vibrant party system, where electors are genuinely more able to make a choice. Hesitancy over a decision does not necessarily indicate dissatisfaction with the available options. We can understand this idea more fully if we think of parties as products to be bought. Let us say, for example, that I was buying a video recorder. I might find that there were three models, each made by different companies which caught my eye. Each model was excellent and all were competitively priced. Even if I had some level of brand loyalty, I might find it difficult to choose which model to buy. This would be purchaser hesitancy. However, what is clear is that my hesitancy does not mean the products are poor. So it is with political parties.

A further indicator of a party decline might be electoral turnout. Low turnout, for example, could indicate alienation from the political

Table 2.2   **Turnout in General Elections 1950–92.**

Year	Turnout (%)
1950	84.0
1951	82.5
1955	76.8
1959	78.7
1964	77.1
1966	75.8
1970	72.0
1974 (February)	78.1
1974 (October)	72.8
1979	76.0
1983	72.7
1987	75.3
1992	77.7

Source: Denver (1994).

and party system. On the face of it, turnout appears to have declined significantly (see Table 2.2). However, the elections of 1950 and 1951 were exceptional years, far above the pre-war average, and without including those elections the trend is small. Also, all cases are not alike. In 1970, for example, the voting age was lowered from 21 to 18 years, increasing the electorate by 3 million. Moreover, while internationally quite low, electoral turnout in Britain is surprisingly high given the number of predictable and safe seats (Denver, 1994:137).

We should also note that turnout is frequently measured by calculating the number of people who voted against the number on the electoral register. This creates inaccuracies. The electoral register is compiled on the basis of household returns every October. It comes into force in the following February and lasts 1 year. Given that there are inherent inaccuracies in the electoral register, Rose calculated a formula to take account of these problems and produce a more accurate view of turnout (Denver, 1994:138–9). Based on Rose's estimations, turnout since 1950 was as shown in Table 2.3.

Using this indicator of turnout there is still some decline, but it is less steep and indeed appears to have recovered from the low point of 1970. Given that there remains turnout of around 80 per

Table 2.3   **Adjusted turnout in General Elections 1950–92.**

Year	Adjusted turnout (%)
1950	84.1
1951	88.3
1955	79.8
1959	85.0
1964	83.3
1966	77.4
1970	75.2
1974 (February)	78.8
1974 (October)	78.6
1979	78.6
1983	75.8
1987	78.6
1992	79.7

Source: Denver (1994).

cent, it is difficult to sustain the argument that parties are failing and are in decline. On the other hand, voting may not be seen as an indicator of support for the party system. There are many other explanations of why people vote. For example, electors may vote from a sense of civic duty. Voting is highly regarded in most democratic societies and persistent non-voting is regarded as socially unacceptable. Secondly, while voting may be seen as a duty, it can also be fun. Moreover, it is relatively 'cost-free' in terms of time spent.

Other research indicates that far more practical reasons may account for non-voting. Studies by Crewe *et al.* (1992) and by Swaddle and Heath (1992) both arrive at similar conclusions: namely that most non-voters do not abstain persistently and that the factors which prompted non-voting were factors such as high residential mobility and living alone. What emerged was a common theme of social isolation: fewer pressures to fulfil civic duty from friends or community. Nevertheless, they also found that low levels of party identification had some effect upon turnout. In Britain, then, it seems as though at general elections non-voting is more to do with temporary, practical reasons for abstention rather than being alienated from the political and party system.

Finally, Webb examines whether there has been any growth in support for anti-party parties, but again finds little evidence to make this case. Beyond the impressive showing of the Green Party in the 1989 European Elections neither the Greens, nor any of the other anti-party parties such as the British National Party or the Natural Law Party, have made any significant impact at national level. While in 1992 there was a record number of minor party or independent candidates, all but one lost their deposit and that candidate was a member of the newly reformed Liberal Party (Butler and Kavanagh, 1992:342–3). To be sure, some of these parties have been successful at local level and one cannot dismiss the repercussions of their success, particularly in the case of the British National Party, who temporarily held a local government seat in East London. Nevertheless, in national terms such parties have not made any significant electoral impact and this becomes more apparent when one witnesses the electoral success of similar parties in other parts of Europe.

In short, we can observe parties in decline by some indicators but, by and large, they remain as important elements of the political scene. In certain areas their roles and functions may be downplayed, such as political communication, which may be said to be more a function of the media. Moreover, the multiplicity of single interest groups may be seen as evidence of dissatisfaction with parties. On the other hand, this may simply be an indicator of a healthy pluralist society. Whatever the case, political parties can at least point to their own mechanisms of accountability, through internal democracy and national elections to which single-issue groups are not subjected.

Conclusions

Political parties are an essential feature of the British political scene, not simply because they exist but because they perform valuable functions. Of course, no party is perfect and each performs the functions with varying degrees of skill and success. Moreover, in the policy making sphere it is apparent that the role of parties may be diminishing to some extent, not only because of the way in which policy emerges, but also because of external factors which restrict any party's actions. Nevertheless, it is clear that parties play important roles and could not realistically be replaced without a fundamental transformation of political life. It is also difficult to sustain the view that parties are in decline. To be sure, there are some indications of decline, not least the low membership figures and the often precarious finances of the parties (which we will explore in later chapters). However, people still like parties. There are barely fewer partisans today than 30 years ago. The fact that the support for parties may be weaker in strength may simply be a reflection that voters have become more sophisticated as electoral consumers. It is much harder to display brand loyalty when there are several good products on the market. If that sounds perversely content and optimistic, it is simply to suggest that indicators of strength or decline are open to more than one interpretation.

3

THE CONSERVATIVE PARTY

In this and the following chapters, we will examine various aspects of the three main national political parties. The layout and topics covered for each will be the same, which will enable easy comparisons.

Introduction

The Conservative Party is the dominant political party in Britain. It has held power for a majority of years this century and since the Second World War has held office continually for two long periods: for 13 years between 1951 and 1964 and, at the time of writing, for more than 16 years since 1979 (see Appendix I). It has the largest individual membership of all the parties, and while it has accumulated significant debts, has access at least to the largest pool of finance. It is in many ways, then, the most successful party in British party political history. Yet, despite this success, the party periodically finds itself in trouble. On occasions it loses elections and within its ranks, there have been deep splits which have led to regroupings. In this chapter, we will examine various aspects of the party and see if an evaluation can be made as to why it has been so successful and why it is sometimes prone to difficulties.

Organisation and internal elections

The Conservative Party is a hierarchical party. All efforts are directed towards the assistance of the parliamentary party and

Figure 3:1   Conservative Party Organisation

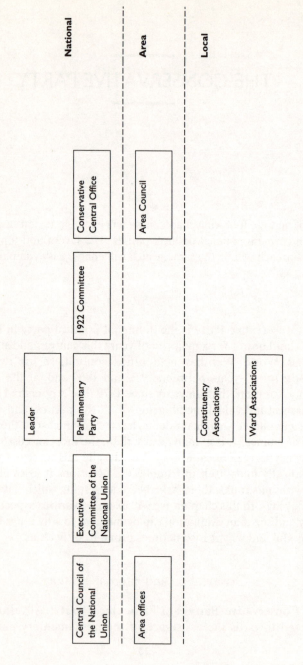

Sources: Webb (1992a:854); Jones and Kavanagh (1994:247).

especially the leader. This, in part, is a reflection of its origins. The Conservative Party emerged from within Parliament. The parliamentary party was therefore established before extra-parliamentary activities had developed in the mid- to late nineteenth century. The parliamentary party was thus paramount. The hierarchy and the pre-eminence of the leader is also a reflection of the party's broad political thought; namely an approval of authority and status, and a willingness to serve. Thus the importance of the leader is clearly a reflection of the wider political creed of conservatism. It also reflects one of the Conservative Party's key objectives which itself helps to shape party thinking: the pursuit of government. While all the mainstream political parties seek power, none do so as single-mindedly as the Conservative Party and, as history has shown, it is rather good at achieving this goal. Constitutionally, then, the Conservative Party is strongly hierarchical, as shown in Figure 3.1.

Formally, there are three levels to Conservative Party organisation: local, area and national. At local level the basic unit is the party member who will be a member of a ward association, which in turn is part of the local constituency party who in some cases employ agents. Local parties are far more independent than is the case in other major parties and guard this status fervently. The local level links to the area offices and council who may offer local constituencies advice on procedures such as the selection of candidates. The area level in turn consults with particular arms of the national association. It is at the national level that we see how the Conservative Party has earned its reputation for hierarchy. At this level there are three principal focuses of power: the leader, the parliamentary party and Central Council of the National Union of Conservative and Unionist Organisations. The leader and the parliamentary party are theoretically independent of the other parts of the Conservative Party although, of course, MPs are subject to reselection by constituencies. The leader has sole responsibility for the drafting of the election manifesto and has direct control over Conservative Central Office, the organisational centre of the party, through the appointment of both the chairman and deputy chairman. Area offices have linkage with the party chairman, but it is through the National Union that grass-roots Conservatives receive formal representation at the national level.

The National Union was set up in 1867 as a means of organising the various Conservative constituency organisations in England and Wales, and represented the beginnings of the modern party system. There are two bodies within it: a central council (comprising representatives from every constituency association, as well as all Conservative MPs, MEPs and Peers and Conservative societies) and an executive committee (which comprises representatives of the area councils as well as the party leader, the leader in the Lords, the Chief Whips and representatives of the 1922 Committee). The council's role is quite limited, meeting only once a year principally to elect officers of the National Union. The executive committee, however, meets more regularly and in addition to resolving party disputes engages in policy discussions which are then offered as advice. It is important to note here that while constituency parties may find representation on these bodies, both contain elite members of the party at the national level. Thus it remains that the key role of the National Union is the organisation of the various party conferences throughout the year and that role is under threat, since the Conservative Party has followed some of its government policies and put the organisation of conferences in the hands of CCO Conferences Ltd.

However, bald constitutional facts do not necessarily indicate the reality of a situation. For example, it may be questioned whether the Conservative Party is as hierarchical as it appears. The party conference is an example of this. Conference has no formal policy making powers. Moreover, popular folklore has it that the annual Conservative Party conference is merely a public relations exercise where senior party members speak to, and receive rousing approval from, a compliant and passive party membership. It is no more than a display for the television cameras, and helps cement the leader and his or her team's authority. This is particularly the case when the party is in power; in a sense the normal situation. The Conservative Party conference exists merely to flatter its leadership.

However, empirical study has suggested otherwise. Kelly, for example, challenged this thesis. He argued that it was inaccurate to consider the main party conference in isolation. Rather, one should also examine the many regional and sectional conferences of the party that are held throughout the year. These include conferences for Scottish Conservatives and the Conservative

Women's Conference. It is here, Kelly has argued, that issues are debated in a much more democratic manner and the results of these conferences will often be reflected in senior party figures' speeches at the main conference. The level of support received by figures at conference is a reflection of how many of the demands of the other conferences had been articulated in the main conference speech delivery. As a result Kelly has argued that the Conservative Party is, in fact, far more consultative, albeit in this informal way, than has been often imagined (Kelly, 1989). Whiteley, Seyd and Richardson (1994) also considered this question in their survey of Conservative Party members. They concluded, on the basis of members' perceptions of their own potential level of influence within the Conservative Party, that the traditional view was misleading. However, while endorsing Kelly's revisionist position to an extent they argue that Kelly had exaggerated the influence of grass-roots members.

In Parliament, also, the notion of the theory of the back-bencher simply playing the role of lobby fodder has come under increasing strain. There are certainly circumstances which assist the maverick back-bencher, not least the size of majority that the governing party enjoys. Logic suggests to us that as the potential votes in Parliament for each party become closer, so the potential for back-bench influence increases. Certainly, back-bench revolt among both Conservative and Labour MPs has increasingly occurred since the 1970s. The governments of both Edward Heath and Margaret Thatcher suffered defeats in the division lobbies because of back-bench revolt. However, in the case of Mrs Thatcher, at least, back-bench cross-voting would often be irrelevant to the final result because the majorities enjoyed by her governments were so large.

Since 1992, however, there have been signs that back-benchers are more willing to flex their particular muscles given that the government was elected with a relatively slim majority, which has been regularly diminished through by-election losses. The debates over the Maastricht Treaty on European integration and the imposition of value-added tax (VAT) on domestic fuel have lead to embarrassing government defeats as a result of Conservative back-benchers exercising a degree of political independence. Indeed, so deeply did the party leadership resent these defeats that those who had consistently voted against the government on the divisions over Europe were, for a time, denied the party whip. Theoretically, this made them non-aligned members and denied the Conservatives their official majority. Eventually these members were readmitted to the party. However, they had clearly demonstrated that back-bench opinion could not be ignored.

In addition to the exercising of dissent in the House of Commons, back-bench Conservatives also find representation through the 1992 Committee. Formed at the Carlton Club in 1922 as a vehicle for urging the leader (Austen Chamberlain) to abandon the coalition with the Liberals, the committee provides the collective focus for back-bench opinion. It elects its own executive committee and provides a means by which the party leadership can be made aware of grass-roots feeling within Parliament. The Committee guards its independence fiercely and has in the past been willing to remind leaders and ministers that their actions have lacked favour on the back-benches. However, we may also see the 1922 Committee in some ways as a means of managing dissent, since it tends to support the leadership publicly despite the discussions that go on behind closed doors. Nevertheless, it seems that the leadership cannot ignore advice from the 1922 Committee, and it is formally charged with the responsibility of conducting elections for the leadership.

The election of the leader

The existence of internal party elections also belies to an extent the wholly hierarchial thesis. The key elections do, however, have a rather select franchise: members of Parliament. That said, these elections serve as an agent of accountability to an extent, so should not be dismissed. Perhaps the most important internal election within the Conservative Party is that for the leadership. Prior to Edward Heath's election in 1965, leaders of the Conservative Party resigned or died and new leaders 'emerged'. Resignation was not necessarily wholly voluntary and gave rise to the popular phrase 'the men in grey suits' who were supposedly senior party figures who would advise a leader that they should resign.[1] In similar circumstances, a successor would emerge to assume the

---

[1] The existence of 'the men in grey suits' may in fact be pure fiction. The account is certainly contested by Bogdanor (Bogdanor, 1994:89).

leadership. The process of succession appeared to be one whereby an individual would emerge after discussions among senior party figures.

On the face of it, this would seem to have been a bizarre process. However, it appears less odd when one considers recent changes in leadership in the Labour Party. Neil Kinnock's resignation was not a surprise and immediately there was talk of his going John Smith emerged as his probable successor. Similarly, after John Smith's untimely death Tony Blair quickly emerged as the front-runner. In both elections the actual vote seemed to be something of a formality.

Nevertheless, while the Conservative Party had appointed their leaders in this informal way for many years the approach came under significant critical scrutiny following the accession of Alec Douglas-Home to the leadership following Harold Macmillan's resignation in 1963. The system had hitherto proved to be successful. Both Eden in 1955 and Macmillan had proved to be electoral assets. Moreover, such a secretive system could at least obscure any in-fighting from public view. The appointment of Douglas-Home was, however, considered to be an error. Home was a peer and was required to renounce his title. Moreover, he appeared less dynamic than the younger Labour leader, Harold Wilson. This dilemma was confirmed when Labour won the 1964 General Election, albeit with a slim majority.

It was decided to change the procedure for appointing leaders radically. Candidates would be nominated and seconded from among the ranks of Conservative MPs and would contest a ballot whose electorate were Conservative Members of Parliament. In order to secure victory, a candidate would require an overall majority against the other candidate(s) plus a 15 per cent lead over his nearest rival.[2] If these conditions were not satisfied, a second ballot would be held where only an overall majority was required. Finally, if this had not resolved the issue, a third ballot would be held of the most popular three candidates using the Alternative Vote method of election. This was amended in 1991 so that the third ballot (if required) is confined to the top two candidates.

When Douglas-Home resigned as leader in 1965, Edward Heath became the first elected leader of the Conservative Party. The

[2] This figure of 15 per cent was apparently arrived at in an arbitrary manner.

results of the first ballot technically required a second ballot, but
the rivals withdrew and Heath was duly elected (see Table 3.1).
This was important as a protracted leadership contest might have
been deemed damaging to the party. The Conservative Party had
then apparently succeeded in reacting to the limitations of its previous system of electing the leader and, despite losing the 1966
Election, Heath was successful in 1970.

However, after a particularly turbulent period of government
Heath lost both elections in 1974 (although the Conservatives did
win more votes in February 1974 than Labour). Under 'normal'
circumstances, Heath might have been expected to resign. He resisted this, however, and as a result changes were made in the
election rules which now allowed Conservative leaders to be challenged, whether in or out of government, so long as a challenger
had the nomination of two fellow Conservative MPs. In 1975, then,
Heath was challenged by Margaret Thatcher and back-bencher
Hugh Fraser. At that time Thatcher, although a Cabinet member,
was not a political 'heavyweight'. Indeed, her principal fame at this
time was as a result of her decision as Education Secretary to end
the provision of free milk to schoolchildren. This earned her the
title of 'Mrs Thatcher: Milk Snatcher!' Nevertheless, in the first
ballot she polled more votes than Heath. Although Thatcher had
not technically 'won' the ballot, Heath withdrew after the igno-
miny of polling fewer votes. At this stage the cabinet 'heavy-
weights' entered the contest. It was expected that one of them
(probably William Whitelaw) would win the second ballot. This
was for two main reasons. First, it was thought that many had
voted for Thatcher because she 'wasn't Heath'. Secondly, it was
not considered likely that a woman would win the leadership
ballot. By this time, however, Thatcher had created something of a
bandwagon effect and was duly elected on a second ballot majority
(see Table 3.1). Just as Heath had risen by the rule changes, so he
fell by them, a pattern to be repeated 15 years later with Margaret
Thatcher.

No further leadership ballots occurred until 1989. This is not
surprising. Notwithstanding early difficulties in Mrs Thatcher's
first government, the party under her leadership won three successive General Elections, each with a substantial majority; but
by 1989 Mrs Thatcher's position was beginning to look less
secure, not least following the resignation of Nigel Lawson as

Chancellor of the Exchequer, ostensibly as a result of Mrs Thatcher's leadership style. In November 1989 Sir Anthony Meyer, a little-known back-bencher, formally challenged Mrs Thatcher in a leadership contest. He was not, himself, a serious contender for office. However, his challenge could be seen in two ways: either as a simple expression of dissatisfaction with Mrs Thatcher's leadership, or as a 'stalking horse' candidate; that is a candidate who wounds his opponent sufficiently and then allows a more serious candidate to move in for the kill. In some ways, this was how Mrs Thatcher's challenge in 1975 was viewed. Meyer's challenge did not wound Thatcher in the immediate short term. She won the ballot comfortably. However, a significant number of Conservative MPs did not vote for her: 33 voted for Meyer while 27 deliberately abstained.

In the long term then, it was clear that there was disquiet in the parliamentary party. Thatcher continued in office but faced a very difficult year as result of the introduction of the 'Poll Tax' in England and Wales as well as the resignation of key Cabinet colleagues, in particular Geoffrey Howe. Sure enough, November 1990 saw Mrs Thatcher challenged again, this time by the heavyweight Michael Heseltine. In the first ballot Thatcher polled more votes than Heseltine, but was four votes short of the required majority. A second ballot was therefore necessary. Thatcher did not immediately resign, however. This might have been expected since so many of her colleagues had voted against her. The prospect of a divided parliamentary party loomed large. In the end she was persuaded to resign after it was predicted that she could not win a second ballot. At that point two of her Cabinet colleagues entered the race: the Foreign Secretary, Douglas Hurd, and the less well-known Chancellor, John Major.

Prior to Thatcher's withdrawal it had been widely assumed that Douglas Hurd would assume the leadership. A respected and able Foreign Secretary, he appeared to be the man that would be able to unite an apparently disunited party. By contrast, John Major was far less well known. He had been elevated to Foreign Secretary very suddenly in the summer of 1989 before becoming Chancellor of the Exchequer 3 months later when Lawson resigned. He appeared to be too lightweight compared with Hurd and Heseltine, yet he emerged quickly as a front-runner just as Hurd's ambitions receded. In the ballot that ensued Major won most votes but was two short of an overall majority (see Table 3.1). However, Heseltine and Hurd withdrew and John Major became the new leader of the Conservative Party and Prime Minister.

The process appeared to have been successful and decisive. Certainly, the opinion poll fortunes of the Conservatives soared and as a party, it appeared to have been able to achieve a remarkable feat – namely that voters perceived the blame for political and economic difficulties to rest with the previous leadership (Sanders, 1992:200). In short, John Major's administration was given a clean slate; but the matter did not come to a close. It was perhaps inevitable that there should be some bitterness within the party as a whole that the most successful Prime Minister in living memory had been removed. While the voters may have given John Major a clean slate, the Thatcher legacy lived on within the Conservative Party, despite the fact that Major had been Thatcher's choice as a successor.

It was thought that Major would suffer from the shadow of Thatcher's leadership as long as he had not won a General Election. When he did lead the Conservative Party to victory in 1992, however, the shadow did not recede and if anything became darker. With Major having won an election he could reasonably claim to have been victorious on his own terms, yet he faced constant and increasing criticism from Thatcher supporters that he was betraying the legacy of the previous administrations. To compound such problems, Major faced at least two major political problems which Thatcher had not and which served to exacerbate his difficulties. First, unlike Thatcher, he did not enjoy a substantial majority in the House of Commons. As a result, it became more important to acknowledge back-bench dissent. Secondly, he was required to negotiate and ratify critical European legislation in the form of the Maastricht Treaty. As a result of these and other difficulties which Major's government had brought upon itself the subject of Major's leadership appeared to be under constant discussion.

Major had the advantage that, after the 1990 leadership contest, it had been decided to make a challenge to an incumbent leader more difficult by requiring not only a proposer and seconder for a challenge, but also for 10 per cent of the parliamentary party to write to the Chairman of the 1922 Committee requesting an election. Given that the Conservatives had 336 MPs after the 1992 election, significant dissent was evidently required to trigger an election and a 'stalking horse' candidate such as Sir Anthony Meyer was less likely to come forward. Nevertheless, there was the constant expectation that a challenge would occur as Conservative fortunes appeared to slide.

In 1994, then, a challenge was widely expected. However, since the whip had been withdrawn from some of Major's sternest critics, opponents were unable to raise sufficiently large numbers to mount a contest. The whip restored, many expected a contest in the Autumn of 1995. Major, however, took an unprecedented step and forced a contest by resigning the leadership in June 1995. Signalling that he would contest any election, he sought to pre-empt a challenge. This was a considerable risk and was greeted with great surprise. In the end there was only one challenger, the Welsh Secretary John Redwood, who was a clear candidate of the Thatcherite right. Many thought that Redwood would gain suffi-cient votes or at least prompt many to abstain, thus wounding the Prime Minister. This would force a second ballot where it was widely assumed there would be contest between the right-wing Michael Portillo and the more leftish Michael Heseltine. Major survived the ballot, although Redwood polled an impressive num-ber of votes and, combined with abstentions, denied Major approximately a third of the votes available (see Table 3.1). Never-theless, there was no need for a second ballot and Major now looked safe at least until the next General Election, particularly since it was decided that there should not be the opportunity for a further contest that year.

We must consider, then, what we can detect from Conservative leadership contests. First, whether the leadership is decided through a ballot or through appointment, one thing seems clear: that the Conservative Party (or at least its parliamentary wing) prizes one thing above all others: electoral success. Leaders who have repeatedly lost elections or who appear to be an electoral liability in future General Elections are removed. The experience of Margaret Thatcher shows clearly that regardless of how suc-cessful leaders have been in the past they must be seen to be an electoral asset in the future. All this assumes, of course, that leaders can have an influence on election results; a point upon which political scientists are in disagreement; for while few would doubt the indirect influence of leaders, through party policy shifts,

Table 3.1 **Conservative Party leadership elections 1965–95.**

Year	First ballot		Second ballot		Leader elected
	Candidate	Votes	Candidate	Votes	
1965	E. Heath	150	Not required		Heath
	R. Maudling	133			
	E. Powell	15			
	Abstentions	6			
1975	M. Thatcher	130	M. Thatcher	146	Thatcher
	E. Heath	119	W. Whitelaw	79	
	H. Fraser	16	J. Prior	19	
	Abstentions	11	G. Howe	19	
			J. Peyton	11	
			Abstentions	2	
1989	M. Thatcher	314	Not required		Thatcher
	A. Meyer	33			
	Abstentions	27			
1990	M. Thatcher	204	J. Major	185	Major
	M. Heseltine	152	M. Heseltine	131	
	Abstentions	16	D. Hurd	56	
			Abstentions	0	
1995	J. Major	218	Not required		Major
	J. Redwood	89			
	Abstentions	20			

Source: (1965–90): Bogdanor (1994:85).

for example, opinion is divided as to whether the personality of a leader has much direct influence on election results.[3]

Secondly, while the Conservative Party is hierarchical in its structure, it is quite straightforward to challenge and even remove the leader. In part because of the narrow electorate (or 'selectorate'), it is probably easier to unseat the leader of the Conservative Party than it is to remove the leader of any other major political party.[4] This may be explained in part by the fact that MPs may have different interests from party members, namely the retention of their seats.

[3] For an excellent attempt to examine this issue see Crewe and King, 1994.
[4] Interestingly, there is strong support for the electorate to be widened to elect the leader; 50 per cent of party members support one member – one vote for this process. See Whiteley, Seyd and Richardson, 1994:266.

The selection of parliamentary candidates

The selection of candidates in the Conservative Party is complex and is an area where constituency parties can have an impact, although central party organisation has the ability to influence the process strongly.[5] In the initial stage prospective candidates apply to Conservative Central Office, who define a 'pool of eligibles' for vacant seats (Norris and Lowenduski, 1995:35). Admission to the approved list is gained through quality of application, then a Central Office interview. Those that survive this process are then required to attend a residential selection board, similar to those employed by the armed forces for officer recruitment. Only after prospective candidates have passed this test are they able to apply to constituencies for vacant seats. The constituencies then select candidates through three stages: the constituency selection committee, then the constituency executive committee, before finally putting the candidates before the constituency members at a general meeting of the constituency association. Candidates can only be presented to the general constituency association after approval from the executive committee. The result of this is that, on occasion, the ordinary members are not presented with a choice, which has caused division in the past.[6] Nevertheless, ordinary party members can have the final say on whether or not a candidate is adopted. That is not to say, however, that the local party is totally sovereign since the centre effectively controls the supply of prospective candidates through its approved list. Moreover, the Standing Advisory Committee on Candidates has the power of veto over any local party selection (Blackburn, 1995:218). What then is the outcome of this selection process on the composition of parliamentary candidates?

The social background of Conservative MPs and candidates

Certain patterns emerge from an examination of Conservative MPs and candidates from the last three elections. First of all,

[5] For an excellent account of British parliamentary recruitment which explores the process both from the parties' and candidates' perspectives, see Norris and Lowenduski, 1995.
[6] Certainly, in the Conservative Party member survey, 41 per cent disagreed with Conservative Central Office having a greater role in candidate selection, while 31 per cent supported the notion. See Whiteley et al., 1994:265.

Table 3.2   Sex, age and ethnic background of Conservative MPs and candidates.

Year	1992		1987		1983	
(%)	Elected	Defeated	Elected	Defeated	Elected	Defeated
Male	94	87	95	89	97	89
Female	6	13	5	11	3	11
20–29	0	13	1	20	3	19
30–39	14	38	19	44	22	50
40–49	38	31	39	25	35	22
50–59	33	14	30	9	29	8
60–69	14	3	11	2	10	1
70–79	1	0	1	0	1	0
Median age	48	39	48	37	47	36
White	99	98	100	98	100	98
Non-white	<1	2	0	2	0	2
n	336	298	376	257	397	236

Note: totals may not add up to 100% due to rounding.
Source: derived from Butler and Kavanagh (1992, 1988, 1984).

Conservative MPs and candidates are largely male. There has been a small growth in the proportion of women MPs, but this is minute compared with the proportion of men. Secondly, while the median age of MPs and candidates has remained fairly stable (47–48 and 36–39 years, respectively), it is apparent that there has been a decline in the proportion of both MPs and candidates under 40 years of age. Finally, the composition of MPs and candidates is almost exclusively white (Table 3.2). Indeed, 1992 saw the first non-white Conservative MP elected.

Much is frequently made of the educational background of MPs. In the period under examination here, it is evident that there has been a decline in the proportion of both public school educated MPs and candidates. Nevertheless, those with such a background still constitute 62 per cent of MPs. There has also been an increase in the proportion of graduates generally. They now constitute 86 per cent of the Conservative parliamentary ranks. Moreover, this increased proportion of graduates tend to have come from non-Oxbridge institutions. Nevertheless, Oxbridge graduates still constitute nearly half of the parliamentary party and tend to be more successful at getting elected than non-Oxbridge graduates (Table 3.3).

Table 3.3   **Educational background of Conservative MPs and candidates.**

Year	1992		1987		1983	
(%)	Elected	Defeated	Elected	Defeated	Elected	Defeated
Elementary	0	0	0	<1	0	<1
Secondary	6	13	7	10	7	12
Public school	8	4	11	5	17	13
Secondary+univ/poly/college	32	51	25	49	23	47
Public school+univ/poly/college	54	32	57	37	53	28
(%)						
Eton/Harrow/Winchester	13	4	15	7	16	8
Other public schools	49	32	53	35	54	33
All public schools	62	35	68	41	70	40
Oxbridge	45	16	44	22	48	22
Other univ/poly/college	41	67	38	63	28	53
All univ/poly/college	86	83	82	85	76	75
n	336	298	376	257	397	236

Note: totals may not add up to 100% due to rounding.
Source: derived from Butler and Kavanagh (1992, 1988, 1984).

Table 3.4   **Occupational background of of Conservative MPs and candidates.**

Year	1992		1987		1983	
(%)	Elected	Defeated	Elected	Defeated	Elected	Defeated
Education	7	8	7	11	5	13
Legal	18	15	17	20	21	15
Other professions	15	13	18	15	19	14
Business	38	44	37	34	36	36
Political activity	6	6	6	5	3	2
Publishing/journalism	8	3	7	5	8	6
Miscellaneous	7	11	8	6	8	9
Manual workers	1	0	2	3	1	5
n	336	298	376	257	397	236

Note: totals may not add up to 100% due to rounding.
Source: derived from Butler and Kavanagh (1992, 1988, 1984).

Education: teachers in higher education, further education and schools.
Legal: barrister, solicitor.
Other professions: doctor/dentist, architect/surveyor, civil/chartered engineer, accountant, civil servant/local government, armed services, consultants, scientific/research.
Business: director, executive, commerce/insurance, management/clerical, general business.
Political activity: politician/political organiser.
Publishing/journalism: publishing and journalism.
Miscellaneous: farmer, housewife, student, miscellaneous white collar.
Manual worker: skilled worker, semi/unskilled worker, miner.

In terms of occupation, Conservative MPs are drawn largely from business and the professions. Business provides the largest proportion of members. Overall, the occupational make-up of MPs has been remarkably stable; yet we can detect an increase in the number of candidates from a business background, possibly as a result of the strongly pro-business stance of the Thatcher government (Table 3.4).

Funding

Few aspects of political parties raise as much vitriol as the ways in which the parties raise their money. It is, of course, a vitally important issue. At the same time, it is an area which provokes numerous attacks and accusations, many of which have no founding in any empirical findings. Innuendo and the reliance on journalistic inference is all too frequently the order of the day. The Conservative Party is generally the most frequent target of these attacks, principally, it must be said, because of the self-imposed secrecy that surrounds its financial affairs, and also because of an apparently international suspicion of the motives of anyone (especially businesses) giving money away. In this section then, we will examine the 'facts' (such as they are available).

While we have long been able to ascertain the proportion of income that comes from the constituency organisations, one has only been able to speculate upon what proportion of donations to the Conservative Party had come from corporate sources and what proportion were from individuals. The reason for this is that published Conservative Party accounts give little detail and do not

Table 3.5 **Estimated sources of Conservative Central Office income.**

	1950–64	*1967/8–1973/4*	*1974/5–1977/8*
Institutions	67.4	62.5	56.3
Individuals	16.9	15.6	14.1
Constituency quotas	11.9	19.2	21.5
Other	3.9	2.8	8.0
Total	100.0	100.0	100.0

Source: **Pinto-Duschinsky (1981:139).**

Table 3.6   Proportion of Conservative Central Office income comprised of institutional and individual funding 1992–3.

	(£000s)	(% of total)
Corporate donations	4,300	37.3
Individual donations	3,516	30.5
Total central income	11,520	100.0

Note: the figures here differ from previous published information in the light of new information.

Sources: oral evidence to the Select Committee on Home Affairs, 16/6/93, Conservative Party Accounts 1993, private information.

distinguish between corporate and individual income. Pinto-Duschinsky, however, made some estimates for the post-war period until 1978 (Table 3.5).

Despite these estimates, it has been difficult to be clear about the extent of the sources of income since company donations have apparently declined in importance in recent years (Pinto-Duschinsky, 1989a; Fisher, 1994a). This trend was confirmed by the Conservative Party in the Select Committee on Home Affairs' investigations into the funding of political parties and it was here that the then Party Chairman, Sir Norman Fowler, revealed greater detail for the financial year 1992–3 (Table 3.6).

The proportions of companies making direct political donations are small. In surveys covering the late 1980s and early 1990s, only around 12 per cent of the top 1000 companies and 6 per cent of the top 4000 companies made a political donation (Fisher, 1995:182). Moreover, British companies do not make large political donations relative to what they could potentially make available. The mean donation during 1991–2 was £16,085 and donations as a proportion of profit have tended to be very small (a mean of 0.1 per cent) (Fisher, 1994b:691).

In recent years there have been important developments in techniques of party fund-raising which indicate not only a shift away from institutional sources of finance, but also possibly a new era of Conservative Party finance (see Table 3.7). First, a trend that has been apparent in recent years has been the re-emergence of personal donations in the finances of the Conservative Party to the extent that some individual donations have exceeded any made by

Table 3.7   Conservative Party central income 1988/9–1994/5.

| | 1988–9 | | 1989–90 | | 1990–1 | | 1991–2 | | 1992–3 | | 1993–4 | | 1994–5 | |
	£000s	% of total central income	£000s	% of total central income	£000s	% of total central income	£000s	% of total central income	£000s	% of total central income	£000s	% of total central income	£000s	% of total central income
Donations	6,718	77.7	7,090	77.5	10,556	80.9	20,044	85.5	7,816	67.8	9,372	66.5	12,729	83.2
Constituency quota income	1,191	13.8	1,211	13.2	1,281	9.8	1,288	5.5	1,051	9.1	745	5.3	865	5.7
Sundry income	736	8.5	851	9.3	1,205	9.2	2,117	9.0	2,653	23.0	3,977	28.2	1,713	11.2
Total central income	8,645	100.0	9,152	100.0	13,042	100.0	23,449	100.0	11,520	100.0	14,094	100.0	15,307	100.0
Net assets (liabilities)	NA		NA		NA		(17,347)		(19,200)		(17,402)		(15,018)	

Notes: donations – all corporate and individual. sundry income – primarily from conferences, sales, services and other. NA – not applicable.
Source: Conservative Party accounts.

a corporation (Pinto-Duschinsky, 1989a:210; Fisher, 1994a). More-over, in 1994–5 the growth in donations was largely brought about by individual direct mail contributions as well as a 'substantial legacy'. This meant that contributions from individuals accounted for two-thirds of all donations (Conservative Party, 1995:8). Additionally, there has been an apparent growth in donations emanating from individuals abroad (Fisher, 1994a).

Secondly, there has been a growth of other forms of income (classified in Table 3.7 as Sundry income) which largely comprises commercial activities manifesting themselves through financial services, conferences and sales. This technique of fund-raising has grown quickly, providing 28.2 per cent of Conservative central income in 1993–4; a growth of more than 300 per cent in 5 years. However, in 1994–5 the amount raised was apparently much lower, although this can be explained partially by changes in accounting practices (Conservative Party, 1995:8).

Thirdly, the proportion raised from constituency quota income has fallen considerably. This is compounded by the continuing and projected fall in Conservative Party membership which, as Whiteley *et al.* note in their study of Conservative Party members, is itself a vague concept (Whiteley *et al.*, 1994). This is illustrated well by the fact that membership of the Conservative Party carries no set fee. Whiteley *et al.* found that 2 per cent of party members paid nothing for their membership. Of the majority that did pay some fee, the median figure was £10. However, members' annual financial input is often greater since local parties indulge in many rounds of additional fund-raising. When that is included the median member's contribution was £20 (Whiteley *et al.*, 1994:75–6).

Ideology

In some ways the notion of a Conservative ideology is an anomaly. Many Conservatives point out that since conservatism offers no abstract notions such as justice or rights, it is debatable whether it should be considered as an ideology (Eccelshall *et al.*, 1984:80). Indeed, many might claim that the fact that it is not an ideology in these terms is one of the strengths of conservatism. Certainly, the party has shown itself to be very adept at shifting ideological position throughout its parliamentary history. Conservatism is fundamentally reactive in its outlook, responding to other ideas, either through resistance or through pragmatic change. Nevertheless, other writers have argued that a broader notion of ideology is preferable, and thus with conservatism and indeed the Conservative Party, one can identify distinct strands of thought which may reasonably called ideological (Eccleshall *et al.*, 1984:81; Goodwin, 1987:139).

The Conservative Party is a traditionalist one. While during some periods it has displayed some reforming zeal, the emphasis has been upon conserving many aspects of the existing order and existing traditions. It has a respect for established practices and institutions. This also takes its form in a strong nationalism. That is not to say that the Conservative Party is opposed to change. Rather, it prefers evolutionary change to revolutionary change. It is an arch pragmatist in that change is adopted when deemed necessary, but only in order that traditions themselves remain. This approach gels very well with a second strand of Conservative ideology, the view of the organic society.

This strand takes the view that society develops as an organism. An analogy would be a tree, developing and growing stronger as each year passes. The implications of such a view are many. First, it emphasises a respect for history by arguing that societies cannot be created, they must evolve over time. Secondly, it is a view that can be used to justify existing orders within society. The growing society relies upon each component playing its role. Any radical diversion from this principle will threaten society's continued development. Thus, the Conservative Party can justify different and often long-term roles and positions in society as being essential for society's health. Inequality is thus inevitable and desirable because each person must play their role in society's development and resultant strength. Moreover, authority is essential for the maintenance of this 'natural' order.

Thirdly, Conservatives are political sceptics. They reject abstract principles in politics such as justice, rights and equality and prefer the practical approach of society developing upon the knowledge of experience. This view is linked to their suspicions of humanity's inherent nature. Conservatives see humanity as flawed. Typically, this has been associated with the doctrine of 'original sin'[7] but

---

[7] The idea of 'original sin' relates to biblical tales which tell us that Eve's succumbing to temptation with the serpent is evidence of man's inherent fallibility. Thus man (humanity) is always flawed in character and will naturally act in selfish and often apparently irrational ways.

secular Conservatives, while rejecting the biblical origins, have nevertheless shared the scepticism about the 'goodness of man'. If humanity is flawed, then abstract theory is unpredictable and potentially damaging.

A consequence of the Conservative Party's emphasis upon organicism and scepticism is the support for capitalism. However, throughout its history the party has approached capitalism in different ways. Perhaps the most well established approach within the party is the so-called 'One Nation' view, espoused first by Disraeli and pursued more recently by Macmillan and in his later period, Heath. This approach, while embracing capitalism at its heart, is one whereby the state takes an active role in attempting to avoid great social disparities. It is a paternalist approach that seeks to involve the state in the welfare of all the nation. In this way it is hoped that one nation will be preserved, thus avoiding the dangers of a deeply divided society.

By contrast other Conservatives have placed greater emphasis on liberalism, especially in the economic sphere. Mrs Thatcher is the person most readily identified with that tradition, but it is one that has periodically surfaced in the Conservative Party ever since Peel's leadership (Garner and Kelly, 1993:75). The economic liberal approach seeks to avoid, where possible, any role for the state in economic life. It rejects paternalism in the economic sphere and seeks to place greater emphasis upon free enterprise, released from state intervention (or interference as it is often referred). Such an economically liberal viewpoint was of course taken by Mrs Thatcher and her mentor, Keith Joseph, but they were not the first to espouse such thoughts in recent times. Edward Heath, while often associated with the principles of One Nation Toryism, espoused strong free market ideas during the period of opposition in the 1960s and came to power upon a platform of proto-Thatcherite policies in 1970. Similarly Enoch Powell, while more famous for his views on race, was a keen exponent of economic liberalism long before Mrs Thatcher had become leader of the Conservative Party; nor were Heath and Powell economic mavericks in the broad history of the Conservative Party.

What is significant is that while there has been a free market element within the Conservative Party since the nineteenth century, and especially since the collapse of the Liberal Party which saw many Liberals turn to the Conservatives, its views have not always been given credence. Just as with other ideas, economic standpoints tend to cycle; or to be more cynical, there are fashions in economics. Thus, when individuals such as Powell were advocating free market solutions during the early 1960s they were largely overlooked, as free market economics had little mainstream credibility at that time. However, 15 years later the economic climate had changed; monetarism was respectable and Mrs Thatcher's approach became dominant, while exponents of One Nation Toryism entered the wilderness.

What distinguishes the economic liberalism of the Conservative Party from liberalism in general, however, is the approach to social matters. It is misleading to consider politics as occupying one issue dimension. Frequently, we talk of *left* and *right* in politics, often referring to stances on broad economic policies. However, there are arguably many other dimensions to political debate, not least that of liberalism and authoritarianism. This dimension refers to views on areas such as public morals, law and order and tolerance. Here, we can clearly distinguish the Conservative Party from liberalism. On many of these issues Conservatives prefer authority to liberty. That is not to give the terms a normative flavour. More to emphasise that the Conservative Party has tended to emphasise strong law and order policies, a very traditional approach to public morals with an emphasis on the family and marriage, and has favoured the established church. Ironically, economic liberals such as Margaret Thatcher and Enoch Powell have been least liberal on this dimension: Powell with his attitudes towards race and Thatcher with hers towards public morals. It is the paradox of Conservative liberalism; where economic *laissez-faire*-ism may be said to be in potential conflict with social paternalism.

Essentially, there are many strands of ideology in the Conservative Party: religious and secular; *laissez-faire* and paternalist. These strands are always present but are emphasised to a greater or lesser extent at different periods of time. Moreover, Whiteley *et al.* (1994), in their study of Conservative Party members, demonstrated that these various strands are apparent at the party's grass roots. They identified four major ideological components within the Conservative Party: traditionalism, progressivism, individualism and moral traditionalism. Traditionalism referred primarily to issues of preservation of institutions and the position of Britain, law and order and immigration; progressivism covered the more paternalistic views, emphasising support for welfare and controls on the free market; individualism, by contrast, displayed support for greater economic liberalism and finally, moral traditionalism displayed opposition to areas such as abortion and divorce.

This is not necessarily to suggest, however, that the Conservative Party has no encompassing ideology. Rather, we may perhaps refer to an ideology of governing. Just as the Conservatives reject abstract theory, so they desire to always be in government; they see themselves as the natural party of government. To that end, the party has been very successful at pragmatic change in order to achieve and maintain power. In true reactive style the party has noted the public mood and the relevant strand of conservatism has come to the fore. Thus, sensing the popularity of many of Labour's policy implementations in 1945–51, the Conservatives vowed to maintain many of these achievements and indeed sought to outdo the Labour Party, promising to expand public house-building. By contrast, in the late 1970s, they capitalised on public disquiet with trade unions and promised reform. Similarly in 1990, sensing the growing unpopularity of some strands of Mrs Thatcher's policies, the party sought to present a more collectivist face in the form of a new leader and apparently less right-wing policy goals.

Measuring ideological change

One way of testing the ideological changes within a party is by examining election manifestos. Manifestos are a statement of a party's aims and values and can often offer an addition to abstract ideological goals, because they are couched in the political circumstances of the day. However, it seems that few citizens actually read even one of the manifestos, let alone all of them, and the result is that the interpretation of the subject matter tends to be conducted by the mass media. The inevitable result is that certain manifesto areas are highlighted more than others and frequently journalistic interpretation of the ideological scope of a manifesto is accepted uncritically.

A more objective approach (although perhaps controversial) is through a technique called content analysis. This technique essentially dissects text into its component parts and in this case, categorises statements and promises as being libertarian, socialist, and so on. Once this process has been undertaken, one can then analyse if *text a* is more libertarian than *text b*. As long as the categorisation is consistent, we can evaluate manifestos (or any piece of text) in a manner which reduces our subjective interpretations. Of course, the initial categorisation is influenced by subjectivity, but this operates at a lower level than simply evaluating text as a whole.

This technique has been used to examine British General Election manifestos since 1979 by the political scientist, Richard Topf (Topf, 1994). In an intriguing article, Topf attempted to evaluate whether there had been ideological consistency in the three main parties' manifestos over time. Topf broke the ideological content of manifestos down into six principal areas, or value clusters. These were egalitarianism, socialism, communitarianism, traditionalism, *laissez-faire*-ism and individualism. He then reduced these into left- and right-wing ideologies; left being the combination of egalitarianism, socialism and communitarianism, and right being traditionalism, *laissez-faire*-ism and individualism. Once this has been done, we can measure whether parties' manifestos have become more right wing, more left wing or remained consistent. We can also compare each party's manifesto with the total for all manifestos which illustrates whether the ideological climate as a whole has remained constant. For example, we might argue that after the 1945–51 Labour government, the political climate as a whole was more left wing than it had been 20 years previously, and perhaps that the experience of the Thatcher governments has shifted the political goalposts to the right. Table 3.8 below reveals the Conservative and total manifesto scores since 1979. The figures are the percentage of the manifesto that is right wing minus the percentage that is left wing. Thus a positive score indicates a right of centre manifesto, and a negative score a left of centre. Similarly,

Table 3.8   **The balance of ideology on Conservative manifestos.**

	Conservative manifestos (%)	*All manifestos (%)*
1979	37	–1
1983	49	24
1987	53	49
1992	56	52

Source: Topf (1994:164).

the greater the figure (positive or negative) the more strong right or left wing the manifesto.

Here we see that from 1979, the Conservative manifestos became increasingly right wing, registering a positive score of 37 per cent in 1979 and one of 56 per cent in 1992. On this basis, then, it would appear that the Conservative Party have become more right wing over this period. However, it is important to compare these results with those of all the manifestos. These scores reveal that in 1979, manifestos as a whole were very slightly left of centre, thus suggesting the radicalism of the Conservatives' manifesto at that election. Similarly, there is a big difference between the Conservatives' position in 1983 and the overall score for that election, again revealing a markedly right-wing position. However, we should also note that the score for all the manifestos has consistently and quite rapidly risen, indicating that the political climate as a whole has shifted rightwards. It is against this backdrop then, that we should consider the Conservatives in 1987 and 1992. While these manifestos were more right wing than their predecessors, there is only a small difference between the Conservatives' position and that of all of the manifestos. The effect of this is that what were essentially very right-wing manifestos in 1987 and 1992 appear moderate in the prevailing political climate. Thus we can say that in absolute terms the Conservatives are more right wing than before, but relative to the wider political picture, they are now far less radical.[8]

Groupings and factions

The notion of factions in such an apparently hierarchial party may be seen as something of an anomaly but groupings do exist within the Conservative Party. This is partly a result of different strands of ideological thought. Indeed, as Barnes notes: 'Because Conservatism is not a fully worked-out ideology, it lays itself open to ideological projects of one kind or another and to the possibility of factionalism' (Barnes, 1994:340). However, the groupings and factions that do exist exert themselves in very different ways and in recent years one issue above all others has precipitated factionalism in the Conservative Party since the crisis of Tariff Reform: Europe.

[8] For further details of the study summarised here, see Topf (1994).

Formal groupings have existed since the last century. The oldest, for example, is the Primrose League, formed in 1883 which sought to encourage the social contact of grass-roots Conservatives. Today for example, there is the Charter Movement, formed in the early 1980s, which campaigns for more conventional modes of democratic involvement within the Conservative Party. The group publishes a regular newsletter, *Charter News*, and has long campaigned for a directly elected policy committee and greater accountability in the financial affairs of the party, among other matters. Essentially, the main thrust of the Charter Movement's campaigns have been the perceived remoteness of Conservative Central Office from the grass-roots of the party. The Charter Movement has been joined in their campaigns by the Party Reform Steering Committee with whom it has strong links, and have campaigned together for the responsibility for party finances to fall within the domain of the National Union rather than Conservative Central Office (Whiteley *et al.*, 1994:32). Both groups have periodically been highly visible, particularly over questions of Conservative Party finance, and have apparently scored some success in the setting up by Conservative Central Office of a committee to oversee party funds (*Guardian*, 4/8/93). However, in all other areas they have consistently been ignored and there may be a case for arguing that their prominence owes more to the fact that they exist as dissenters within the Conservative Party than anything else. Certainly, within the Conservative Party they are not considered to be a powerful force, although as Whiteley *et al.* argue, greater democratic involvement in the party may be a necessary development if the Conservative Party is to arrest its membership decline (Whiteley *et al.*, 1994: 237–8).

Most other groups have had an ideological edge to them. The Monday Club, for example, represents the traditionalist wing in its support for and concern about Britain's world role. Typically, the Monday Club has taken a very nationalist approach to matters such as defence and immigration. Other ideological groups in the party have been largely concerned with the paternalist and libertarian debates within the Conservative Party. The Bow Group and the Tory Reform Group represent the paternalist 'One Nation' tradition and have been largely on the defensive since the election of Mrs Thatcher to the leadership. Both have members from Parliament although the Bow Group also has a grass-roots membership and policy groups as well.

Economic libertarians within the party have been represented since 1973 by the Selsdon Group. The group was set up as a response to Heath having apparently abandoned the free market policies of 'Selsdon Man', a phrase coined to describe Heath's original proto-Thatcherite approach partly developed at a Shadow Cabinet meeting in the Selsdon Park Hotel in Surrey. Other libertarians were sufficiently committed to Mrs Thatcher's policies to form another group: the No Turning Back Group. This was set up in 1988 in order to preserve the changes that Thatcherism had brought about and has become more significant since Thatcher's demise. It is committed to continuing the pressure for cuts in taxes and public expenditure and counts many prominent MPs among its membership. Certainly, it is continuing pressure from this group which has helped fuel continuing speculation about the leadership of John Major. Indeed it was one of its number, John Redwood, who stood against John Major in 1995. Importantly, many of this group have also continued to support Thatcher's *latterday* stance upon Europe. I stress latterday because, although Thatcher had always taken a stance opposing the level of Britain's financial contribution to the EC, she did support Britain's entry in 1973 and more importantly, signed the Single European Act of 1987 which precipitated the extension of European integration.

It is the issue of Europe which has most exposed divisions and factions within the party. It was the partly the question of Europe which precipitated Thatcher's fall from grace and it has been Europe that has presented John Major with so many difficulties. There are many dimensions to the European issue, but the principal one which divides Conservatives (particularly MPs) is the issue of national sovereignty.[9] Sovereignty is itself a thorny and potentially vague issue which can lead to a variety of interpretations. Indeed, so vague can the notion be that politicians may take apparently contradictory positions. A good example is Mrs Thatcher's support for the European Single Market, which was not seen as a threat to national sovereignty, despite its opposition to national tariffs, while opposing other challenges to national sovereignty such as extensions of the powers of the European Parliament. Nevertheless national sovereignty, as it is generally interpreted, is

[9] For an excellent investigation into Conservative divisions on the question of Europe, see Baker, Ludlam and Gamble (1993) and Baker *et al.* (1995).

the ability for a nation's government to act unconstrained by other nations or institutions and to retain the decision making processes and veto over issues which directly affect that nation. Of course, no nation has complete national sovereignty in as much as the economy and the decisions that flow from it, including taxation and interest rates, for example, are to an extent influenced on a global scale through financial markets. What is clear in debates about national sovereignty and Europe is that while some threats are seen as inevitable, others are deemed worthy of resistance.

Questions of national sovereignty have divided the Conservative Party in a variety of areas, such as the powers of the European Parliament, the harmonisation of workers' rights, the retention of the veto in the Council of Ministers through Qualified Majority Voting and the power of the European Court of Justice. However, perhaps the most heated divisions have arisen over currency harmonisation through the Exchange Rate Mechanism (ERM) and European Monetary Union (EMU). The Exchange Rate Mechanism was a device whereby currencies within the European Union were maintained within a pre-set band. That is to say, governments and their central banks were committed to intervene in the currency markets in order to ensure that the value of a domestic currency did not vary a great deal in relation to other currencies within the Exchange Rate Mechanism. Britain had long resisted entry into the ERM and the issue sparked strong divisions between Nigel Lawson (then Chancellor) who supported entry and Mrs Thatcher who, for a long period of time, did not.

Ultimately, Britain did enter the ERM just prior to Mrs Thatcher's downfall, but by September 1992 Britain could no longer sustain membership at the rate at which it had entered and withdrew. The failure of Britain's period in the ERM is cited by so-called Euro-sceptics as an example of the failure of the EU to operate beyond the basic free market. It is, however, the second stage of currency harmonisation, EMU of which the ERM is a precursor, which highlights such divisions. Under EMU there are plans for some or all member states of the European Union to develop a single currency and abandon their own. This is seen by Euro-sceptics as not only an economic question but also a constitutional one, since nation states would lose at least some of their ability to determine economic and fiscal policies. It is an issue which has bitterly divided Conservative MPs, resulting in so-called

Euro-rebels voting against their own party on the issue of Europe in the House of Commons. This resulted in these MPs losing the whip of the Conservative Party for a period of time, which technically denied the Conservatives of their overall majority. It is also a source of division among those who have continued to support the government; it was, for example, a key issue highlighted by John Redwood in his leadership challenge to John Major. Moreover, among party members, while many share Euro-sceptic views, a substantial minority (perhaps up to a third) are ardent Europeanists (Whiteley et al., 1994:56–8); thus it is clear that divisions over Europe extend from the elite of the party to the grass roots.

Recent history

The recent history of the Conservative Party has been both triumphant but at times quite desperate. It should be set against three key factors: continued electoral triumph at national level, the fall of Mrs Thatcher and the challenge of Europe. In one sense, it might be surprising to speak of problems for the Conservative Party given their success in General Elections. Under Mrs Thatcher, it took government from Labour in 1979 and embarked upon radical and at times unpopular, changes, to British political and economic life. It won the next election with a very large majority, continued with its radical changes and then won the next election, also with a very comfortable majority. Then, when the party appeared to be in trouble, it chose a new leader who was able to win a fourth General Election victory, albeit with a reduced majority. The lesson from this period could easily be that the Conservatives are so adept at winning elections that problems can always be overcome. Moreover, the continuing success of the Conservative Party has allowed it to pursue its ideas for a long period of time, thus giving many of the changes that have been made an impression, at least, of permanence. It has not been forced to interrupt its programme of change with the inconvenience of the alternation of government.

That is perhaps to paint the party too rosy a picture. Two shadows continue to fall over the future success of the party. The first is the fall of Margaret Thatcher from the leadership of the party. As we have seen, Thatcher was a very successful leader in terms of winning elections; yet, when it seemed to the elements of the parliamentary party that her leadership might become an electoral liability, she was removed in one of the most dramatic periods of British politics in recent years. However, the period when she was removed was not the first time she had been very unpopular. The early years of Thatcher's premiership were also difficult, but she survived. The key significance of Thatcher's downfall in 1990 was that after 11 broadly successful years in office and three election victories she had developed significant support, not only among the party in general, but among many members of the parliamentary party and those who were selected as candidates for subsequent elections. The result has been that while Thatcher may be gone from the House of Commons (she retired at the 1992 Election and was elevated to the House of Lords), her legacy lives on among many MPs who wish to see her political agenda remain. This has caused continuing problems for John Major. Despite the fact that he has, at the time of writing, been Prime Minister for almost half the time that Thatcher was, he and his government are still subject to attack from those who view his government's policies as having drifted too far from those of Mrs Thatcher. This might have been expected during the period following his election as leader until the 1992 election, because that administration had been elected on the basis of the Thatcher leadership, but if anything the attacks have become more severe after Major won the election. Thus, he has had to face strong opposition within the fields of economic policy and the issue of Europe in particular. This has resulted in significant defeats in the House of Commons and a challenge for the leadership of the party. Despite his 5 years in power the legacy of Mrs Thatcher has often made Mr Major appear a temporary leader living on borrowed time.

This has been strongly reinforced by divisions within the party over the issue of Europe. As we have seen, the role of Britain within Europe has been a continuing problem for Major and the Conservative Party. In some ways, he was handed a poisoned chalice. It was Mrs Thatcher, after all, who signed the Single European Act which was a precursor to many of the factors that have so divided the party. Major then did not initiate many of the European problems. In fact, Europe has on occasions been a source of strength for Major. His negotiations in the arrangements for the Maastricht Treaty, where he secured options for Britain to opt out of legislation such as the Social Chapter, were widely praised yet by and large he has been attacked for his stance upon Europe largely by Eurosceptics. The result has been that the Conservative Party appears to be deeply divided on the issue. Moreover, the party has suffered electorally for its unclear stance on the European question. Notwithstanding the protest element of European elections, the Conservatives gained only 41 per cent (see Appendix II) of the European seats in 1989 and by 1994 this had fallen to 21 per cent.

Conclusions

In conclusion, we may observe a number of key aspects of the Conservative Party. First, while the party may appear to be firmly hierarchical it is not quite as it seems. There are democratic elements of consultation within the party but these are largely informal. The party in that sense is like a family, where discussion may exist and even be heeded, but where it is always clear that the head of the family is in charge. Moreover, just as informal democratic expression can be extended, so it can easily be withdrawn. Secondly, as we have noted, the party is nevertheless very successful. Indeed, its success may partly be due to these less formal manifestations of party democracy. The party has therefore been able to change and adapt its stance with relative ease. Indeed, the party's ability and willingness to change has been part of its key to success. To an extent, it has appeared to be a party that will adapt to change and thus generally be able to offer a good electoral alternative. Of course, this might mean that the party has less in the way of a consistent ideology, yet it does display certain ideological strands which reassert themselves at different periods in time. If the party has a consistent stance, however, it is one of governing and the ruthless pursuit of government.

At the start of 1996, the party appears to have great problems. The question of Europe threatens to cause deep divisions within the party and opinion polls for a long period have seemed to suggest that it may suffer electorally at the national level as well as at local level. Perhaps the problem for the party is that it has been in power for such a long period. If that seems perverse, it is simply to suggest that the party may have been denied ideas to react against. Without this classic position, the party can appear to be ideologically at sea.

4

THE LABOUR PARTY

Introduction

If the Conservative Party is the dominant political party in Britain, then Labour is its chief challenger. Although not nearly as strong as the Conservatives in terms of General Election victories and individual membership, the Labour Party has nonetheless attained significant success. The Labour government in the immediate post-war period, for example, implemented certain policies such as the introduction of the National Health Service which despite various reforms have become a firm part of the British political scene. Indeed, following Labour's landslide victory in 1945, many saw it as the 'natural' party of government. This was the case again after the victory in 1966. Yet Labour has not now won a General Election since 1974 and even then, its parliamentary majority was so slim that it had ebbed away within 2 years. Moreover, in the last three general elections, it has failed to gain the share of the vote that it enjoyed when the Conservatives were returned to power in 1979 (see Appendix I). In many ways one might be tempted to argue that electorally, at least, Labour is a spent force. Yet, it continues to be the principal opposition party; it has attained impressive electoral success at the European and local levels and, in 1992, it seemed to have a realistic chance of forming a government. Moreover, opinion polls since 1992 have suggested that it may attain electoral success at a future General Election. It is an intriguing party.

Organisation and internal elections

Constitutionally, the Labour Party is less hierarchical and more democratic than the Conservative Party. Individual members may vote in internal elections including that of the leader and also at conferences. Moreover, party conferences are designed to determine party policy. The party also consists of affiliated organisations, including trade unions and various societies. These organisations are also granted an input into the Labour Party through votes just as individual members. On the face of it, the Labour Party is internally democratic and accountable to its membership. This is largely a legacy of the fact that unlike the Conservatives, or indeed the Liberals, the Labour Party developed outside of Parliament. It was created in a bottom-up fashion rather than top-down, as was the case with the Conservatives and Liberals. However, just as it is misleading to examine the Conservative Party solely in terms of its constitution, so it is the case with the Labour Party. Appearances can be deceptive. Indeed, in his classic study in the 1950s Robert McKenzie argued that the Labour Party was in fact very similar to the Conservatives in terms of its oligarchic tendencies (McKenzie, 1955). We will examine first the formal position (Figure 4.1).

We can identify three distinct levels of Labour Party organisation, within which there are a variety of bodies which interact both with each other and across levels of organisation. The three levels are local, regional and national. At local level, the difference between the Labour Party and the Conservatives and Liberal Democrats becomes immediately apparent. Whereas in the latter two the individual member is the core unit, in the Labour Party there are both individual members as well as trade union branches and various socialist societies affiliated to constituency parties. However, whereas members belong to ward branches which in turn are part of the constituency party, trade union branches affiliate directly at constituency level. At regional level there is a layer of organisation through which constituency parties operate. This layer in turn reports to the national level. The exception to this is the direct relationship that constituency Labour Parties (CLPs) have with their MPs. This is, perhaps, the key function of CLPs in that it is constitutionally they who select and reselect prospective parliamentary candidates.

Figure 4:1 Labour Party Organisation

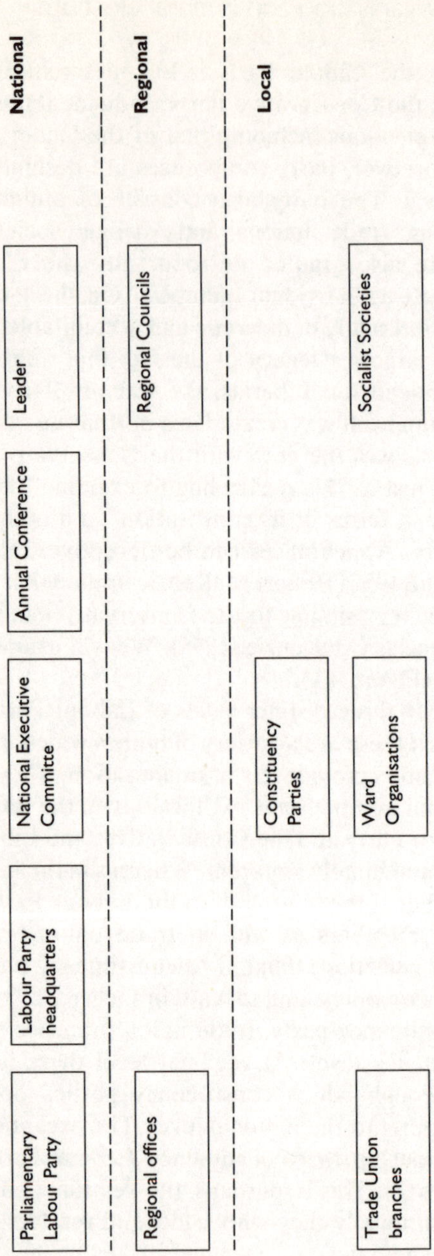

National

| Parliamentary Labour Party | Labour Party headquarters | National Executive Committe | Annual Conference | Leader |

Regional

| Regional offices | | Regional Councils |

Local

| Trade Union branches | Ward Organisations | Constituency Parties | Socialist Societies |

Sources: Webb (1992a:851); Jones and Kavannagh (1994:252).

At national level there are five elements of organisation: the Parliamentary Labour Party (PLP), the party headquarters, the National Executive Committee (NEC), the annual conference and the leader of the party. Of these, the NEC and leadership are the most powerful. Technically, since the NEC is elected by the party conference, it is subservient to it; yet the relationship is such that the NEC appears to be the dominant party. This is largely because of the fact that most aspects of party policy originate from within the NEC. Motions can be put to conference by unions or CLPs but the main debates focus upon proposals put forward by the NEC. It is, in some ways, a reflection of procedures in the House of Commons, whereby most business originates from the government although debates may be sponsored by private members. The NEC also has joint responsibility with the leadership for drawing up the party's manifesto, although this role has declined in recent years. This is partly as a result of the establishment of such bodies as the Shadow Communications Agency, which were initially developed to improve the party's public image but have since taken a stronger role in policy initiation. Such bodies have been linked closely to the leadership which has exercised its power increasingly. Nevertheless, it is the NEC and not the leader that is responsible for the party organisation itself.

Theoretically, then, the NEC could act as a check upon the power of the leadership. However, while this may have posed a problem in the past for Labour leaders, since Kinnock's leadership the NEC has been increasingly loyal to its leader and opponents on the NEC have become increasingly marginalised. During the late 1980s NEC votes consistently supported the leadership with the exception of two members, Tony Benn and Dennis Skinner. However, since then both Skinner and Benn have lost their seats and whilst Skinner regained his seat, it remains the case that the NEC is now largely a leadership supporting body.

The role of the trade unions

One of the enduring arguments about the Labour Party has been that it is controlled by the trade unions on account of their constitutional role within the party and because of their financial input. It is not difficult to see why such claims have been made. However, empirical evidence is often in stark contrast with perceived truths. First there is the assumption that trade unions and the Labour Party are inherently linked. The assumption has been, first, that all trade unions are Labour supporters. In fact, only around 11 per cent of 300 or so trade unions in Britain are affiliated to the Labour Party. Admittedly, this represents around 53 per cent of trade union members, but the link is anything but absolute (Fisher, 1992:112–14). Secondly, even where the absence of this absolute link has been acknowledged, the other assumption has been that all trade union political action is Labour Party related. In fact, only around two-thirds of trade unions with political funds are affiliated to the Labour Party, and those that are only use on average two-thirds of their political funds for Labour Party purposes (Fisher, 1992:114–17). Nevertheless, those trade unions that are affiliated would appear to wield considerable power within the Labour Party through their constitutional position. We can test this thesis by examining a number of areas where trade unions might be said to have influence in the Labour Party.

The principal source of debate regarding trade unions and their relationship with the Labour Party concerns the party conference and the block vote. The system of block voting has its origins in the Nonconformist churches. It is a system of 'regulating the affairs of a confederal organisation' (Coates and Topham, 1980:319) whereby each affiliate votes in accordance with its own input of money and members.[1] Under the block vote system, affiliated unions declare a number of affiliated members, which may or may not correlate with the actual number of political levy payers. Unions can affiliate for any number of members they choose up to the amount of members who have not contracted out of paying the political levy. Many unions affiliate on the basis of fewer members than they are permitted either to save money or so as not to appear that they are attempting to dominate conference.

Supporters argue that the practice is wholly in keeping with the Labour Party's traditions and notions of representative democracy, whereby decisions are reached both collectively and are collectively adhered to. Opponents of the block vote argue that it is undemocratic, that votes are cast on behalf of people who have

---

[1] Crouch compares the block vote to a shareholder voting in limited liability companies. Crouch in Kavanagh, 1982:177.

Table 4.1 Union representation on Labour's NEC, 1964–92.

Year	Unions	Non-unions
1964	9	13
1966	11	12
1970	12	13
1974	12	13
1979	12	14
1983	12	14
1987	12	14
1992	11	14

Note: Totals do not include Chair and Vice-Chair of the party, the Leader and Deputy Leader, the General Secretary and the Treasurer.
Sources: Webb (1992b) and Norris *et al.* (1992).

little or no say in the decisions that these votes are intended to reflect and that it does not allow for minority representation. More fundamental criticism emerges from those who argue that the effective *purchase* of votes by affiliated unions is essentially corrupt (Pinto-Duschinsky, 1981:302–11). Those who are neither supporters nor opponents argue that while the system may appear unattractive, it does militate against extremist control of the party by equally unrepresentative constituency activists.

Until the 1990s the block vote accounted for 90 per cent of conference votes. In 1992 the block vote was reduced to 70 per cent. The following year, however, conference recommended that unions be able to split their vote in future and union voting strength is soon to be reduced further to 50 per cent. Some argue that in fact Conference is not the real decision-making forum it appears to be; many have also argued that in government, Labour leaders effectively ignore conference decisions. In opposition too, it seems that the practice of debate and voting gives a somewhat misleading impression of events. A further reason for the claim that Conference is not the premier decision-making forum is the claim that the real power in the party is held by the NEC. Certainly, the trade unions are strongly represented on the Labour Party's NEC. Additionally, the NEC has a number of permanent subcommittees upon which unions have a significant presence (Table 4.1).

Some take the view that although unions could, in theory, control the entire Labour Party, they have systematically refrained from doing so. This attitude dates back to the formation of the Labour Party which entailed an acceptance of the separate nature of politics as distinct from trade unionism. Thus direct control has never really been attempted (Minkin, 1991). This reticence has been driven by two principal considerations: first to ensure that constituency activists are not alienated and secondly, the view that Labour is a 'trade union party' is considered to be electorally unattractive (Walsh and Tindale, 1992:10). In essence the situation is likened to the governance of Britain, whereby everything is done in the name of the Monarch, who technically is the all-powerful Head of State, whereas all decision making is actually conducted from Downing Street.

A number of recent instances have further illustrated that unions do not control the Labour Party in the manner that is frequently suggested. The Policy Review undertaken after the 1987 General Election defeat addressed a number of 'sacred cows' of party policy – nuclear weapons, public ownership and trade union reform, as well as internal constitutional changes. While the passage of reforms was not always smooth, in mathematical terms they nonetheless required the consent of the unions in order for the changes to succeed and this was broadly achieved. In more recent years, two radical policies have been passed by the Labour Party despite significant opposition from some quarters of the union movement. The passing of one member – one vote (OMOV) for the selection of candidates and the rewording of Clause IV of the party's constitution are themselves strong indications that trade unions do not control the Labour Party.

From another perspective, some writers have argued that in fact trade unions in general have very little power (Taylor, 1989:188–94; Minkin, 1991; Rosamund, 1992) and that unions have rarely arrived at a 'single view' except in the area of industrial rights. Even then, the experience of the Policy Review illustrated strong divisions on the question of what proportion of Conservative employment legislation might be repealed by a future Labour government. Similarly, trade unions were clearly divided over the abolition of Clause IV. Moreover, trade unions are also unlikely to seek other political bedfellows, thus reducing any power they may be said to hold over the Labour Party. In essence, the unions' problem is that the likelihood of any sizeable group of unions being able to reach an agreement on a political switch is so small as to make it dismissible as an option.

The election of the leader

The leader and deputy leader are elected by an electoral college comprising of the PLP, affiliated organisations (largely trade unions) and individual members. The votes are calculated so that a third of the votes are each allocated to the PLP, the affiliated organisations and the constituencies. Prior to 1993, the proportions were 40 per cent to the PLP and 30 per cent each to the affiliated organisations and constituencies. A candidate must score more than 50 per cent of the vote or a second ballot is held. This system was adopted in 1980 and replaced the election by PLP alone. This was part of the constitutional changes spearheaded by the left wing of the party during this period which also included the mandatory reselection of sitting MPs. However, before a contest can take place a challenger for the leadership must have the support of at least 20 per cent of the PLP (this was increased from 5 per cent in 1988). Moreover, if the Labour Party is in government, this requirement must be accompanied by the approval for the contest by at least two-thirds of the annual conference. These stipulations have led many to observe that despite Labour's stronger democratic credentials, it is easier to unseat a Conservative leader than it is to unseat a Labour one.

So far, of course, this system of electing the leader has only taken place outside government and moreover, of the four times there have been leadership contests, there has only been one where there was a challenge to the incumbent (Tony Benn's challenge to Neil Kinnock in 1988 which prompted the increase of the PLP threshold to 20 per cent). The other three contests have been brought about by the resignations of Michael Foot and Neil Kinnock, and the death of John Smith. Moreover, all the contests have produced a decisive result, which importantly were largely expected before voting even took place (see Table 4.2).

The contests for the deputy leadership have, however, often proved to be closer affairs and despite the relatively limited role of the deputy leader, have often proved to be very politically significant. The first such contest, in 1981, was just that. This required two ballots after the more right-wing candidate, Denis Healey, won the first ballot although he fell short of the 50 per cent threshold. The subsequent second-round contest with the left winger, Tony Benn, was so close that the candidates were separated by less

Table 4.2   Labour Party leadership and deputy leadership elections 1981–94.

Year	Leadership			Deputy leadership		
	Name	Total %	Leader elected	Name	Total %	Deputy leader elected
1981 (First ballot)	No election			D. Healey	45.4	
				T. Benn	36.6	
				J. Silkin	18.0	
1981 (Second ballot)				D. Healey	50.4	Healey
				T. Benn	49.6	
1983	N. Kinnock	71.3	Kinnock	R. Hattersley	67.3	Hattersley
	R. Hattersley	19.3		M. Meacher	27.9	
	E. Heffer	6.3		D. Davies	3.5	
	P. Shore	3.1		G. Dunwoody	1.3	
1988	N. Kinnock	88.6	Kinnock	R. Hattersley	66.8	Hattersley
	T. Benn	11.4		J. Prescott	23.7	
				E. Heffer	9.5	
1992	J. Smith	91.0	Smith	M. Beckett	57.3	Beckett
	B. Gould	9.0		J. Prescott	28.1	
				B. Gould	14.6	
1994	T. Blair	57.0	Blair	Prescott	56.5	Prescott
	J. Prescott	24.1		Beckett	43.5	
	M. Beckett	18.9				

Source: Butler and Butler (1994:136–7).

than 1 per cent of the electoral college. Healey won, but that election showed how powerful the left had become in the Labour Party. In subsequent contests the results have been decisive, although much closer than those for the leadership (see Table 4.2). Nevertheless, the deputy leadership contest has often been a way of uniting different wings of the party. Thus, when the right-wing Hattersley was elected deputy in 1983, this was seen as a balance to Kinnock who had come from the left of the party (although he subsequently moved more to the right). Similarly John Prescott, with his strong trade union connections and more traditional Labour approach, is seen as a balance to the modernising and less traditional Tony Blair.

The selection of parliamentary candidates

Since 1993, candidates have been elected on the basis of one member – one vote (OMOV), a system which, as the phrase implies, gives each CLP member an equal vote in the selection process. This contrasts with previous selection processes whereby trade unions affiliated at local level possessed a block vote. However, while it may appear as though this aspect of party recruitment is completely in the hands of local members, the actual position is rather less clear-cut.

CLPs are presented with various lists from which to short-list candidates. These include trade union nominees; CLP nominees; Co-operative Society nominees as well as an all-women list which includes women who may be on other lists as well. Additionally, branches may also nominate candidates for short-listing. While the power to short-list then falls to the CLP for ultimate selection, there are certain criteria which restrain a free hand. Most obvious of these was the decision taken in 1993 that, in half the parliamentary seats where Labour was the incumbent or where it stood a good chance of victory, there should be all-women short-lists of candidates. This represented a continuing trend within the Labour Party to attempt to increase the number of women in Parliament. Potentially this had every chance of success, but led to some resentment among CLPs. As a result, the policy was challenged and found to be illegal at the beginning of 1996.

Once the candidates are formally short-listed, there is then a vote of CLP members. However, there is further evidence here that the constitutional position may not be all that it seems, since elected candidates must then be approved by the NEC. The NEC has always had the power to veto any candidate selection, but has largely abstained from using it. Since the mid-1980s the NEC has displayed a far greater willingness to exercise its prerogative; this extended to the imposition of favoured candidates in by-elections replacing the choice made by the local party as well as expelling two incumbent MPs at the 1992 election who were supporters of Militant. The effect of this willingness to intervene is that CLPs have become more conscious of the NEC's potential role and have liaised with it over short-lists more than was the case beforehand. For the NEC's part, the veto has been exercised or at least threatened in an effort to ensure that candidates are seen as electoral maximisers. So far, the policy has proved to be successful.

Sponsorship of candidates and MPs

Trade unions sponsor MPs under the conditions of the Hastings Agreement, which specifies that an affiliated union can pay no more than 80 per cent of the maximum election expenses permitted by law. Many unions pay the full 80 per cent, although this is rarely very expensive given that constituency expenditure is limited by the Representation of the People Act. In 1987, for example, the average total expenses for a Labour candidate was £3,900. The first point to make about sponsorship is that the relationship is not between the individual and the union, but the constituency party and the union. This has been a development during the last 25 years whereby unions have ceased personal payments or frozen them at very low levels. This is significant, because it distinguishes the practice as payment to the *party* rather than payment to an *individual* which is characteristic of areas such as MPs acting as consultants.

Research has indicated that the relationship between unions and their sponsored MPs is not particularly strong (Webb, 1992b; Minkin, 1991) and although it is still the case that different unions take slightly different positions on the exact nature of the relationship, the underlying position is that sponsorship is certainly not central to the overall relationship, nor is it one that is exploited to any significant degree. Indeed, many MPs receive requests from unions to sponsor them and can effectively 'shop around' for the best deal (Minkin, 1991:261). This is a reflection of recent trends in union sponsorship. First of all there is the growth of 'co-option', a practice whereby unions adopt sitting MPs. The constituency party then receives assistance and the MP fights the next election as a sponsored candidate (Minkin, 1991:244).

When elected, sponsored MPs form the Trade Union Group (TUG) within Parliament. The group was revived in 1954 in the context of the ideological struggle between left and right wingers over the party's future (Minkin, 1991:258). However, despite brief bursts of activity over the Wilson government's trade union proposals in the White Paper *In Place of Strife* in 1969 and Heath's Industrial Relations Act in 1971, the TUG has become fragmented

Table 4.3 **Trade union-sponsored MPs 1945–92.**

Union	1945	1970	1979	1992
AEU	3	16	17	13
Apex	—	3	5	—
(ASTMS)MSF	—	3	8	13
COHSE	—	—	3	6
EETPU	1	3	4	3
GMB	8	12	14	17
NCU	—	1	3	3
NUM	35	20	16	14
NUPE	—	6	7	12
NUR(RMT)	12	5	12	12
Sogat(GMPU)	—	—	—	5
TGWU	17	19	21	38
TSSA	9	4	3	2
UCATT	5	2	2	—
UCW	—	1	2	0
USDAW	6	9	5	3
Others	25	8	8	2
Total	121	108	126	143
PLP	393	288	269	271

Sources: *Guardian* 13/8/92 p.2; Butler and Kavanagh (1992:227).

both politically and industrially. Trade union-sponsored MPs are not, therefore, a collective force in Parliament and in the case of a clash of loyalties an MP would have to support the party. Moreover, sponsored MPs have often voted or acted in ways counter to union policy, often over a period of years, yet few have had sponsorship withdrawn (Minkin, 1991:262–7).

Despite the apparent lack of power enjoyed by sponsors there were more union-sponsored MPs following the 1992 election than at any time since the war, although there was strong evidence of a shift away from manual unions towards the general and health ones (see Table 4.3).

The social background of Labour MPs and candidates

There is evidently a number of factors influencing the selection of parliamentary candidates. Let us then examine the profile of those selected by the Labour Party. First, like the Conservative Party, Labour's MPs and candidates are dominated by men, although not to quite the same extent. Moreover, there has been an apparent and quite rapid increase in the proportion of women MPs and

Table 4.4   **Sex, age and ethnic background.**

Year	1992		1987		1983	
(%)	Elected	Defeated	Elected	Defeated	Elected	Defeated
Male	86	72	91	82	96	84
Female	14	28	9	18	4	16
20–29	0	6	0	9	<1	13
30–39	13	36	19	49	15	46
40–49	42	42	41	31	30	25
50–59	30	12	28	10	36	15
60–69	15	3	12	1	16	2
70–79	0	0	<1	0	2	0
Median age	49	42	47	38	51	38
White	98	99	98	98	100	99
Non-white	2	1	2	2	0	1
n	271	363	229	404	209	424

Note: totals may not add up to 100% due to rounding.
Source: derived from Butler and Kavanagh (1992, 1988, 1984).

Table 4.5 **Education.**

Year	1992		1987		1983	
(%)	Elected	Defeated	Elected	Defeated	Elected	Defeated
Elementary	3	0	5	<1	13	4
Secondary	13	17	14	16	16	16
Public school	0	1	<1	1	0	<1
Secondary+univ/poly/college	69	73	66	71	56	68
Public school+univ/poly/college	15	9	14	12	14	11
(%)						
Eton/Harrow/Winchester	1	0	1	0	1	0
Other public schools	14	10	13	13	13	11
All public schools	15	10	14	13	14	11
Oxbridge	16	9	15	12	15	12
Other univ/poly/college	68	74	64	71	58	67
All univ/poly/college	84	83	79	83	73	79
n	271	363	229	404	209	424

Note: totals may not add up to 100% due to rounding.
Source: derived from Butler and Kavanagh (1992, 1988, 1984).

candidates although evidently there is still some way to go before a more equal distribution is achieved. Secondly, again as with the Conservatives, the median age of MPs and candidates has remained fairly stable (47–51 and 38–42 years, respectively) but again, we can detect a decline among the under-40s. Finally, Labour's MPs and candidates are largely white, although have been joined by non-white MPs since 1987 (Table 4.4).

Regarding educational background, the picture is one of an increasingly educated parliamentary Labour Party (Table 4.5). Eighty-four per cent of Labour MPs are now graduates. Of these graduates there has also been an increase in non-public school and Oxbridge MPs.

Unlike the Conservative Party, however, the occupational make-up of Labour MPs and candidates has been less stable. There has been a decline in the proportion of MPs drawn from manual occupations, and while they constitute 22 per cent of MPs today, they are no longer the largest occupational group in the parliamentary Labour Party. That position has now been taken by MPs drawn from education, who now constitute nearly 30 per cent of the parliamentary party (Table 4.6). Moreover, this group also dominate the defeated candidates. Finally, we can also detect a growth in the ranks of those drawn from a life of political activity.

Table 4.6   **Occupational background.**

Year	1992		1987		1983	
(%)	*Elected*	*Defeated*	*Elected*	*Defeated*	*Elected*	*Defeated*
Education	28	31	24	36	25	35
Legal	6	6	8	4	8	6
Other professions	8	15	9	12	9	11
Business	8	12	10	9	9	9
Political activity	9	5	5	5	3	2
Publishing/ journalism	5	4	6	2	4	3
Miscellaneous	14	19	10	17	8	19
Manual workers	22	9	29	14	33	15
n	271	363	229	404	209	424

Note: totals may not add up to 100% due to rounding.
Source: derived from Butler and Kavanagh (1992, 1988, 1984).

Education: teachers in higher education, further education and schools.
Legal: barrister, solicitor.
Other professions: doctor/dentist, architect/surveyor, civil/chartered engineer,
    accountant, civil servant/local government, armed services, consultants,
    scientific/research.
Business: director, executive, commerce/insurance, management/clerical, general
    business.
Political activity: politician/political organiser.
Publishing/journalism: publishing and journalism.
Miscellaneous: farmer, housewife, student, miscellaneous white collar.
Manual worker: skilled worker, semi/unskilled worker, miner.

Funding

As with the Conservative Party, the funding of the Labour Party
provokes controversy. Certainly, the trade unions contribute a significant proportion of Labour's finances and help fund the party in
a number of ways, including affiliation payments, grants and *ad
hoc* donations, sponsorship of candidates and MPs, advertisements
in Labour Party publications, stands at party conferences and a
wide range of payments in kind including the provision of both
resources and personnel. This variety of techniques is in part explained by the long-term institutional links between the Labour
Party and affiliated trade unions.

However, Labour has been successful in recent years in diversifying its fund-raising, although traditionally it has been less successful in attracting large individual donations because of the
sociodemographic make-up of its supporters. Nevertheless, one of
the most recent initiatives, the Labour Party Business Plan, is

Table 4.7 Labour Party central income 1988–93.

	1988		1989		1990		1991		1992		1993	
	£000s	% of total central income	£000s	% of total central income	£000s	% of total central income	£000s	% of total central income	£000s	% of total central income	£000s	% of total central income
General fund	5,808	99.9	6,285	80.6	6,463	69.4	7,181	57.9	8,565	52.8	8,182	63.9
General Election fund	2	<0.1	1,075	13.8	1,915	20.6	3,532	28.5	3,846	23.7	2,339	18.3
Business Plans	—	—	434	5.6	930	10.0	1,692	13.6	3,816	23.5	2,275	17.8
of which												
Trade unions	4,133	71.1	5,359	68.8	6,384	68.6	7,855	63.3	8,631	53.2	6,962	54.4
Individuals	836	14.4	821	10.5	806	8.7	1,266	10.2	2,226	13.7	1,852	14.5
Commercial	—	—	73	0.9	177	1.9	461	3.8	467	2.9	510	4.0
Other	841	14.5	1,541	19.8	1,941	20.1	2,823	22.8	4,903	30.2	3,458	27.0
Total central income	5,810	100.0	7,794	100.0	9,308	100.0	12,405	100.0	16,227	100.0	12,796	100.0
Net assets (liabilities)	(1,085)		(374)		680		1,111		(242)		2,551	

Note 1: trade unions – affiliation fees, donations (calculated from donations from fund-raising for the General Fund and donations to the General Election fund.

individuals – membership dues, membership campaigning and donations, high value donor activity, General Election high value donors.

commercial – commercial unit, conferences, financial services.

other – PLPs Parliamentary Grant, fund-raising, legacies, by-election fund, sundry, standing orders, interest, all other.

Note 2: Total Labour Party central income calculated from income from general fund, Business Plans and General Election fund, gross fund-raising used for general fund.

Source: Labour Party accounts.

Table 4.8   Income of the Labour Party Business Plans.

	1989	1990	1991	1992	1993
Amount raised (£000s)	434	930	1,692	3,816	2,275
% Increase from preceding year	—	114	82	88	−40

Source: Labour Party accounts.

largely financed by individual donations from members and supporters or activities, such as high profile dinners, which attract
money from individuals rather than institutions. Since the Business
Plan was established, it has been very successful in continually
increasing its fund-raising capacity such that it now provides
around 18 per cent of Labour's central income. Additionally, Labour's newer forms of fund-raising (classified as 'Other' in Table
4.7) have also shown remarkable growth, nearly doubling in the
proportion (14.5–27 per cent) of Labour's central income between
1988 and 1993. In general, then, it is clear that the Labour Party is
diversifying its income base, and while trade unions continue to
play a very important role financially, Labour has been successful
in harnessing significant income from individuals, either through
donations or through activities concerned with the Business Plan
(Table 4.8). Labour is still heavily reliant upon the unions for
income, but the base of that income has widened.

Ideology

The Labour Party is identified with the ideology of socialism. Socialism itself is generally seen as having developed as an important
strand of political thought during the nineteenth century. The first
recorded use of the word was in the 1820s (Wright, 1993:80) and
the ideology itself developed from early utopian socialists through
the 'scientific' socialism of Marx and Engels. There were also
strong British influences in the form of the Fabians. There is no
shortage, then, of theoretical foundations.

Early socialism can, according to Wright, be traced back far
beyond the nineteenth century. He argues that early socialist
thought can be identified wherever people have questioned

inequality, which can partly explain why many see socialism as being more fundamentally based in the social application of Christianity (Wright, 1993:79). More conventionally, however, the roots of modern socialism are to be found in the rational and French revolutions of the late eighteenth century. As a burgeoning doctrine it was developed in England by Robert Owen with his social engineering experiments and in France by the technocratic Saint-Simon and the communitarian Fourier. While these thinkers were very different in one sense, they have generally been grouped together under the heading of utopian socialists, because they concentrated upon what socialism should achieve (the reduction or elimination of poverty and inequality) rather than the means by which it could be achieved.

This can be contrasted with the 'scientific socialism' of Marx and Engels. Marx essentially viewed society as having its own internal dynamic, the constant antagonism between the ruling class and the ruled. He saw capitalism as inevitably doomed to be logically succeeded by the socialist epoch and then ultimately, communism. Interpretations vary as to how the socialist epoch was to be realised, but most favoured a revolutionary path since Marxists viewed the state as existing in the interests of the ruling class. Thus a key chasm emerged within socialism, even in its formative years, principally between those who saw socialism as a form of reformism to be achieved within the confines of democratic sovereignty and those who viewed it as an ultimate event which although theoretically inevitable, would rely upon the fundamental mechanisms of the state being overthrown.

There was also a distinctively British influence upon socialist thought, which is largely credited to the Fabian Society. The Fabians were certainly in the reformist camp, but they shared with Marxists the view that change in society had an element of inevitability about it, based upon historical precedent. However, the Fabians differed from the former groups in that they viewed the process as inevitably gradual and basing their aims upon what could be achieved within the constraints of practicality. The Fabians were well aware that ideology was one thing, but implementing it was another. Moreover, the Fabian vision was one not only of economic change, but of cultural and social change as well. It was in many ways an ethical form of socialism which sought to change society through an appeal to its morals.

The Labour Party, then, has had a rich vein of socialist thought from which to draw and the broad thrust of socialist thought gives a clue as to why there has been much disagreement about what constitutes socialist goals. Indeed, there is a famous quotation which states that 'Socialism is what a Labour government does' (Herbert Morrison). If this quotation holds some truth, it reveals two important things: first, that rigid ideology plays little role in British political parties and secondly, that the Labour Party has been pragmatic and adept at changing its emphasis in a manner similar to the Conservatives.

If the quotation is largely fictitious, however, it still alludes to an important consideration: namely that there is no one definitive notion of socialism. And so it is with the Labour Party: there are different and distinct strands of thought, each laying different emphases and each laying claim to being 'socialist'. It is perhaps this fact that has led to so much internal factionalism and fighting. Many a long hour has been spent between groups arguing that the other is not 'socialist' or that their aims are 'truly socialist'. In a sense, perhaps this is inevitable given that Labour is a party that has always been the party aiming to change society and its institutions.

Perhaps this heavy concentration on socialism and the Labour Party's adherence to it has itself been something of a red herring. The quotation above alludes to this. Moreover, former General Secretary Morgan Phillips claimed that '. . . the Labour Party owed more to Methodism than to Marxism', a claim reiterated by former leader, and last Labour Prime Minister, James Callaghan (Callaghan, 1988:36). Tony Benn, also, has been keen to emphasise roots other than Marxist ones in Labour's development (Callaghan, 1989). Certainly, as we have seen, the organisation of the Party Conference owes more to the party's religious roots than anything else. Others claim that the trade union roots of the party have had a long-standing effect on the party's political thought or general ethos (Webb, 1992b; Drucker, 1979a, 1982; Harrison, 1960). The unions have dominated the Labour Party virtually from the time of its inception, consequently being in position to influence strategy, doctrine and ethos (Webb, 1992b; Drucker, 1979a, 1982; Harrison, 1960). Such writers have described the Labour Party not as 'socialist' but as 'labourist', defined thus:

Labourism . . . [refers to] the dominant definitions of 'the political' enshrined in the political philosophy and practice of the Labour Party since 1900 . . . A 'Labourist' reading of working class political interests emphasises their discrete and limited nature, their attainability within capitalism, and their capacity for realisation through parliamentary channels. (Coates, 1989:36)[2]

Thus labourism is distinct from many forms of socialism because there is no attempt to remove the economic superstructure of capitalism, and defines working class (and therefore trade union interests) as those which can be achieved within the existing economic and political order.

Whatever the Labour Party is, socialist or labourist, we can still detect and define distinct strands of ideological thought. First, the Labour Party is committed to parliamentary democracy. Despite appeals from the party's left on occasions for extra-parliamentary action to be taken, the party has committed itself to seeking change through the established institutions of the state. This represents a rejection of the Marxist view that the state cannot be considered as neutral. The Labour Party has used the state in a number of ways in order to attempt to achieve its goals, the two principal ways being through public ownership of certain industries and the development of and commitment to the welfare state.

Public ownership of certain industries has commonly been linked to the recently abolished Clause IV of the Labour Party's constitution which read:

To secure for the producers by hand or by brain the full fruits of their industry, and the most equitable distribution thereof that may be possible, upon the common ownership of the means of production and the best obtainable system of popular administration and control of each industry and service.

The principal technique for public ownership has been nationalisation, which essentially entailed the state assuming ownership of certain industries while retaining the corporate structure of those organisations (Callaghan, 1989). Since this has been the practice it has been largely assumed, therefore, that the Labour Party stood

---

[2] Coates goes on to point out that Keir Hardie in fact defined a similar concept of Labourism at the founding conference of the Labour Party in 1900 (Coates, 1989:36).

for nationalisation. However, nationalisation is simply a tool. Nothing in Clause IV committed the Labour Party to this particular technique and this misconception dogged the party for many years. Moreover, its abolition from Labour's constitution in 1995 does not necessarily imply that nationalisation or indeed any other technique of public ownership will not be attempted in the future. Nevertheless, the party has been committed to public ownership as a means by which essential services can be harnessed in the interests of the nation, although during the inter-war years it was advocated more as a means of wealth re-distribution. Public ownership, then, has formed a cornerstone to Labour's collectivist vision.

The second key area of Labour's use of the state has been in the field of welfarism. The party is committed to maintaining the state's role in the provision of a wide range of areas, principally including health, education and provision for those in need. This includes areas such as pensions and unemployment benefit. By using the state, the party has attempted to eradicate inequalities in opportunity and develop greater social equality in general. This has been combined with progressive fiscal policies designed not only to fund these objectives, but also to assist in an element of wealth redistribution. This has frequently led to the party being associated with high levels of direct taxation, even if that assess-ment itself has been wide of the mark. For example, in order to draw a clearer picture of the income tax burden, one should also consider the effects of tax thresholds. Tax allowances may be eroded by inflation, and thus in spite of cuts in the rate of income tax the taxation paid may be the same or even greater than before. Research has shown that any party political effect on income tax is unclear (Hogwood, 1992:89–101).

It has been this strand of collectivism that dominated Labour Party policy from the 1950s onwards, since it was argued by many that once the extreme aspects of capitalism, such as poverty, had been eliminated then socialism should concentrate upon improv-ing welfare provision. Such views were associated with Anthony Crosland and his followers, the so-called 'revisionists' (see the next chapter on social democracy for further discussion). Moreover, the view was that capitalism had been permanently reformed to ac-commodate collectivist ideals and thus the focus of Labour's vision should change. Nevertheless, there have been many within the

Labour Party who have disagreed and have preferred the route of more extensive public ownership as a means of reforming society.

Moreover, as we have noted, the Labour Party abolished the old Clause IV in 1995. This was not the first time that this had been attempted. In 1959 the leader, Gaitskell, attempted to abolish it, seeing it as an electoral albatross. His view was that although few in his party expected or desired large-scale nationalisation (as it was conceived) to be implemented, its presence within the constitution served as a hostage to fortune. Gaitskell lost his battle having underestimated the symbolic esteem in which Clause IV was held. Tony Blair took the same view as Gaitskell and was successful, although the groundwork had already been laid by Neil Kinnock and John Smith by their acceptance of the market. In many ways, Blair faced the same problems as Gaitskell, not least the symbolism of abolishing a commitment made 77 years previously. While it was clear to many that nationalisation might have been an effective, if not blunt, tool in the 1950s, the situation in the 1990s was very different. Blair won relatively easily, although not without some disagreement with key supporters.

Tony Blair's socialism is much more a reflection of the ethical tradition. He reflects many of the concerns of the Croslandites in the 1950s, yet importantly rejects the idea that welfare provision can always be funded through sustained economic growth. His emphasis, too, is more upon the ethical and moral aspects of life rather than the elimination of social divisions such as class. Indeed, the socialism that Blair advocates has a strong flavour of communitarianism. It stresses that humans are interdependent and owe a duty to one another and to a broader society. Blair sees this as social-ism (Blair, 1994:4). His view, therefore, is that global economic changes have rendered many of the old Labour economic policies unworkable and stresses that Labour should concentrate upon building partnership with private industry, rather than materially opposing it. In short, the socialism currently pursued by Labour centres upon equality of opportunity and quality of life, and not upon redistribution of wealth. It is well within the traditions of Labour Party thought, but very much in one camp.

In their study of Labour Party members, Seyd and Whiteley (1992) also found that various ideological strands were present. They identified a number of factors where members' attitudes displayed some consistency. These were attitudes such as views on the free market, nationalisation, international and environmental concerns and the role of trade unions (Seyd and Whiteley, 1992:120–6). Clearly, then, it is not only elites in the party that differ ideologically. All the ideological traditions of the Labour Party are also apparent in the membership.

Measuring ideological change

Using the same techniques as for the Conservative Party, we can assess the ideological position of Labour manifestos since 1979. As before, a positive score indicates a more right-wing manifesto and a negative score a more left-wing one. Similarly, the greater the score, the more left or right wing the manifesto. The results for Labour and the manifestos overall are shown in Table 4.9.

Examining the Labour manifestos in isolation, we can see that the left-wing flavour declined significantly between 1979 and 1987 before recovering somewhat in 1992. Thus in 1979, the manifesto was quite significantly left wing; by 1987 it had become almost evenly balanced between left and right, leaning very slightly to the left. What is also significant is the score that 1992's manifesto records. Written after the Policy Review which was widely inter-preted as introducing a greater right-wing element in Labour pol-icies, it was still significantly more left wing than its predecessor and of a similar score to the 1983 manifesto which had been widely interpreted as being very leftist. Moreover, this result is all the more fascinating for the fact that the 1992 Labour manifesto did not even use the term *socialist*!

We should also place Labour's manifestos within the context of all other manifestos. In this way we can assess just how far Labour

Table 4.9   **The balance of ideology on Labour manifestos.**

	Labour manifestos %	*All manifestos %*
1979	−29	−1
1983	−12	24
1987	−4	49
1992	−15	52

Source: Topf (1994:164).

differed from the norm. This approach paints a slightly different picture. For example, examining Labour's position in isolation suggests that 1979 was the most left-wing manifesto. However, the overall score reveals that in that election, all the manifestos were largely balanced. Thus Labour were able to fashion a fairly left-wing manifesto against a relatively sympathetic political climate. One should contrast this with the overall position in 1983, when there had been a clear shift to the right. Against this backdrop, it is easier to fathom why 1983's Labour manifesto was perceived as being so radical. Moreover, the political climate continued its rightwards march in 1987 and so while Labour's manifesto on its own might appear mild, it was nevertheless comparatively left-field. However, this second analysis serves to underline how 1992's manifesto could be viewed as radical since the difference in position of this manifesto and all manifestos was so marked. Despite the consolidation of right-wing values in all manifestos, Labour nevertheless took a significant move leftwards.

Groupings and factions

It is not surprising given the broad church of Labour ideology that there have always been groupings and factions within the Labour Party. At its formation, for example, it was an alliance of ethical socialists, the Independent Labour Party (ILP), (who nonetheless offered a 'scientific' approach to socialism), the gradualist and elitist Fabians, the quasi-Marxist Social Democratic Federation (SDF) and trade unions, some of whose sympathies had formally been with the Liberals. Even at its outset, then, Labour was divided in ideological terms. Moreover, it did not frame its ideology as such until the drafting of the 1918 Constitution.

Factionalism within the Labour Party has tended to revolve around two broad themes: the extent of state activity within the economy and the democratic procedures within the party itself. That said, these two broad themes have often found themselves campaigned upon in conjunction with each other. In the inter-war years, for example, the collapse of the Labour government in 1931 led to a questioning of Labour's gradualism and a stressing of the need for the state to control the power of financial capital.

It was during the 1950s, however, that strong ideological factions began to emerge, principally in the form of the Bevanites, 'led' by Aneurin Bevan, who urged greater state ownership of industry and the 'revisionists' whose views were reflected by Crosland and who were supported in the party's hierarchy, who wished to see Labour concentrating more upon social policy and calling a halt to further state economic activity. Divisions between the left and right of the party were also visible in the field of nuclear weapons, which were opposed by the Bevanite left. The revisionist right tended to have the ascendancy, although not without problems as the defeat over Clause IV in 1959 illustrated. Nevertheless, the revisionists emerged as the more powerful faction when Wilson broadly pursued their policies in his governments of the 1960s.

Factionalism around these themes has not, however, disappeared. It emerged strongly in the early 1970s when the left were successful in promoting the Alternative Economic Strategy which promoted more extensive nationalisation than any previous Labour government had ever come close to attempting. Then, after the Labour government of 1974–9, there were again attempts to take the party leftwards, which culminated in the split of certain revisionists to form the SDP and the 1983 Election where Labour campaigned upon a fundamentalist agenda. Since the election of Neil Kinnock to the leadership in Autumn 1983, the revisionists have again been more powerful, yet divisions remain and explain the historic and continuing factionalism in the Labour Party.

Factions or groupings formed around the question of internal democracy within the Labour Party have also tended to reflect the revisionist/fundamentalist divisions, although ironically in recent years it has been the fundamentalists who have resisted further democratic shifts within the Labour Party. Most prominent among these groups was the Campaign for Labour Party Democracy (CLPD), set up in 1973, which sought to reduce the power of the Labour parliamentary leadership and increase that of the party conference. This came to prominence during and after the 1974–9 government, when the Labour leadership had clearly ignored conference 'instructions'. The campaign also sought to introduce mandatory reselection of MPs by constituency parties, widen the electorate for the leadership from simply the parliamentary party (PLP) and place sole responsibility for the drafting of the manifesto with the National Executive Committee (NEC). In the period from 1979 to 1983, the CPLD was successful in its aims; after the election of Kinnock as leader, real control of the party gradually returned to the leadership.

Ironically, Kinnock's, Smith's and now Blair's own attempts to give grass-roots members a greater say in the party's affairs have often met with opposition from those that wish to extend participation in the party in earlier years. These leaders have sought to reduce the voting power of trade unions at conference and in internal elections in favour of votes from individual members. However, opponents of such changes have viewed such moves with cynicism and have decried the apparent decline of trade union power in the party.

It is against this backdrop, then, that we should examine the various groups and factions within the Labour Party. The revisionist/fundamentalist division is well represented. In the revisionist or reformist wing, we can readily identify the Fabian Society. One of the founding organisations of the party, it not only has a large individual membership, but also around half of the parliamentary party as members. Traditionally, Labour leaders are also members. Although it has a small constitutional role in the party, its main activity involves debate and policy initiation through regular pamphlets. These pamphlets, which are frequently well reported in the national press, are often arenas for policy kite-flying.

The fundamentalist wing has been more active in forming groups and factions, which is probably due to the fact that it views the right of the party as frequently having power anyway. A number of groups have emerged in the party which campaign for Labour to take a more leftish stance, often in the tradition of the Bevanites. Most famous has been the Tribune Group, begun in 1966, which had its roots in the Keep Left Group, Victory for Socialism and the Unity Group, which had campaigned for greater state intervention and a tempering of the pro-US foreign policy that had been pursued by the Labour leadership after the war. Tribune, named after the left-wing journal, attracted considerable support in the 1970s, particularly in the pursuit of the Alternative Economic Strategy and opposition to the European Community and nuclear weapons. It was the identifiable face of the left wing in the Labour Party and a counterbalance to the revisionists in terms of intellectual debate.

Since the early 1980s, however, the Tribune group has become far more moderate. This was first signalled by the election of Michael Foot to the leadership of the party. Himself a Tribune supporter, Foot was required to play a balancing game in the early 1980s in order to try to keep the party together, particularly after the defection of key figures to the SDP. Some Tribune members shifted to the centre in an effort to support Foot. This process was cemented when Kinnock was elected leader. Kinnock was another former left winger who had shifted to the centre, and largely took Tribune with him.

Seemingly denied left-wing representation, fundamentalists set up the Campaign Group in 1982, which now forms the key focus for left wingers in the party. Campaign reflects many of the previous concerns of left-wing groups but has also adopted calls for sweeping constitutional change such as the abolition of the House of Lords. One of the key figures in Campaign is Tony Benn, a veteran and charismatic campaigner within the Labour Party, who has been associated with many of its fundamentalist campaigns. He has provided a focus for the left in the same way that Bevan did before him, thus promoting many to refer to the Bennite tendency. Benn is still a key figure in the party, although his influence appears to have waned following the loss of his NEC seat in 1993. Nevertheless, he remains the key left-wing intellectual and campaigner in the party.

Recent history

The recent history of the Labour Party has been turbulent and dramatic. Inevitably, it has been strongly influenced by four successive General Election defeats, which has forced the party to re-examine itself and decide in which direction it wants to go. Not all election news has been so bleak, however. The party made very impressive showings in the European Elections of 1989 and 1994 and 'won' both elections. Indeed, in 1994 it won its highest share of the national vote since 1970 and holds 62 of the 84 British European seats (see Appendix II). Moreover, at local level, Labour continues to do well to the extent that it is the main party in local government. Nevertheless, despite the importance of these successes, local and European elections are not as critical for the party as General Elections, although they have served to illustrate the growing popularity of the party.

Labour has then examined itself largely in the light of continuing failure at national level. It has done so in three principal areas: party policy in the shape of the Policy Review, the role of the trade unions within the party and the role of the leadership. The policy review was begun after the 1987 General Election defeat. Instigated by Neil Kinnock, it was the strongest indication that he wanted to reappraise many of Labour's policies which many considered to be electorally unattractive. The result was a far more moderate stance on areas such as nuclear weapons, the European Community and economic policy. Labour abandoned its unilateralist stance on nuclear weapons, embraced the European Community with far more vigour and began to relax its traditional hostility to elements of the private sector. While many of the changes brought about by the policy review had their roots prior to its commencement, the review did at least crystallise many of the changes that Kinnock had envisaged after becoming leader. Kinnock set Labour in a direction which was later taken up by John Smith and then Tony Blair and it is not unreasonable to argue that both Smith and Blair would have been unable to pursue their ideas if the groundwork had not been laid by Kinnock. In short, he may not have been electorally successful in the short term, but the effects of Kinnock's leadership of the Labour Party continue to be felt.

The party has also examined the role of the trade unions in its organisation. Despite little confirmatory evidence, the role of unions in the Labour Party's affairs has long been held to be an electoral liability. John Smith, therefore, attempted to alter the relationship with the unions, first by reducing the size of unions' voting strength at conference and secondly by removing the block vote in candidate selection. Of course, it may be that Smith was simply attempting to reform the party for the sake of increased participation within the party by members. Certainly, many members appeared to agree, although at the same time they were mindful of apparent electoral disadvantages (Seyd and Whiteley, 1992:51). Nevertheless, the point is worth making that if voters were so concerned with the quality of internal party democracy, they would surely never vote Conservative.

The third area of note has been the way in which the power of the Labour leadership has appeared to develop. This should be viewed, of course, against the backdrop of the constitutional changes that were made in 1981 which sought to limit, to an extent, the leader's power. Kinnock began by developing his own team of advisers who were not democratically elected by the party. Similarly, John Smith and now Tony Blair have appeared to build a close team around themselves which is less penetrable from outside. This has led to claims that the leader is not responsive and fairly remote from the party. Whatever the reality, it does seem as though successive leaders have been keen to take a very active role in all key decisions. On the other hand, this is not to suggest that previous Labour leaders were weak or beholden to the mass party. Rather, it is that Labour leaders today have formalised what was the actual position.

The final point worthy of note in Labour's recent history has been the quick succession of leaders since the 1992 General Election. Neil Kinnock resigned shortly afterwards, and was succeeded by John Smith. Smith's period of leadership was generally cautious, which helped cement the foundations of reform initially laid by Kinnock. However, Smith's period of leadership cut short by his untimely death in the spring of 1994. Tony Blair succeeded him and has embarked on what seems radical reform of the party. Importantly, his reforms have been carried out relatively smoothly, although by mid-1995 some within the party were complaining that Blair had become too powerful. Nevertheless, he has appeared to enjoy the support of the electorate, with Labour's opinion poll standings since his election to the end of 1995 being comfortably above those of the Conservatives.

Conclusions

A study of the Labour Party then tells us a number things about it. First, history plays a strong role in the party. The importance of Clause IV is a good example since many supported its retention, not so much for what it said, but for its huge historic symbolism. Secondly, while the party is constitutionally democratic it is clear that the leadership plays a much stronger role than the constitution suggests. Partly through control of bodies like the NEC and partly through the compliance of the party, the Labour leader clearly plays a vital role in the party's affairs. This further illustrates that arguments about the role of the trade unions in the party's affairs, while not quite being a red herring, are wide of the mark when considering where power lies in the party.

In terms of ideology the ideas advanced by Kinnock and his successors have illustrated a more pragmatic approach, similar to that practised by the Conservatives. Whether or not this means that Labour will enjoy similar levels of electoral success is open to question, of course. However, since 1983, it has clearly made attempts to improve its electoral prospects through ideological shifts and while not yet winning a General Election it seems more plausible that it may do so in future.

5

THE LIBERAL DEMOCRATS

Introduction

The Liberal Democrats are Britain's newest mainstream party. They were launched in March 1988, although did not adopt their current name until October 1989. This gives a clue to the problems that a new party encounters and to the significant developments that have occurred in the party's brief history and its attempts to develop its own identity. In constitutional terms, the Liberal Democrats began life as a formalised merger of the parties of the SDP–Liberal Alliance which had fought two General Elections with some degree of success. However, the merger itself was often far from harmonious, and debate continues as to whether the Liberal Democrats are a genuine new party or perhaps essentially the old Liberal Party operating under a new name. Certainly, the early years of the party were very difficult. The merger process proved to be more protracted than many had hoped and contributed to the initial electoral unpopularity of the party. Confusion reigned over such basic issues as the party's name, which did nothing to inspire the voters (or probably the party) with confidence. The party underwent two changes of name before Liberal Democrats was finally chosen. Initially, they were to be known as New Liberal and Social Democratic Party (which could be shortened to the Alliance), then they were renamed the Social and Liberal Democrats (which could be shortened to The Democrats). While with hindsight this may seem trivial, it nevertheless delayed and hampered the launch of this new party and it was common to hear individuals joking about the obvious confusion surrounding the party name.

One suspects that this confusion contributed to the low point in Liberal Democrat fortunes, the European Elections of 1989. In that election, the Liberal Democrats trailed behind the Green Party in terms of the national share of the vote. It secured less than 6 per cent while the Greens gained an impressive 15 per cent (although did not win any seats). Of course, there are many other contextual factors which contributed to that result: the sudden rise of apparent environmental concern at the end of the economically strong 1980s (which withered away just as quickly in electoral terms) and the protest element of second-order elections. Nevertheless, the result was highly symbolic and from that low point the Liberal Democrats have undergone a strong recovery, although not perhaps to the level that they might have hoped. In addition to their frequently sensational by-election victories, they re-established themselves at national level in the 1992 General Election and have been remarkably successful in local elections. The Liberal Democrats, then, have had a dramatic history. However, the signs are that they now hold a permanent place on the British political landscape, even if they appear destined to be the major minor party in national politics.

Organisation and internal elections

As we have noted, the Liberal Democrats were formed as a result of a merger between members of the Liberal Party and the Social Democratic Party (SDP). That merger did not satisfy everyone in either party and thus the SDP continued as a party in its own right until 1990. Similarly, a small group of individuals reconstituted themselves as the Liberal Party in opposition to the merger, and while they were the most successful minor party in the 1992 Election, securing an average of 1.7 per cent of the vote, only one candidate (Michael Meadowcroft, a former SDP/Liberal Alliance MP) saved his deposit.

The merger of the two parties resulted in elements of each party's components being reflected in the new party's organisation. Thus, while on one hand the party retains the strong federal structure of the Liberals, the national conference is theoretically

Figure 5:1 Liberal Democratic Organisation

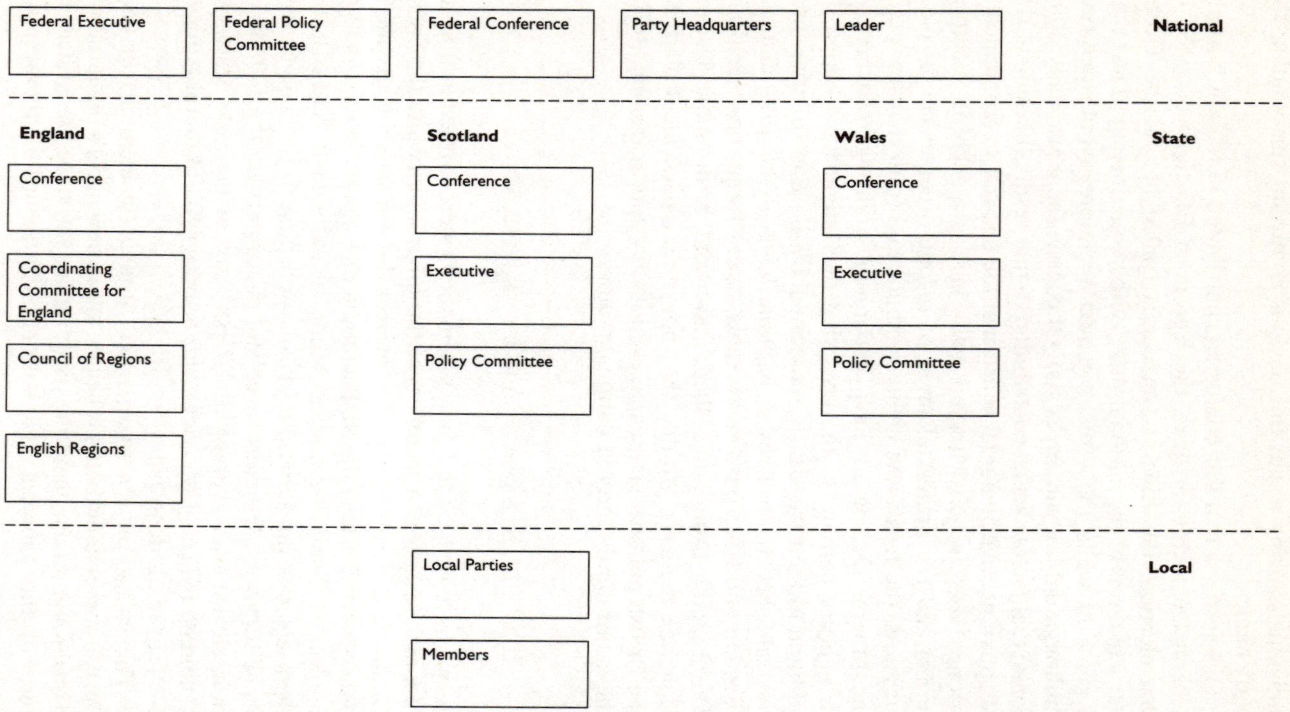

National

Federal Executive	Federal Policy Committee	Federal Conference	Party Headquarters	Leader

State

England

Conference

Coordinating Committee for England

Council of Regions

English Regions

Scotland

Conference

Executive

Policy Committee

Wales

Conference

Executive

Policy Committee

Local

Local Parties

Members

Sources: Webb (1992a:853); Jones and Kavanagh (1994:265).

sovereign in policy formulation. This reflects the greater centralised structure that was a feature of the SDP. There are three levels of organisation in the Liberal Democrats. The national level includes the leader, party headquarters, the federal executive, policy committee and national conference. The state level comprises separate organisations for England, Scotland and Wales each comprising a state conference. In Scotland and Wales there is an executive and policy committee, while in England there is a regional council and co-ordinating committee, reflecting a regional structure within England. Finally, at local level, there are the local parties and the basic unit of the party, the individual members (Figure 5.1).

The federal structure remains the basis for party membership, with members joining the state party. A levy (currently 20 per cent, but likely to be raised) is then paid by the state parties to the centre. This element helps to ensure that a degree of autonomy is retained by the state parties. Moreover, the practice of national conferences suggests that the federal bodies may be more powerful than the constitution suggests. Most policy proposals are put to conference after consideration by the federal policy committee, which in turn scrutinises any amendments made by conference. conference is then invited to consider the revisions of policy documents. While this might suggest that Conference does possess considerable power, it also important to point out that this procedure allows the federal policy committee an opportunity to offer alternatives to any policy decisions to which it is opposed. Moreover, conference only elects 13 of 27 places on the committee, the other places including the leader, president, four MPs and a peer. Finally, the federal committee may insist that final decisions on policy matters be delayed for consideration and has the responsibility with the parliamentary party of drawing up the election manifesto.

Thus, while the national conference is theoretically supreme, it is clear that the federal policy committee maintains a considerable amount of power which can be harnessed by the leadership. Moreover, that power is enhanced by the federal executive, on which the leader, president and three MPs, among others, sit. This executive allows a ballot to be called among the whole membership should it be faced with an issue it considers to be sufficiently important. This device could be used to overturn a conference decision. Nevertheless, such devices cannot altogether prevent the independence of the national conference. In 1994, for example, much media coverage was given to the fact that the Liberal Democrat conference had voted in favour of legalising cannabis, a move which clearly embarrassed the leadership.

Within the Liberal Democrats there are a number of official organisations which can have a policy input. There are two types, Specified Ancillary Organisations and Associated Organisations (McKee, 1994:1009). These include groups such as Green Democrats and Liberal Democrat European Group, which are Associated Organisations, and Liberal Democrat Agents Association and Liberal Democrat Youth, which are Specified Ancillary Organisations. The difference between the two groups is largely one of type. Associated Organisations campaign upon particular issues, while Specified Ancillary Organisations represent various organisational wings of the party. Both groups enjoy consultation in policy-making, although McKee argues that it is more accurate to see them as 'interest lobbyists more than policy campaigners' (McKee, 1994:1011).

Significantly, Associated Organisations gain their recognition and status from the party, thus indicating a tolerance of their activities. It can also lead to partial regulation since the sanction of withdrawal of official status remains with the party leadership. Thus, in general such groups can be relied upon to avoid serious challenges to the leadership (McKee, 1994:1010). The position of Specified Ancillary Organisations is slightly more secure given that they are listed in the Liberal Democrat constitution. Nevertheless, as McKee points out, with the exception of the Association of Liberal Democrat Councillors (ALDC) all groups are headed by figures from the party's hierarchy, which can result in tacit regulation (McKee, 1994:1011). The exception to this, the ALDC, derive this autonomy from, first, the strong Liberal Democrat presence at local government level and secondly, the fact that there has been a similar organisation in existence since before the Alliance was born.

In general, the organisation of the Liberal Democrats owes something both to the rank and file sovereignty of the Liberals and the leadership control of the SDP (McKee, 1994:1006). Its constitution has accommodated both internal democracy and leadership authority so that on one hand, the indiscipline of the Liberals has been averted and on the other hand, the centralised authority of the SDP has been tempered.

The election of the leader

As far as internal elections are concerned, a system of one member – one vote exists for elections for the leadership, presidency, the selection of parliamentary candidates and the election of conference representatives. The leadership has so far been contested only once. In that election in 1988 there were two candidates, Paddy Ashdown and Alan Beith. Both were former Liberals and sought to take over from David Steel, the former Liberal leader and a driving force behind the merger, who had decided not to stand. Ashdown secured 72 per cent of the vote and was duly elected. This process owes more to the legacy of the Liberals than the SDP. In the latter, the parliamentary party was more powerful, for although the leader was elected by the membership he could only be removed if, first, he was not Prime Minister and secondly, if an election was called for by more than half the parliamentary party. In the Liberal Democrats a leadership election is held 2 years following a General Election or if more than half the parliamentary party demand it, or if there is such a call from 75 local parties.

The selection of parliamentary candidates

The selection of candidates in the Liberal Democrats follows a similar path to that of the Conservatives, although the responsibilities for selection reflect the party's greater emphasis upon regional organisation (Norris and Lovenduski, 1995:79). Prospective candidates make initial applications to candidate committees at state level (that is, England, Wales and Scotland). Once initial applications are approved candidates are then required to attend a selection day similar to that of the Conservatives. Those that pass this stage are then placed upon regional approved lists. At this stage, approved candidates may apply to constituencies where vacancies arise. Candidates are then short-listed by the local executive committee before being presented to local members for selection. Often, local members may not be provided with a choice of candidates due to a lack of applicants, but where they are the party urges, but unlike past practice in the Labour Party does not enforce, candidates from both sexes. In fact, the Liberal Democrats face difficulties in supplying sufficient candidates and on occasions simply supply candidates from their approved lists to constituencies where there is no candidate in order to ensure that there is a candidate in every British seat (Norris and Lovenduski, 1995:80–1).

The social background of Liberal Democrat MPs and candidates

When drawing conclusions about Liberal Democrat MPs one must proceed with caution given the small numbers involved. Nevertheless, some patterns are clear. The MPs are largely male, in their 40s and all are white. True, there are now some women MPs where there were none among the Alliance in 1983, but that number is still small. Given the small number of MPs it is perhaps more

Table 5.1 **Sex, age and ethnic background.**

Year	1992		1987*		1983*	
(%)	Elected	Defeated	Elected	Defeated	Elected	Defeated
Male	90	77	91	83	100	88
Female	10	23	9	17	0	12
20–29	5	10	9	9	9	11
30–39	15	27	18	39	30	40
40–49	45	35	41	32	30	30
50–59	35	21	27	17	22	15
60–69	0	7	5	3	9	2
70–79	0	0	0	0	0	<1
Median age	45	43	46	40	44	39
White	100	99	100	99	100	99
Non-white	0	1	0	1	0	1
n	20	612	22	611	23	610

* SDP/Liberal Alliance.
Note: totals may not add up to 100% due to rounding.
Source: derived from Butler and Kavanagh (1992, 1988, 1984).

Table 5.2 **Education.**

Year	1992		1987*		1983*	
(%)	Elected	Defeated	Elected	Defeated	Elected	Defeated
Elementary	0	<1	0	<1	0	<1
Secondary	10	13	18	9	17	9
Public school	0	2	0	2	13	2
Secondary+univ/poly/college	40	67	36	57	30	57
Public school+univ/poly/college	50	18	45	31	39	31
(%)						
Eton/Harrow/Winchester	0	1	0	4	0	4
Other public schools	50	19	45	30	52	30
All public schools	50	20	45	33	52	33
Oxbridge	30	12	27	23	30	23
Other univ/poly/college	60	74	55	66	39	66
All univ/poly/college	90	85	82	89	70	89
n	20	612	22	611	23	611

* SDP/Liberal Alliance.
Note: totals may not add up to 100% due to rounding.
Source: derived from Butler and Kavanagh (1992, 1988, 1984).

sensible to examine the candidates in order to gain a picture of the outcome of the selection process. The first thing that is apparent is that there has been a significant increase in the proportion of women, although they still constitute less than a quarter of the candidates. Secondly, the median age of candidates is increasing. As with other parties, we are seeing a decline in the proportion of those under 40 years of age. Finally, even among such a large number of defeated candidates, there are only a handful of non-whites (Table 5.1).

Regarding educational background, we see that most Liberal Democrat MPs and candidates are graduates and increasingly these are drawn from non-public schools and non-Oxbridge institutions (Table 5.2). Moreover, as with other parties, there has been a decline in public school educated candidates in general.

There is quite an even spread of occupational backgrounds amongst Liberal Democrat MPs, although there are no manual workers among them. If there are any trends here, it is that the legal profession is most represented in Parliament, but overall there are many more candidates derived from educational and business backgrounds. Again, however, manual workers are almost entirely unrepresented (Table 5.3).

Table 5.3 **Occupational background.**

Year	1992		1987*		1983*	
(%)	Elected	Defeated	Elected	Defeated	Elected	Defeated
Education	20	26	18	24	13	26
Legal	30	5	27	10	22	12
Other professions	10	18	14	16	26	17
Business	10	28	9	26	4	21
Political activity	10	2	5	4	4	2
Publishing/journalism	15	3	14	5	22	7
Miscellaneous	5	15	14	12	9	11
Manual workers	0	2	0	3	0	2
n	20	612	22	611	23	610

* SDP/Liberal Alliance.
Note: totals may not add up to 100% due to rounding.
Source: derived from Butler and Kavanagh (1992, 1988, 1984).

Education: teachers in higher education, further education and schools.
Legal: barrister, solicitor.
Other professions: doctor/dentist, architect/surveyor, civil/chartered engineer, accountant, civil servant/local government, armed services, consultants, scientific/research.
Business: director, executive, commerce/insurance, management/clerical, general business.
Political activity: politician/political organiser.
Publishing/journalism: publishing and journalism.
Miscellaneous: farmer, housewife, student, miscellaneous white collar.
Manual worker: skilled worker, semi/unskilled worker, miner.

Funding

With few or no sources of institutional income other than through conferences where companies may take out stands, the Liberal Democrats are far more dependent upon their membership for funding. Income from membership fees accounts for 23 per cent of central income. Moreover, that figure has been growing throughout the Liberal Democrats' short history. The largest proportion of central income, however, still comes from direct mail appeals, although that technique has been in steady decline. A potential replacement are standing orders, which have been introduced in recent years and already account for 10 per cent of central income. This technique of raising income, which removes to an extent the voluntary aspect of donations and direct mail, could prove to be a far more reliable form of income for the Liberal Democrats. Indeed, this technique has also been adopted by the Labour Party.

Table 5.4 Liberal Democrat central income 1989–93.

	1989		1990		1991		1992		1993	
	£000s	% of total central income	£000s	% of total central income	£000s	% of total central income	£000s	% of total central income	£000s	% of total central income
Direct mail income	399	62.6	355	48.2	465	40.6	382	41.4	266	27.1
Donations	18	2.8	286	38.8	356	31.1	155	16.8	189	19.2
State parties levy (20% of member's subscriptions)	34	5.3	–	–	157	13.7	170	18.4	230	23.4
Standing orders	–	–	–		–	–	100	10.8	98	10.0
Commercial	97	15.2	50	6.8	96	8.4	90	9.8	100	10.2
Other	89	14.0	45	6.1	70	6.1	25	2.7	100	10.2
Total central income	637	100.0	736	100.0	1,144	100.0	922	100.0	983	100.0
Net assets (liabilities)	(202)		(106)		(149)		(122)		(81)	

Notes: State party levy – 20% of membership subscriptions paid to English, Scottish and Welsh parties.
Commercial – financial services, conferences.
Other – interest and other.

Source: Liberal Democrat accounts.

Ideology

Given that the Liberal Democrats grew from two parties it is not surprising that different ideological traditions exist within the party. Not only can we identify the broad thrust of liberalism and social democracy, but within those traditions there are themselves distinct subgroups of opinion also reflected in the membership of the party.

The liberalism within the Liberal Democrats has two broad origins: classical liberalism and social liberalism. At the formation of the Liberal Party in 1859, it was classical liberal thought that dominated, principally expressed through unrestricted competition in the economic sphere. This strand of political and economic thought found its roots in Adam Smith and essentially advocated that the market was the most efficient distributor of goods. It was regulated by the so-called 'invisible hand'. In other words, markets would adjust themselves through their own dynamic, producing levels of costs based upon movements within the economy.

Many nineteenth-century liberals rejected intervention in the economy which would distort what they saw as its natural equilibrium. Intervention found its forms in tariffs and import duties which had been introduced in order to advantage some producers of goods. For example, corn producers in the early part of the century had been protected from foreign competition by import levies being applied to foreign corn. Such intervention in the economy, for whatever reason, was deemed unacceptable by classical liberals, not least since it meant that the price of basic foodstuff of much of the population was maintained at artificially high levels.

Classical liberalism, however, is not only a strand of economic thought. This element of liberal thought argues that a free market allows free expression by individuals and that any intervention in that market is therefore an impediment to an individual. Thus, the freedom of an individual bound up the freedom of the marketplace. By placing restrictions upon the market, restrictions are placed upon the individual. This strand of liberalism, while historic to a degree, is still apparent in the Liberal Democrats. There remains a commitment to private enterprise as the principal economic operator within the state. However, there has been some tempering of the harder edges of classical liberalism from early theorists such as Spencer, which accepted poverty if it had been created by the market (Bellamy, 1993:37). While this strand of liberalism has been resurrected in more recent times by theorists such as Robert Nozick, it has not found favour in the Liberal Democrats or its modern predecessor.

The more common strand of liberalism which can be found among the Liberal Democrats is that of social liberalism, reflected in the nineteenth-century writings of John Stuart Mill. While Mill reflected the classic liberal premise that the individual was paramount in any discourse and that the imposition of restrictions from authority should be restricted or viewed with scepticism, he acknowledged that the unregulated market could serve to deny individuals freedom to pursue their own interests, principally through the poverty that was evident in Victorian Britain. Mill, therefore, advocated that states should intervene in order that individuals should be provided with the opportunity for self-development. It was essentially a recognition that the unregulated market could not guarantee such provision. What Mill and later liberals developed was an alternative type of freedom, for while classical liberals were concerned that individuals should have freedom *from* restrictions, social liberals were more concerned with providing individuals with freedom *to* pursue their own interests. In many ways this forms the basis of the notion of equality of opportunity since it is concerned with providing equal chances for each individual. What is significant, however, is that there is no concept of equality of outcome.

Mill's writings also concerned themselves with liberalism beyond the economic sphere. He was concerned with the liberty of the individual to pursue his own interests without the interference of the broad morality and intolerance of society. Thus, he advocated tolerance in lifestyle and religious matters, provided that an individual's actions did not harm another. Such concerns were also apparent among the Nonconformist pressure groups, which were important in the establishment of the modern Liberal Party.

The Liberal governments of the early part of the century reflected this reformulation of liberalism. This was manifested through the social reform programmes which included schemes such as national insurance and pensions, and were predecessors of the more comprehensive welfare state. It was taken further by Keynes who, while supporting capitalism, advocated economic intervention in order that inequalities in society be reduced. The moral aspects of liberalism were also apparent in legislation such as David Steel's Private Members' Bill which led to the legalisation of abortion in 1967.

These two strands of liberalism have logically struggled throughout the Liberal Party's history for, on one hand, the party has been committed to the individual, while on the other hand it has recognised the need to restrict the unregulated consequences of the free market. It is an area which the party has emphasised to a greater or lesser degree at differing times. In the post-war period, for example, the Liberal Party tried to grapple with this problem and decided that it should advocate welfare but that welfare should be distributed by the market and voluntary sector, rather than the state. By contrast, the Liberal Democrats today are more committed to the state as a means of welfare provision and indeed advocated an increase in income tax at the 1992 General Election in order to pay for improved educational provision.

In part because of the entrenched nature of welfarism on the political landscape, liberalism has concerned itself more with notions of citizenship, again in part a reflection of Mill's ideas. There has been an emphasis upon individual rights and their entrenchment in law and stemming from that, attempts to reform the British political system in order that those rights be guaranteed or enhanced. Thus the Liberals and later the Liberal Democrats have advocated a Bill of Rights, electoral reform and the devolution of government as means by which citizens might be better able to preserve personal rights.

A third strand of liberalism apparent within the heritage of the Liberal Democrats is that of community liberalism. Community liberals were concerned much more with ethical values, reflecting Mill's approach more than that of the classical liberals. There was a greater emphasis upon participation together with criticisms of representative democracy. Community liberals argued that within communities, individuals should have a greater opportunity to become involved in decision making and advocated single-issue campaigning. Thus, they sought to involve communities in political participation both within and outside conventional political institutions. This strategy, which the Liberal Party adopted at their 1970 Conference, proved to be very successful at local government level and is reflected in the fact that while Liberal fortunes may have fluctuated at a national level, they have enjoyed an enduring strength in local politics. This community approach did have its pitfalls, however. First of all, it often resulted in clashes between the grass-roots activists and the leadership. The leadership were seen as remote while some of the more radical policies of the community liberals such as the opposition to nuclear weapons on occasions presented the leadership with problems, particularly during the collaborative period with the SDP. The strong communitarian approach also served to emphasise the somewhat anarchic features of the party's affairs, which again presented problems for the leadership.

The second main strand of political thought which forms part of the Liberal Democrats' ideological heritage is that of social democracy. Social democracy did not emanate solely from the Social Democrats, although that party did provide its own distinctive strand of this tradition. It has been a long-established tradition in British political thought which in some ways has its roots in the liberal adoption of welfarism. Essentially, social democracy is an attempt to combine the best elements of the state with the distributive and responsive characteristics of the market. Its development as a strand of British political thought owes much to the Fabians and early socialists whose emphasis was more upon ethical concerns than economic ones. Like the Fabians, there was a recognition that an unjust society could not be resolved by economic redistribution alone. As Behrens notes: 'This scepticism and rejection of grand theory arose out of a recognition that the challenge of democratic socialism was to reconcile the competing values of individual liberty and social equality' (Behrens, 1989:75). Here, then, social democrats differed from social liberals, for while they both shared a desire to promote individual liberty ostensibly by the use of state intervention, liberals were not concerned with social equality. Early social democrats were concerned as much with equality of outcome as equality of opportunity.

Unlike some other socialist groups, the social democratic tradition was resolutely parliamentary in as much as there was a rejection of revolution as a means of social change. This was confirmed after the Second World War, when the Labour government supported the Western defence organisation the North Atlantic Treaty Organisation (NATO) in opposition to the Soviet-dominated Eastern bloc which, for the most part, eschewed conventional liberal democratic norms. Indeed, it was during the decades immediately after the war that British social democracy really developed as a distinct form of political thought, notably through the writings of the Labour politician Anthony Crosland, who published *The Future of Socialism* in 1956.

Crosland called for a re-examination of socialism in the light of the post-war experience. Essentially, he argued that the policies of the Labour government between 1945 and 1951 had rendered arguments about class politics obsolete. By introducing the widespread nationalisation of many key industries together with the welfare state and near full employment, he argued that there had been a comprehensive shift in economic control. Moreover, the willingness of subsequent Conservative administrations to broadly maintain these policies gave these shifts an element of permanence. Crosland's conclusion therefore was that there was no longer a need for intervention in the economic sphere; rather, that the state should now concentrate upon social policy concerns in order that genuine equality of opportunity could be promoted. In some ways, Crosland's arguments had an element of inevitability about them. First, nationalisation was a controversial issue which did not enjoy continual public support. Moreover, it was clear that by the end of the Labour period of government it had exhausted its obvious candidates for public ownership. The attempt to nationalise the sugar industry in retrospect appears to be a clear example of this. Secondly Crosland assumed, not unreasonably, that economic growth would continue so that such social policy programmes could be financed.

Crosland's view of social democracy appeared eminently viable until the 1970s, when economic conditions began to challenge the Keynesian orthodoxy that had been the bedrock of British economic policy. With steady growth no longer a reality and the combined effects of rapid inflation and the oil shock, the idea of the state being able and willing to finance the continuing development of social policy looked increasingly vulnerable. Against this backdrop, then, we should examine the strand of social democracy that one can detect as having emanated from the SDP.

The founders of the SDP (Roy Jenkins, David Owen, Shirley Williams and William Rogers) were of the view that social democracy could no longer be pursued within the Labour Party, particularly after the troubled period of the 1974–9 government and the party's lurch to the left following the election defeat of 1979. Thus, unlike previous social democrats they urged a far more centrist approach, free of the producer pressures within the Labour Party. They wished to distinguish clearly between social democracy and democratic socialism by accepting and promoting the private sector within a mixed economy. Beyond that, there was a desire to decentralise many elements of decision making in order that they be more responsive to changing needs. Moreover, they wished to avoid appeals to class politics. Here we see some differences between this approach and that of Crosland, whose approach was far more predisposed to central bureaucracy in its attempts to ensure that all had equal access to provision. Perhaps inevitably, this had led to bureaucratic expansion with its subsequent impact upon the taxpayer. Beyond the elements of reformulation of social democracy, the new SDP also offered a resolutely internationalist approach within the EEC, NATO and the United Nations.

We can also detect elements of the SDP which were to become apparent in the Liberal Democrat outlook. While the SDP was founded by four individuals, it became increasingly dominated by David Owen after he became leader in 1983. Helped by the very centrist structure of the SDP, Owen shifted the party seemingly to the right. While he acknowledged the electoral advantages of the Alliance he clearly had little time for the more radical policies of the Liberals, particularly in the sphere of defence policy. Moreover, he began to embrace the idea of the 'social market' which supported minimal welfare and minimal state intervention in the economy. Thus we can detect a second aspect of social democracy emanating from the SDP which we might term 'Owenism', which can be classified as a managerial approach to politics with a strong emphasis upon market-led efficiency.

What then of the Liberal Democrats? Given that we can detect a fairly broad ideological heritage, we must consider whether there is a distinct Liberal Democrat ideology. This can be done in two distinct ways. On one hand we can examine the party's positions on certain issues and on the other hand we can examine the views of members. From the point of view of the party, there is much influence of the social liberal tradition and more classical social democracy. The party takes a more centrist approach in economic matters rather than a radical liberal one, promoting some state

intervention in the economy and an emphasis on the small business, which links well with its positions on social policy and welfare
provision. In social policy terms it takes a more leftist view than
had been the case previously reflected in particular concerns for
education, housing and health. In constitutional terms, however,
the party has reflected some of the community liberal agenda in its
promotion of decentralised government and in local decision
making.

In international terms the Liberal Democrats take a strongly
pro-European stance, a reflection of the heritage of both the Liberals and the SDP. The Liberals had long advocated international
economic and political co-operation, while the founders of the
SDP had all been committed supporters of the European Community. The support for Europe from the Liberal Democrats was
clearly demonstrated in the House of Commons when the Government avoided defeat upon an early vote on the Maastricht Treaty
as a result of the support of Liberal Democrat MPs.

The Liberal Democrats have, however, emphasised one area
more than have previous incarnations through its promotion of
rights, citizenship and the reform of political institutions. The party
has emphasised this area as one that is of particular importance,
thus shifting the debate away from traditional left–right concerns.
This in part may be accounted for by practical considerations for as
McKee points out, the fact that the Liberal Democrats (and indeed
their predecessors) have been kept at the edges of parliamentary
life has generated a need to develop a distinct party identity
(McKee, 1994:1008). Whether or not this will generate mass appeal, however, is another matter.

Broadly speaking, it is the liberal tradition that is more prominent in the new party. There is none of the nostalgia for the 1950s
and 1960s that characterised the early Social Democrats and its
support for private enterprise is tempered with a view that individual rights and freedoms must be protected. In other areas, however, the Liberal Democrats seem to have taken on board
elements of the SDP. In particular, while retaining many elements
of a devolved party structure there has certainly been a shift in
emphasis toward centrist policies, both ideologically and in terms
of presentation and organisation. There is less of the element of
community politics in evidence and more of the managerial elements of the SDP. If one was to caricature such developments, one

might say that the party is now less beard and sandals and more estate car with electric windows!

In terms of the membership, we can also analyse the party's ideological profile, examining data from a membership survey, undertaken by John Curtice, Wolfgang Rüdig and Lynn Bennie (Rüdig, Curtice and Bennie, 1995; Bennie, Curtice and Rüdig, 1995). They have sought to examine these very points, highlighting similarities and differences between members that are new to the party, among formers Liberals and also among former Social Democrats. Their conclusion is that in terms of membership, at least, the Liberal Democrats are much closer to the old Liberal Party that the SDP. They found this by examining two broad sets of attitudes which may be said to have differentiated the old Liberal and Social Democrats, views on socialist/*laissez-faire* values and the question of nuclear weapons. They then compared the views of former Social Democrats and Liberals who had not joined the new party, and current Liberal Democrat members. In this battery of questions, current Liberal Democrats were more in keeping with the former Liberals. In some ways we should not be surprised. Within the new party, former Liberals outnumber former SDP members by three to one. Nevertheless, it is worth noting that even Liberal Democrats who were not members of either the Liberals or the SDP are still more similar in political outlook to the Liberals. For the membership at least the Liberal Democrats are more Liberal Party and less SDP.

Measuring ideological change

Using the same techniques as for the Conservative and Labour Parties, we can also assess the ideological position of Liberal Democrat, Alliance and Liberal manifestos since 1979. As before, a positive score indicates a more right-wing manifesto and a negative score a more left-wing one. Similarly, the greater the score, the more left or right wing the manifesto. This will allow us to assess whether the political 'centre' has remained ideologically consistent over a period where it has been represented by three different organisations. The results for the centre parties and the manifestos overall are shown in Table 5.5.

Examining the Liberal, Alliance and Liberal Democrat manifestos in isolation, it appears that the Liberals' relationship with

Table 5.5   The balance of ideology on Liberal Democrat, Alliance and Liberal manifestos.

	Lib/Alliance/Lib Dem manifestos %	All manifestos %
1979	–9	–1
1983	–13	24
1987	0	49
1992	11	52

Source: Topf (1994:164).

the SDP and subsequent merger has shifted the main centre party from a moderate left of centre party to moderate right of centre one. A fairly clear pattern emerges where by 1987, the Alliance was totally balanced in terms of left- and right-wing policy clusters and 1992's manifesto continued this trend. However, it is also clear that the initial Alliance manifesto took the parties to a more left-wing position than the Liberals had occupied in 1979. In some ways this might be expected, given that in 1983 the SDP partner was young, apparently dynamic and comprised largely of disaffected former Labour elites at its helm. Nevertheless, what is striking is that in these aggregated left/right scores, the Alliance manifesto was as left wing as Labour's. This is perhaps counter-intuitive, but can be explained by the fact that Labour stressed a stronger individualist aspect in their manifesto (which gives a positive score) while the Alliance were more keen to press communitarianism (which gives a negative score) (Topf, 1994:162). The aggregate effect of the admittedly broad left/right clusters defined in these terms is that Labour and the Alliance overall were fairly ideologically similar in 1983.

This surprising finding, however, is to obscure what appears to have been the growing influence of 'Owenism' which took the Alliance rightward and the subsequent continuation of this trend even without the presence of the former SDP leader. Moreover, if we examine the Liberal, Alliance and Liberal Democrat manifestos in the context of the wider political values, we can see that the Liberal Democrats have remained moderate by shifting their moderation with the political tide. Thus, while their manifesto of 1992 might have seemed quite right wing had it been published in 1979, by 1992 the political climate had shifted so that it might be described as moderate or even slightly left-field.

Groupings and factions

One might expect that in a political party so young that there would be scant opportunity for factions to emerge. This might be the case particularly with the Liberal Democrats since the merger was so protracted and unity would seem to be the overriding objective. On the other hand, within a merged party it is perhaps inevitable that factions should exist and, moreover, it may indicate a more mature political party which is capable of absorbing tendencies within it without threatening the broad organisation. Thus within the Liberal Democrats there are a number of factional interests, although as research illustrates, the membership of the various factions is generally very small (McKee, 1994:1012–19).

The ideological factions are based around the traditions of the party's core ideological heritage, liberalism and social democracy, although the tradition of liberalism is rather better represented. Liberal thinking is promoted by groups such as the Liberal Information Network (LINK), the Liberal Philosophy Group, the Beveridge Society and the Gladstone Club. LINK was established in 1983 and has been dedicated to promoting the cause of liberalism both within the Alliance and the new party. It has enjoyed patronage from many senior figures within the Liberal Democrats (including Paddy Ashdown) but did lose a number of key individuals, such as Michael Meadowcroft, who were opposed to the merger. Nevertheless, it remains the most prominent grass-roots liberal faction, by far larger and more established than the northern-based Liberal Philosophy Group, which wishes to develop a distinctly liberal agenda for Liberal Democrat policy. The other liberal factions within the party are the Beveridge Society and the Gladstone Club, which are characterised by elite memberships. The Beveridge Society, formed in 1992, is a group committed to the promotion of social liberalism through welfarism, while the Gladstone Club pursues liberal economic goals.

The social democratic tradition is promoted primarily by Social Democratic Voice and the Chard Group. Social Democratic Voice is a product of the merger and represents an attempt to redress the perceived imbalance of liberal ideas within the new party. However, it proved to be largely unsuccessful because first there were far fewer Social Democrats in the new party and secondly it did not receive the patronage of many prominent former Social

Democrats. More effective has been the Chard Group, which while comprising both former Liberals and Social Democrats, has pursued a clear Social Democrat path by emphasising wealth redistribution and public welfare.

While ideological groups clearly exist within the Liberal Democrats, it would be misleading to argue that it was riven by factionalism. Groups such as the Beveridge Society, for example, may be said to represent a shared agenda with the various groups which would find favour in the other camps. Moreover, the membership of these groups is small in relation to the wider party, so one should not overemphasise divisions. Nevertheless, McKee argues that the ideological struggle between the various groups has led to a lack of ideological clarity within the Liberal Democrats (McKee, 1994:1020). This is probably a slight exaggeration and belies that fact that in such a short period of time the Liberal Democrats have developed a stronger identity than is commonly acknowledged. After all, the apparent lack of ideological clarity has been apparent in all parties at various points in time and the Liberal Democrats lack no more clarity than their predecessors.

Recent history

In a sense the history of the Liberal Democrats is all recent, given the party's youth. However, there are certain factors which are especially worthy of note. First, while the party continues to have minority status in Parliament, it is a major force in local government. It continues to build on its strength at local level so that it now is the Britain's second party (behind Labour) at this level of government. Secondly, while the party performed notoriously badly at the 1989 European Elections, it gained its first two seats in 1994 (see Appendix II). Indeed, the likelihood is that the party would have gained another seat were it not for a candidate standing as a *Literal Democrat* in the Euro constituency of Devon and Plymouth East. That candidate, an unknown, picked up an unprecedented number of votes which, on the assumption that electors cast their vote for him by mistake, would have given the seat to the Liberal Democrats.

Thirdly, the party is now firmly established on the political landscape and has succeeded in making the issue of electoral reform a salient electoral issue. Labour's flirtation with the topic in the 1992 election and beyond is clear evidence of this. Moreover, Paddy Ashdown seems to be a popular leader. Indeed, opinion polls have often suggested that he is the most popular of all the party leaders; yet David Steel was also popular. Moreover, one might reasonably say that it is far easier to indicate approval of a leader with little chance of taking government than it is to choose between two more realistic candidates.

Conclusions

Despite the party's disastrous launch it is now firmly established. Indeed, even the launch must be placed in some form of context. The Labour Party, after all, existed as the Labour Representation Committee for a full 6 years before its current name was adopted. Moreover, it did not become a major player in the political process until the 1920s. Against this backdrop the Liberal Democrat's short history may look all the more impressive.

However, the party still faces some problems. First, the current electoral system would seem to be a barrier to sustained growth. Moreover, the majority of constituency contests in 1992 were primarily fought between two parties: Conservative–Labour (413 seats) rather than Conservative–Liberal Democrat (151 seats). This represents a continuation of the move back toward Conservative–Labour contests from the Alliance highpoint in 1983 (282 Conservative–Alliance seats as opposed to 287 Conservative–Labour ones) (Johnston, Pattie and Fieldhouse, 1994:261). Secondly, the party faces the risk of its ideological identity being threatened by the moderate policies emanating from the Labour Party. The Liberal Democrats may find themselves 'squeezed' to a certain extent. That said, the party has succeeded in placing some aspects of constitutional reform firmly upon the political agenda.

The Liberal Democrats, then, are an important part of British political life. The merger, although initially traumatic, has cemented the relationship between the Liberals and SDP in a far more coherent manner and moreover has taken the party to heights at all levels of government that the old parties never achieved during the post-war period. It is against this backdrop that we should assess the party.

6

THE 'OTHERS' IN THE BRITISH PARTY SYSTEM

Introduction

It is fair to say that the British party system is no longer a rigid two-party affair. With the obvious addition of the Liberal Democrats, there are MPs returned from nationalist parties in Scotland and Wales. Moreover, in Northern Ireland there is a unique party system reflecting the special circumstances of that part of the United Kingdom. However, it is misleading to argue that Britain is therefore a multiparty system since there are so few electoral contests that are more than two-party affairs. Britain does not have a multiparty system, but it can be argued that there are a number of different party systems at work in different parts of the United Kingdom. It is fairer to say, nationally, that Britain has a two-and-a-half-party system. For example in 1992, of the 634 seats contested at the General Election, 65 per cent were primarily Labour–Conservative contests; 24 per cent Conservative–Liberal Democrat and 2 per cent Labour–Liberal Democrat. Only 9 per cent of seat contests did not fall into these categories (Johnston, Pattie and Fieldhouse, 1994:261).

Nevertheless, despite these facts which may be argued to be partial products of the electoral system, the other parties are still vitally important to the landscape of the British party system. This chapter will examine the 'other parties' that hold seats in the House of Commons. Thus there will be an examination of the

Scottish National Party (SNP); Plaid Cymru (PC), the Welsh Nationalists and the parties that constitute the quite different party system in Northern Ireland.

Nationalist parties in Britain

Perhaps the first question one should ask when looking at nationalist parties is why they exist. The existence of a nationalist party implies dissatisfaction with the existing arrangements of the nation state and is likely to appeal to some form of regional identity. In the case of both the Scottish and Welsh National Parties, there is at least a partial rejection of the political system which is seen to be dominated by England and English interests. Much of this resentment results from the often difficult task of nation building which invariably results in a strong centre and weaker peripheries. Such problems can be overcome should national identity be generated and regional differences diffused. However, where distinct cultures and identities remain, the potential for political conflict lingers. It is no coincidence that Wales and Scotland have nationalist parties, while England does not. Further explanations include first that the growth of nationalist parties reflect in some way the alleged decline of the two-party system in Britain. The suggestion is that the nationalist vote can be explained as a form of protest. Secondly, there is a view that when regions suffer relative deprivation compared with the centre, then discontent will manifest itself in nationalist sympathies (McAllister, 1979:5–6).

That said, the existence of these factors need not necessarily imply that nationalist sympathisers will take the conventional electoral route. They must decide whether to form a political party or take other routes. The choices are outlined in Figure 6.1. Beyond forming a distinct political party, sympathisers can still follow an

Figure 6.1   **Choices facing minority leaderships.**

	Differentiated organisation	Communal permeation
Electoral	Political party	Entryist group
Non-electoral	Pressure or protest group	Social movement

Source: **McAllister (1979:3).**

electoral route by practising entryism into existing political parties. If they take the non-electoral route, the choice may be organisational in that a pressure group can be formed which seeks to advance one or more interests. Alternatively, nationalists can attempt to mobilise common identities of groups, such as religion or ethnicity and create a broad social movement. These movements will not have anything like an organisational base, but will be concerned with broad aims such as the defence of certain traditions such as language, for example (McAllister, 1979:3–4).

The distinct identities of Scotland and Wales have not been lost upon the state or the main British parties. There are separate governmental structures in the forms of the Scottish and Welsh Offices, for example. Scotland and Wales are also overrepresented in Parliament on the basis of a calculation of the mean number of electors per parliamentary seat. In 1992 the mean constituency population in England was 71 676; in Scotland it was 60 408 and in Wales 59 174. Moreover, both the Conservative and Labour Parties have Scottish and Welsh organisations and the Liberal Democrats, with their strong federal structure, have distinct Scottish and Welsh identities. Nevertheless, there is a clearly felt need for nationalist parties.

The Scottish National Party

The case for Scottish nationalism rests upon the argument that Scotland is a separate nation which is dominated by English political and economic interests. Scotland became part of Britain after the Union of 1707, but still retained a number of distinct practices, not least legal, administrative and educational. Nevertheless, nationalists have argued that governance from Westminster has failed to acknowledge Scottish interests and that English interests have dominated the political and economic spheres.

The SNP is the main political focus of nationalism in Scotland. It was formed in 1934, but had its modern roots in the period immediately after the Great War. Scotland was badly affected by the economic slump that occurred after the war. It had been heavily dependent upon its traditional heavy industries during the war but, at its end, it was apparent that the industrial base was increasingly outdated and was being overtaken by changes in technology. The

Table 6.1   **SNP seats and votes in General Elections since 1966.**

Election	Share of Scottish vote (%)	MPs elected
1966	5.0	0
1970	11.4	1
1974 (February)	21.9	7
1974 (October)	30.4	11
1979	17.3	2
1983	11.8	2
1987	14.0	3
1992	21.5	3

Sources: Kellas (1990:129); Butler and Butler (1994:166).

result was that although Britain was suffering economic trauma in general, Scotland was relatively more deprived (Mullin, 1979:110).

A parallel growth occurred in intellectual nationalism as a result of a Scottish literary renaissance. Moreover, nationalists were frustrated that Ireland had gained Home Rule, but parliamentary delays had prevented similar provision for Scotland (Mullin, 1979:110–11). Scottish Nationalists wished to avoid the violent conduct of the Irish Nationalists and so in 1934 formed the SNP from a merger of the National Party of Scotland and the Scottish Party (Mullin, 1979:111).

Following the Second World War, however, the electoral prospects for the SNP looked poor. Just as in the period after the Great War, post-war reconstruction required considerable centralised state economic activity. With such moves being seen as a necessity, the appeal of a party that was naturally hostile to this centralising state was not ripe for widespread support. Moreover, the party itself had experienced divisions, first from those that emphasised cultural over political aims, and secondly from those that did not support the electoral approach with a differentiated organisation. However, by the late 1940s the SNP had at least clarified its identity and future direction, by establishing the ascendency of political rather than cultural aims and by finally committing itself wholeheartedly to electoral politics with its own party (McAllister, 1979:11).

In the late 1950s and early 1960s, the appeal of the SNP began to flourish as intellectual critiques of state centralism gathered pace. Not only was Scotland affected by the actions of the centralised British state, it was also affected by those of large firms, thus the 'small is beautiful' critique of authors such as Schumacher, combined with the growth of grants of independence to former colonies, had particular poignancy in Scotland (Mullin, 1979:112–13).

In more recent years the arguments claiming overcentralisation of governance misrule from England have been drawn into sharp focus both by the beginnings of production of North Sea Oil in the 1970s in Scottish waters and the electoral geography of Scotland since 1979, which has had only a handful of Conservative MPs and yet has been ruled by a Conservative government. Additionally there is, it is claimed, a distinctive 'Scottishness'. Certainly, Scotland has its own language, although it is not widely spoken. Gaelic is the first language of only around 1.5 per cent of Scots. The SNP, as a result, does not emphasise cultural factors in its appeals for support.

Organisation and ideology

Although the SNP was formed in 1934 it was not a party in the modern recognisable form until the 1960s. Since then, it has grown into a political party in the more conventional sense. It operates at three levels: national (Scotland), intermediate and local. At national level there is an assembly, a council, an executive and an annual conference. The intermediate level consists of regional councils and constituency associations while the local level has groups and branches.

Formally, the various levels have the following responsibilities. The annual conference is theoretically supreme, suggesting a high level of internal democracy. Beyond that, the national executive is most powerful while the national council provides an interim policy making mechanism between annual conferences (Levy, 1994:155). The national assembly is a consultative forum with no formal powers. At intermediate level, constituency organisations have a certain amount of formal control over the group or branch. At local level are the party's members. There is no corporate membership as in the Labour Party through trade unions or socialist societies. Membership estimates vary widely, not least since membership is dealt with at a local level. However, recent estimates put the figure at around 16 000, although academic studies have put the figure much lower.[1]

As with other parties, however, the constitutional and actual positions in terms of organisation are often at variance. While early studies of the SNP suggested a degree of disorganisation, later studies suggested that the centre was actually more powerful than previous studies or indeed the constitution had suggested. This was largely because mass membership had not really occurred until the 1960s and therefore local organisation was a comparatively new phenomenon. Moreover, as with other parties, it appears as though the membership was relatively content to allow the central elite to make decisions. That is not to say, however, that members have not become involved in policy initiatives, but to say that while the party may be committed to internal democracy, the reality is that the central organisation is more powerful than its constitutional position suggests. That said, there has been much interaction between the elite and the grass roots in the past through a heavy programme of social activities designed to raise party funds (Mullin, 1979:116). However, in recent years the party has employed more modern techniques of fund-raising, such as direct mail (Lynch, 1995:12), and thus the opportunity for informal interaction has declined.

One of the areas where ordinary members have exercised influence within the SNP is through the growth of clear factions within the party. The spur for the most clear of these factions was the 1979 referendum result on Scottish devolution. In that referendum, while 52 per cent supported devolution, it was not granted because the positive votes had not met the stipulated 40 per cent of the entire electorate required. The problem was that 36 per cent did not bother to vote so the pro-devolution votes counted for only 33 per cent of the electorate. The result was that the SNP withdrew support for the minority Labour government and the 79 Group was established to press for a more radical and left-wing programme, although remaining committed to devolution as a step towards ultimate independence. By 1981 the radical wing of the party had succeeded in gaining conference support for civil disobedience, which was reaffirmed in 1988 when the party supported a campaign of non-payment of the Community Charge (poll tax)

---

[1] Brand estimates 8000 (see Levy, 1994:154).

which was introduced in Scotland a year prior to that of England and Wales. Ultimately, the radical sections of the party also moved away from the pragmatic approach to independence, rejecting the devolutionist approach in the late 1980s.

The factionalism that has on occasions appeared in the SNP gives a clue to its ideology. Prior to 1979 the SNP had been a relatively moderate party, concentrating primarily upon the achievement of independence which was envisaged to be likely to occur after a period of devolution. Ultimately, the moderate wing of the party dominated until the early 1980s and sought to be a party that was 'good for Scotland'. The experience of Thatcherism and the referendum defeat, however, has shifted the party ideologically towards a far more left-wing position, although one that is pro-European. To that end, as Brand *et al.* (1994) point out, the SNP in many respects has become barely different from the Scottish Labour Party.

> Indeed, apart from the constitutional question, the rhetoric of Labour and SNP is barely distinguishable – anti-Tory, interventionist, statist, egalitarian and socially conservative. (Brand, Mitchell and Surridge, 1994:225)

Another notable policy shift has been a reversal of opposition towards the European Community. Indeed, like Labour the SNP has seen aspects of European policy, such as the Social Chapter, as a means of achieving policy goals in spite of a hostile Conservative government. Moreover, the growth of the EC has seen the possibility of the promotion of a policy of independence within a European context, although this policy has angered some fundamentalists who have retained their opposition to the EC having been taken into it by the British government. If Scotland is to be a member, they argue, it should be so on their own terms. Nevertheless, the official policy has been one of 'Independence in Europe' and has been seen as a compromise position between those that actively seek Scottish independence and those that are sympathetic, but fearful of the consequences. Importantly, this policy has proved to be popular among the majority of SNP members and to a lesser but still significant extent, among SNP voters (Brand, 1992:86).

The overall result of these policy shifts is that a new strategic consensus has emerged in the party, largely as a result of the party's gradualist wing becoming dominant (Lynch, 1995:7). There are four strands to this new consensus: increasing electoral support, establishing institutional support for independence, promoting independence and undermining the union and establishing the SNP as a European social democratic party (Lynch, 1995:7–9). It has sought to increase its electoral support by broadening its message including campaigning upon nonconstitutional issues. That said, it is still pursuing independence by attempting to gain support for the idea from broad groups such business and trade union organisations as well trying to gain more mainstream recognition for the negative aspects of the current constitutional position. Finally, the party has sought to develop a far clearer centre left identity, particularly since its core support stems from that tradition and the SNP is seeking to effectively replace the Labour Party in Scotland. Moreover, by offering a coherent ideological platform it is hoped that this will in turn generate greater support for independence itself (Lynch, 1995:7–10).

Selection of candidates

Candidate selection in the SNP, as with the Conservatives and the Liberal Democrats, begins with application to the national approved list. Admission to this list involves a selection board similar to that held by the above. Constituency associations then consider applications and nominations for candidates from this list. If there are sufficient numbers, short-listing occurs and then ordinary party members vote for candidates accordingly. Importantly, however, the result must then be approved by the national executive committee, who can veto the proposal. Moreover, if a by-election is held the selection process must be repeated, which reflects the great importance of by-elections to the SNP (Norris and Lovenduski, 1995:82).

Conclusions

The recent history of the SNP has been a mixture of trauma and success. It has not reached the heights that it did in October 1974, when it scored 30.4 per cent of the Scottish vote, but the 1992 election did see it improve significantly upon its 1987 vote share. Nevertheless, it still managed to secure only three seats; but in the

1994 European Elections the SNP managed to gain a second seat, having gained its highest vote share in these elections. Indeed, it is Europe that has provided much-needed life to the party and its shifts towards European support have proved to be popular. The party has also developed more of an ideological identity. The adoption of a broad social-democratic ideology has provided the party with more potential electoral appeal. Modernisation has also occurred in the area of political communications, with the party adopting many modern techniques such as PR in a similar way to the approach taken by the Labour Party (Lynch, 1995). In one sense it seems that the SNP is highly unlikely to secure a majority of seats in Scotland, especially since the Labour Party are promoting at least the development of a Scottish Assembly. On the other hand, the SNP looks strong enough to retain its identity and residual strength for many years to come. Moreover, the establishment of a Scottish Assembly would give the party added prominence.

Plaid Cymru

Plaid Cymru (PC) shares many similarities with the SNP. Both resent their perception that they are governed by a state dominated by English interests. Unlike the SNP, however, PC places greater emphasis upon cultural independence. There is an economic platform as well and this is formalised through constitutional means in the form of an endorsement of community socialism (of which more later). Wales lost its independence in 1536 but, unlike Scotland, did not retain many distinct internal structures. Culturally, PC reflects the fact that Welsh nationalism is closely linked to Welsh language speaking. While in the majority of Wales English is spoken, a substantial minority of nearly 20 per cent can speak Welsh, and indeed in the north west of Wales, Welsh speakers are in the majority. It is no coincidence that PC has fared electorally better in these areas.

Plaid Genedlaethol Cymru (later renamed Plaid Cymru) was formed in 1925. Although nationalism had long been a force in Welsh politics, the formation of a nationalist party was prompted by number of factors of significance at that time. First, there was a continuing and steady growth of English culture and language, particularly as a result of the increasing commercial penetration of

Table 6.2   Plaid Cymru seats and votes in General Elections since 1966.

Election	Share of Welsh vote (%)	MPs elected
1966	4.3	0
1970	11.5	0
1974 (February)	10.7	2
1974 (October)	10.8	3
1979	8.1	2
1983	7.8	2
1987	7.3	3
1992	8.8	4

Sources: Kellas (1990:129); Butler and Butler (1994:165).

Wales in the late industrial revolution. Secondly, there was disillusionment in Wales that Home Rule policies had not been applied successfully to Wales, and the establishment of the Irish Free State merely served to underline the possibilities for such ideas (McAllister, 1979:14). However, its main objectives when formed focused more on language than self-government. Essentially, the main aim of Plaid Cymru at its inception was to maintain the prominence of the Welsh language (McAllister, 1979:14).

These primarily cultural objectives dominated until after the Second World War and the more pressing economic circumstance of the period no doubt contributed to the party's singular lack of real electoral success. Indeed, while Plaid Cymru (PC) had some of the features of a political party, it is probably more accurate to speak of it during this period as a social movement. After the war, however, the party began to broaden its campaign to include non-cultural issues, notably post-war reconstruction and a devolved assembly. However, its activity still bore more of the hallmarks of a non-electoral movement. During the 1950s, however, PC saw increasingly promising electoral performances at by-elections and there was much anticipation for the outcome of the 1959 General Election. The party fielded more candidates than ever before, yet it attained no electoral successes. The result was that the party developed strong internal tensions between those whose primary concern remained with the language and those, primarily younger members, whose concerns were more focused upon economic and social matters (Balsom, 1979:133–4; McAllister, 1979:17). The latter group were also more concerned with electoral prospects than the former and wished to broaden the appeal of PC to areas of Wales such as the South, where the language was less commonly spoken.

It was the younger radicals that became dominant and thus in the early 1960s, PC appeared to become a political party in the more recognisable sense. This process was aided considerably by the formation in 1962 of *Cymdeithas Yr Iaith Gymraeg* (the Welsh Language Society). This group was committed primarily to campaign on the language question and served to defuse the issue within PC. Moreover, those that were primarily committed to the language issue diverted their energies to the new group rather than the party. PC now became a party dedicated increasingly to social and economic issues and electoral breakthrough came with a by-election victory in 1966. Electoral success was, however, spasmodic and it was not until the General Election of 1974 that PC became firmly established as an electoral force. That said, the electoral support that PC received was not lost on Labour governments at least, who responded by passing the Welsh Language Act 1967, giving the language greater prominence in road signs and official circles and establishing, among others, the Welsh Development Agency in 1974.

Organisation and ideology

Organisationally, PC shares similarities with the SNP. It too has national (Wales), intermediate and local levels of organisation and the member is the core unit. At local level there is the branch (or *Cangen*); at intermediate level, district and constituency committees and at national level, a national council, executive committee, national sections and the annual conference. Unlike the SNP, however, branches are afforded a greater degree of autonomy so long as their programmes are in line with conference decisions. This reflects the notion of co-operation with small communities which is at the heart of much of PC's political outlook (McAllister, 1979:18).

At national level, the National Executive is afforded wide powers and is responsible for the whole organisational structure of the party and implementing council and conference resolutions. As with the SNP, the national sections perform a largely consultative role, while the national council performs policy making functions between the ultimately sovereign annual conference. Studies of PC have suggested, however, that in fact the central elite tends to be more powerful than the constitutional position suggests. This is partly due to the absence of a large parliamentary or assembly party and, again, as a result of the fact that the parties were in place before the advent of genuine mass membership. Moreover, there is also a lack of grass-roots activity to counter elite influence (Levy, 1994:156). Certainly, Conference is seen as a largely managed affair which acts more as a rally than its constitutional position suggests (Broughton, 1995:14). This serves to emphasise that the local branches' main role is in reality raising funds for the party (Balsom, 1979:145–6; Broughton, 1995:13). Membership of PC is said to be around 8000–9000 although it is difficult to be accurate about this figure, since while membership details are maintained centrally there is still a reliance upon local provision of this information. In short, despite constitutional appearances and occasional decentralising efforts, PC is a centralised party with real influence residing with a small elite (Broughton, 1995:14).

While grass-roots members appear to occupy a less powerful role, nevertheless there have been factional groupings within the party. Principally, these have revolved around the themes of fundamentalism and gradualism, socialism and anti-socialism and civil disobedience. As with the SNP, the spur for many of these clashes was the overwhelming referendum rejection of devolution in 1979 and the experience of the Thatcher administration. This renewed tensions largely between those who called for a socialist response and those whose interest was primarily of a single-issue nature, the protection of the Welsh language and identity.

Largely because of the tensions within the party regarding nationalist aims, the ideology of PC has been characterised by elements of compromise and pragmatism. This has been particularly the case over issues such as the language, which are potentially divisive in a country where the majority do not speak Welsh. Thus, PC has sought to safeguard Welsh language and culture rather than focus entirely upon it. Beyond the cultural and socio-economic aspects of PC ideology, we can also identify other aspects. First, PC is constitutional and resolutely non-violent, partly as a reaction to the violence propagated by more extreme forms of nationalism often practised by fascist groups. The non-violent stance of PC has been part of a conscious attempt to disassociate their nationalism from the more unsavoury and frequently racist forms. Nevertheless, PC has sometimes struggled to maintain this image in the face of violence and bombings carried out by nationalist extremists and has suffered some 'guilt by association' in the past (Broughton, 1995:9).

PC is also decentralist and wishes to pursue self-government rather than outright independence. As with Scotland, the influence of 'small is beautiful'-type philosophies have been influential to PC. Since 1981 PC has constitutionally committed itself to socialism and has adopted other areas of concern such as ecology, the role of women and an anti-nuclear stance. However, this has not been without its difficulties. Although the broadly socialist programme is no longer subject to much disagreement, there remain certain residual tensions between the socialist wing and the more liberal, landowning sections of the party who prefer the party to concentrate more on 'Welsh issues'.

These tensions became particularly apparent during the 1980s and early 1990s when PC made alliances with other parties. First, a formal link was established with the SNP just prior to the 1987 general election. This was an agreement as to what both parties would do in the event of a hung parliament. While the link provided both parties with increased media exposure, there were some in PC who opposed the arrangement on the grounds that it was felt the SNP lacked ideological clarity. Most supported the link, although it has now expired (Broughton, 1995:12). A second controversial link was with the Green Party which followed the Greens' impressive showing in the 1989 European Elections. Those that opposed the link did so largely on the basis that the Greens were opposed to PC's nationalist aims and also because they doubted the Green Party's prospects in the long term. Nevertheless, an alliance was struck for collaborative arrangements in seven seats and in one (Ceredigion and Pembroke North), PC was successful in winning the seat. In all other seats, however, the arrangements yielded little if any success. Despite the success in winning a fourth seat under these arrangements with the Greens, there is little enthusiasm within the party for maintaining the arrangement since many feel that nationalist concerns are more important that those propagated by any party with whom PC wishes to make electoral pacts (Broughton, 1995:12–13).

While PC is now constitutionally socialist, its commitment is to 'community socialism' rather than the state form that they claim is advocated by the Labour Party, although the idea of 'community' has rarely been clearly defined. Plaid Cymru is also more gradual-ist that the SNP. This is rooted in the fact that PC's concerns have traditionally been more with cultural preservation rather than sov-ereignty *per se*. Coupled with the rejection of devolution in 1979, PC has been more receptive to proposals for a Welsh Assembly and promotes self-government as its goal. Moreover, since 1990 PC has embraced Europe and sees it as an avenue towards which Wales can gain at least a degree of independence from England. As with SNP, however, there is also continuing opposition to EC membership from some sections of the party.

Candidate selection

The process of candidate selection by Plaid Cymru is unlike the other parties we have examined. There is no centrally approved list, no shortlisting and no formal role for ordinary members (Norris and Lovenduski, 1995:81). Prospective candidates are nominated by branches and appear before a selection committee of branch representatives, constituency officials and regional rep-resentatives. Voting then takes place among the selection commit-tee. The leadership is not involved in this process, although when by-elections occur it is represented on a joint selection board with constituency representatives; an indication, as with the SNP, of the importance of by-elections to the party and of the ability of the leadership to intervene.

Conclusions

Like the SNP, Plaid Cymru enjoyed its greatest electoral successes in the mid-1970s and its share of the vote has been in gradual decline, despite a slight surge in 1992. Indeed, it now has more MPs than ever (four) but shows little sign of extending its appeal beyond the core areas of its support. This is partly due to the resilience of the Labour Party in Wales. Perhaps PC's key electoral problem is that its support is characterised so much by the Welsh speakers. This, Denis Balsom has argued, stems from the fact that Wales is not homogeneous, despite its small population, and can be divided into three distinct groups: Welsh Wales in the industrial south, where English is spoken but identity is Welsh rather than British; *Y Fro Gymraeg* in the Welsh-speaking west and north west, where again Welsh identity is paramount, and British Wales in the east and south west, where identities are British rather than Welsh (quoted in Levy, 1994:149; Broughton, 1995:16). Plaid Cymru has only generally scored well in *Y Fro Gymraeg* where Welsh speaking is most prominent. In other areas it has trailed as a minor party. Nevertheless, PC has enjoyed some notable although sporadic successes at local level. Indeed, in Welsh local elections in 1995 PC came second to Labour in terms of seats, although their support was heavily concentrated and PC won only one seat (of a possible 187) in the three main urban areas in the south of Cardiff, Newport and Swansea.

PC also faces the dilemma of its electoral strategy. Its main electoral rival is the Labour Party, yet Labour is the only party likely to be able to deliver an elected Welsh Assembly. As a result, while PC has attacked Labour in local government, it has tacitly acknowledged that the success of Labour in national politics is essential to attaining PC's own ideological goals. As a result, since PC's electoral success seems to rest heavily on the success of Labour at the national level, it is argued that a political 'dependency culture' characterises party competition in Wales (Broughton, 1995:3).

From a different perspective, PC faces the problem that representation at Westminster is not enough for most committed activists. In the absence of a Welsh Assembly where PC could exercise more influence, the case for supporting the party may be questioned. Moreover, as Balsom has suggested, there is also the danger that PC MPs may become 'institutionalised' by the very conventions of British political life that PC MPs are seeking to alter (Balsom, 1979:149).

The parties of Northern Ireland

The party system in Northern Ireland is quite unlike that of the rest of the United Kingdom. Until 1989 none of the parties on the mainland fielded candidates there, and it now remains only the Conservatives who do so. The party system of Northern Ireland is a reflection in one sense of the special circumstances of the area, but also reveals divisions among the two main forces of political opinion in Northern Ireland; those that support the existence of Northern Ireland and those that wish to see it reunited with the rest of Ireland. Around 90 per cent of votes cast are for parties that are committed to these positions and this division is bolstered by the strong partisan identities of Protestants and Catholics. The party system in Northern Ireland, then, is a greater reflection of its social base than is now the case in mainstream British politics. There are, however, deviations from this dichotomy; the communities themselves harbour different interpretations of the political situation and in the past there has been some evidence of class co-operation which crossed religious boundaries (Connolly, 1990:99). Moreover, there is also the existence of two political parties which attempt to appeal to both communities in Northern Ireland: the Alliance Party and the Worker's Party.

Nevertheless we can, in contemporary terms, talk of two broad 'sides' in Northern Irish politics: the Unionists who support the separate status of the North (although debate exists as to whether this should be within the United Kingdom) and the Nationalists, who support reunification with the rest of Ireland. While there are deep divisions within the two 'sides' to which we will return, Unionist support comes overwhelmingly from Protestants and Nationalist support from Catholics. Indeed, the strong divide is well demonstrated by the fact that since 1970 around 10 new parties have emerged. All, however, have had a brief lifespan and parties that focus on the divisions have enjoyed more enduring support (Connolly, 1990:99).

Unionist parties

In order to appreciate the differences between the Unionist parties, it is important to understand that within Unionism itself there are some significant ideological divisions. The principal division is between what has been termed Ulster British and Ulster Loyalist. Among the Ulster British the primary loyalty is to the United Kingdom, with a secondary loyalty to Northern Ireland itself. This group has tended to be more liberal in its outlook and while supporting the Union, is less sectarian in its approach than Ulster

Loyalists. This second group identify primarily with Northern Ireland, and Protestantism in particular. It is committed to the dominance of loyalists in the province and its loyalty to Britain is not only secondary, but is conditional upon the British monarch remaining Protestant and the British government acting in a favourable manner (Connolly, 1990:99–100). From this more extreme tradition have also emerged paramilitary groups, some of whom have had informal links with Unionist politicians.

There are two main Unionist parties, the Ulster Unionist Party (UUP) and the Democratic Unionist Party (DUP). Both sit within the Ulster Loyalist tradition and are suspicious of both Ireland and the political role of the Catholic Church. They are generally distrustful of the British government and wish to see devolved government restored to the province so as to ensure the loyalist majority are in control. Notwithstanding those similarities, the UUP does not share some of the more extreme positions of the DUP.

The UUP is the oldest party in Northern Ireland and has its origins in the Home Rule debate in the late nineteenth century. It is conservative and very much the party of the establishment. This is not surprising since for the most part, it has had strong links with the British Conservative Party, which itself is strongly committed to the Union. These close ties have been reflected in the political sympathies of the UUP and convention until the 1970s meant that UUP MPs took the Conservative whip. Since the 1970s, when Britain imposed direct rule on Northern Ireland, UUP relations with the Conservatives have been less formal and this was particularly the case following the signing of the controversial Anglo-Irish Agreement 1985 by Margaret Thatcher, which gave Ireland a consultative role in governance of the North. As a result, formal organisational links were severed. Nevertheless, while the UUP has organised itself as a distinct party at Westminster since the 1970s it has continued to support the Conservatives in general, although UUP MPs sit on the opposition benches of the House of Commons.

The UUP supports Northern Ireland's position within the United Kingdom and is in that sense loyalist. In this way, while it attracts middle class voters with its conservative respectability, its strong links with Protestantism through the Orange Order serves to broaden its appeal across classes among the Protestant population. Moreover, there is a far greater range of opinion within the party than is the case within the DUP, which has allowed for more liberal opinion to exist, although these sections are very much in the minority. Like the British Conservative Party, it has succeeded in securing support from all social classes even though its rhetoric is one of the middle classes.

By contrast the Democratic Unionist Party (DUP) is less conservative. It was born in 1971 and presents itself as a radical Protestant alternative to the UUP. It is radical in the sense that it does not attempt to be respectable in the way of the UUP, but rather is more populist in approach, generally finding support among the working class and fundamentalist Protestants. As a party formed in part through disaffection with the UUP, it has tended to thrive in periods when Unionism has been seen as being under threat. Like the UUP it supports the existence of Northern Ireland but frequently with more zeal: a reflection of the strong influence of the Free Presbyterian Church and its leader, the Reverend Ian Paisley. This influence has tended to manifest itself in particular hostility to the Catholic Church and a notably more fundamentalist position towards the position of Ulster.

While the DUP shares the UUP's support for the existence of Northern Ireland, it has nevertheless seen the UUP as a form of opposition, and relations between the two parties have often been far from co-operative. In the early 1980s the rise of Sinn Fein (the political wing of the Irish Republican Army, more commonly known as the IRA) and the development of co-operation between the British and Irish governments which produced divisions within the UUP, led to the DUP being able to capitalise on what it saw as a polarisation of public opinion in Northern Ireland, given its absolute commitment to opposition to a united Ireland. It was initially successful, securing an impressive vote in the 1981 local elections which exceeded that of the UUP. However, its apparent dominance in Unionist politics was short-lived, and the UUP regained its prominence the following year and in the 1983 General Election. This status among the Unionist electorate was partly cemented by the electoral pact between the DUP and UUP following their collective opposition to the 1985 Anglo-Irish Agreement. This lasted from 1986 to the General Election of 1992.

It is also worth noting the existence of the Alliance Party, which is the most prominent example of the liberal strand of Unionism. Although it has never won a seat at Westminster, it has had some success at local level. More significantly, it has maintained a credible share on the vote in General Elections since its formation in 1970. While its high point was 11.9 per cent in 1979, it still received 8.7 per cent in 1992. Although formed largely from Unionist ranks its support has been drawn from both communities, although from the wealthier socioeconomic groups. Its stance has been one of power-sharing and while its position has been hindered by direct rule from Westminster it remains an important symbol of the potential for co-operation between the two communities in Northern Ireland.

Nationalist parties

The Nationalist case lies in the first instance that Northern Ireland should not form part of the United Kingdom, but should be politically united with Ireland. In the second instance, there is the widespread view among the Catholic population of Northern Ireland that it suffers discrimination and as the minority group in the province, this is unlikely to change. While these factors have formed the basis for the nationalist cause the responses have not been uniform, differing between violent and non-violent approaches. Like the Unionists, the Nationalists in Northern Irish politics are themselves split in party terms, although at present only one party holds any seats in the House of Commons: the Social and Democratic Labour Party (SDLP). Formed in 1970, it grew from the older Nationalist Party and was developed as a more modern party organisation than its predecessor. In fact, it is argued that the old party was not really a political party at all (McAllister, 1979:22–3; Connolly, 1990:112–13). First, since Nationalists refused to recognise the legitimacy of Northern Ireland itself, Nationalist activists and MPs tended to abstain from conventional political activity. Secondly, the party had only one real policy goal, Irish unity; and finally, there was no party organisation to speak of either within Parliament or outside.

However, this lack of a coherent party organisation led other groups, notably the non-electoral and violent Irish Republican Army (IRA), to offer alternatives to the Nationalist community, particularly since the Nationalists were unclear about their position upon political violence. This led to the formation of the SDLP, with its commitment to the electoral process and clear rejection of violence. The SDLP is a broad church in terms of Nationalists, drawing its support from Catholic Nationalists, those that had participated in the civil rights campaigns in the 1960s and the (Catholic) urban working class (Aughey, 1994:173). Initially, it promoted a broadly left-wing platform, advocating state intervention in industry and welfare. However, its principal political stance is towards the position of Northern Ireland itself.

The SDLP is Nationalist but, critically, it is Nationalist by consent. While the SDLP seeks to reunify Ireland it wishes to do so only with the consent and co-operation of the Protestant population. To that end, it has sought to involve the Unionists in power-sharing arrangements between Ireland and the United Kingdom, both in the 1970s, in the Northern Ireland Assembly and the Council of Ireland, and in the current peace settlement in the province. Nevertheless, while the SDLP has sought to reach consent upon the future of Northern Ireland, its frustration with what it saw as the obstructive actions of the Unionists and the continuing violence in Northern Ireland has led it on occasions to seek to compel the Unionists to concede certain positions by excluding them from negotiations. An example was the 1985 Anglo-Irish agreement, where the SDLP sought to reach a settlement between the British and Irish governments which it hoped would be forced upon the Unionists, who would not otherwise have accepted the arrangements.

The SDLP has been the most successful Nationalist party partly because of some very adept leadership, notably from John Hume. It has been seen as the legitimate face of Irish Nationalism, and Hume's ability to negotiate between the frequently entrenched positions in Northern Irish politics has made its position even stronger. Nevertheless, the SDLP has not been without political opposition among Nationalist sympathisers, most notably from Sinn Fein.

Sinn Fein came to electoral prominence in the early 1980s. It represents a more hard-line form of Irish Nationalism and has close contacts with the IRA. Certainly, many of its senior figures have been members of the IRA, but Sinn Fein has denied that they are simply its electoral arm. Hard-line Nationalism was not a feature at the ballot box until the early 1980s. The IRA had traditionally opposed involvement in electoral politics as this was seen as a diversion from their ultimate aim of uniting Ireland. Moreover, there was also the view that participating in any election in the divided Ireland was to imply the legitimacy of the partition.

However, as with the DUP, Sinn Fein sought to offer an alternative to the more established SDLP by opposing the consensual and constitutional approach that the SDLP had hitherto taken. In doing so, it sought to supplant the SDLP as the principal party of Irish Nationalism.

Sinn Fein's entrance into the electoral arena was prompted by the campaign of hunger strikes among Republican prisoners. This campaign in the early 1980s served to cement Nationalist feeling in the Catholic community and this was well illustrated when the most prominent hunger striker, Bobby Sands, was elected to the House of Commons in 1981 in a by-election. Seeing the political capital that could be made, Sinn Fein began to develop an electoral strategy which could be viewed as legitimising the non-constitutional approach to Irish Nationalism.

Sinn Fein's electoral success continued. In the 1983 General Election the Sinn Fein president, Gerry Adams, was elected to the House of Commons for the seat of Belfast West after defeating the former leader of the SDLP, Gerry Fitt. He retained the seat in 1987, although with a reduced majority, and the seat was regained by the SDLP in 1992. By this election the SDLP had clearly regained any initiative it may have lost and increased its vote in every seat in which it stood, gaining 23.5 per cent of the Northern Ireland vote. By contrast, Sinn Fein gained only 10 per cent of the vote and had a decreased vote share in almost all the seats in which it stood. That is not to say, however, that Sinn Fein has ceased to be a political force in Northern Ireland. The peace process is likely to involve its significant participation, particularly given Gerry Adams's prominence in these negotiations.

Conclusions

At the time of writing, politics in Northern Ireland is in an entirely new phase. There was a 'ceasefire' from the paramilitary groups for more than a year and the presence of the British army was progressively reduced. The peace process has held, however, and all sides are preparing for talks to determine the future. Of course, this is just the beginning and it is very difficult to predict the outcome of the process. However, assuming that the peace process is maintained, it is quite possible that the party system may undergo some change. For example, in the absence of political violence Sinn Fein may well move to become a mainstream party instead of one largely of protest. Similarly, if some form of power-sharing agreement does emerge, then Unionist parties will presumably be forced to examine their position. This, of course, is all speculation, but if the radically changed circumstances in Northern Ireland can be maintained it seems probable that this must herald new developments in its party politics.

Conclusions

The 'others' in the British party system are clearly of importance and are an established part of the British political landscape. From one perspective, they offer representation to those that share their broad political outlook. However, from another, the importance of the 'others' is truly underlined. Minority parties have the potential to have influence in Parliament through support for governments with small majorities. To be sure, this was not really an issue during the Thatcher administrations. However, during the Labour administration of 1974–9, minority MPs became critical when the government became a minority. Similarly, since 1992 the Conservative majority has been slim and decreasing with each by-election defeat. Thus John Major has required the support of Unionist MPs to survive some votes in the House of Commons. Small parties also help to shape the political agenda to an extent. While they themselves may not enjoy a decisive electoral breakthrough, by mobilising electoral support and public opinion they can lead other parties to respond, either by adopting similar policies or by formulating ones that oppose those of the minority party (Smith, 1991:40).

Beyond the clear relevance of small parties, we can also highlight some common trends. First, for successful electoral mobilisation to take place, minority groups need to adopt the structure and policies that characterise a conventional political party. However, in the second place this inevitably has implications for the aims of groups. Entry into the electoral arena tends to lead to the prospect of political bargaining and compromise and the necessarily slow pace of electoral change leads to the acceptance that the goals of minority parties must become transitional. Thirdly, the electoral and transitional compromises are likely to compel parties to widen their electoral appeal in order to maximise support at the ballot box. In most of the Nationalist parties discussed here, for example, there has been an attempt to widen their electoral appeal beyond the realm of national sentiment. The SNP, Plaid Cymru and the SDLP have all sought to develop a distinct ideological identity beyond their initial ideological remit. Moreover, it is notable that all have adopted left of centre positions. In short, it seems that in electoral terms nationalism is not enough and parties require a far broader platform. Of course, this does not suit all those who support the aims of minority parties and the evidence suggests that factionalism can occur, even in small parties. However, the frequent lack of a credible conventional political alternative leads factions to remain as such and not become permanent schisms. As a result, while the 'others' in British politics may find political progress frustratingly slow, they are likely to remain as an important part of British political life.

7

THE PARTY MEMBERS

Introduction

It is perhaps one of the great mysteries of British political science that party members have not been examined more closely. Prior to the early 1990s there were only a few studies, most of which were of the case study type. For a long period of time, sweeping statements about the type of person who joined a political party were made without any real evidence to support these claims. Assumptions were maintained and even party policies pursued, mindful of the membership that parties thought they had. Such views had their academic origins, at least, in three key works. As early as the turn of the century when the modern party system was in its infancy, Ostrogorski expressed concern that the development of mass-party organisations would compromise the political judgement of leaders and MPs, whom he feared could become beholden to the unaccountable extra-parliamentary organisations (McKenzie, 1955:8–9). Secondly, Michels suggested that the opposite may be true; that in fact, organisations such as political parties were subject to an *iron law of oligarchy*, whereby power tended to reside with a small elite at the head of an organisation, in spite of any mass democratic conventions that might exist (McKenzie, 1955:15–17). For Michels, then, the role of the party member was a minor one.

Finally, McKenzie suggested that Michels' iron law might have relevance to the Conservative and Labour Parties and significantly, that party members should be content to simply play the role of supporting candidates. Indeed, he argued as early as 1955 that even those roles were declining in importance and that the mass media 'and, above all . . . television' would become the most important means of electioneering (McKenzie, 1955:581–91). Remarkably, McKenzie's views were largely maintained and reinforced by political scientists for more than 30 years, leading Seyd and Whiteley to remark that party members and activists were generally seen as either extremists or unquestioning foot soldiers. They were the *Cinderellas* of British politics (Seyd and Whiteley, 1992:1).

During the early 1990s, however, evidence began to emerge from path-breaking studies of the membership of political parties in Britain. A number of studies were undertaken, although, at the time of writing, full evidence is only available for the Conservative and Labour Parties. The evidence was devastating. The long-held myth that Labour Party members were largely radical and were restrained only by the 'moderating bulwark' of the trade unions was laid to rest. Similarly, the view that Conservative members were the grass-roots guardians of Thatcherism was also challenged. For the first time, we were able to see on a large scale what type of people were members of parties and how active (or inactive) they actually were.

The role of party members

While McKenzie had not dismissed totally the activity of party members, he did nevertheless stress a minimal role both in descriptive and prescriptive terms. His view was not shared by those who had surveyed party members, however. They identified, or more accurately emphasised, six important roles played by party members, which suggested that their importance had been understated, both descriptively and prescriptively (Seyd and Whiteley, 1992; Whiteley, Seyd and Richardson, 1994).

First, party members, as we have seen, play an important role in selecting candidates and leaders. Not only that, they provide a population from which most candidates, councillors and MPs are recruited. Secondly, they play an essential role in party fundraising efforts. As we have seen, while the main two parties are able to generate significant funds from a variety of sources, the income derived from ordinary members is still very important.

Indeed, in the case of the Liberal Democrats the absence of corporate or trade union income makes this role all the more significant.

Thirdly, party members have a role as representatives of their party within the wider community. They are, in a sense, the parties' eyes and ears on the political ground and without such representatives, some argue that political parties will lack electoral legitimacy within communities (Whiteley *et al.*, 1994:4). Moreover, this role of party representative allows the members to play an important fourth role in the way of political communication. This operates in two ways. First, party members play a part in communicating the ideas of the party to the wider public. This may be done through formal methods such as canvassing or through more informal ones such as simple conversation. Secondly, through their day to day involvement in community life members can provide an important source of communication to the leadership regarding the popularity, feasibility or otherwise of policy ideas. This, in turn, can lead to a fifth role for the party member; that of policy initiation. As we have seen, the actual operation of party machines can militate against bottom-up models of policy initiation. Nevertheless at local level, at least, the ideas for policy can emanate from party members.

Finally, party members have a role in mobilising the vote. This certainly runs counter to the arguments that McKenzie expressed and that have been generally echoed in much work on the electoral process, namely that local campaigning had negligible effects upon national electoral outcomes. More recent evidence, as we shall see, suggests that local campaigning by parties may indeed play some role in mobilising the vote and more importantly influencing the result (Seyd and Whiteley, 1992; Denver and Hands, 1993; Whiteley *et al.*, 1994; Johnston and Pattie, 1995).

According to these arguments party members are indeed important and worthy of study. Let us examine the party members in order to assess who the members are, what their political views are and how politically active they are. In this way we can attempt to answer such questions as how representative parties are of the wider public in social terms, whether they are extremist or radical in political terms, and what proportion are committed activists.

Who are the party members?

In the following tables we examine the main social characteristics of the party members. As the surveys were conducted during the early part of the 1990s, the profile of members is also compared and contrasted with voters in the 1992 General Election. While there are data on all areas for the Conservative and Labour Parties, they are only partially available for the Liberal Democrats as the full findings for that survey have yet to be published. There are also certain data available for the Greens. The sources for all tables in this chapter are as follows:

Conservative Party	Whiteley *et al.*, 1994
Labour Party	Seyd and Whiteley, 1992
Liberal Democrats	Curtice, Rüdig and Bennie, 1993
Green Party	Rüdig, Franklin and Bennie, 1991, Curtice, Rüdig and Bennie, 1993
Voters	*British Election Survey 1992*

What is apparent first of all is that all parties are more male in their composition than voters. Notably, however, the Conservatives are almost evenly split, a possible reflection of the long-term female participation in the party which dates back to the early role of the Primrose League. The Labour Party is the most male dominated with a split of around 60:40. Nevertheless, the parties overall are broadly even in the distribution of sex of their membership (Table 7.1).

Regarding age, there are much greater differences. What is most apparent is the relative old age of Conservative members and relative youth of the Greens. More than 40 per cent of Conservative members are over the age of 66 and fully 67 per cent over 55. By contrast, 41 per cent of Greens are under 36 and 69 per cent under 46. In fact, as a general trend, all parties have some age bias

Table 7.1 **Sex.**

%	Voters	Con	Labour	Lib Dem	Green
Male	46	51	61	54	56
Female	54	49	39	46	44

Sources: as above.

Table 7.2 **Age.**

%	Voters	Con	Labour	Lib Dem	Green
0–25	10	1	5	4	12
26–35	20	4	17	8	29
36–45	20	11	26	16	28
46–55	16	17	17	21	14
56–65	15	24	16	19	9
66+	19	43	19	33	9

Sources: see p.142.

in their membership (Table 7.2). With the exception of the Greens, all parties under-recruit among the under-35s, although Labour has had more success here than the other two main parties. Such figures present a dilemma for the Conservatives as, should this profile broadly remain, their membership would simply 'die out'. It is not a problem for a party to have large numbers of elderly members if there is renewal among the young. This, however, does not appear to be happening for the Conservatives. On the other hand, of course, it may be that people tend to join the Conservatives in later years for a number of reasons. If this is the case then there is less of a problem. Certainly, while many young people joined the Conservative Party in the 1950s for largely social reasons, this is clearly not the case today.[1] This is also a problem, to an extent, for the Liberal Democrats. Fifty-two per cent of their membership is over 55, although they have had better experience of recruiting younger members (under 35s) than the Conservatives. The Labour Party, by contrast, has a much more evenly spread membership in terms of age.

Table 7.3 **Ethnic origin.**

%	Voters	Con	Labour
White	97	99	96
Non-white	3	1	4

Sources: see p.142.

[1] It is often argued that in the 1950s, many joined the Conservative Party as it was a good way of finding a respectable marriage partner.

Table 7.4 **Class.**

%	Voters	Con	Labour
Salariat	29	55	49
Routine non-manual	24	18	16
Petty bourgeois	7	13	4
Foreman/technicians	5	6	5
Working class	35	8	26

Sources: see p.142.

Finally, in terms of ethnic origins, like voters the parties are dominated by whites (Table 7.3). However, we can detect that the Labour Party has a marginally greater ethnic mix than the Conservatives.

In terms of class the two main parties are in some ways very similar (Table 7.4). Both draw a disproportionate share from the salariat and are clearly far more middle class than the electorate as a whole. Where the two parties differ is among the petty bourgeoisie, who are more attracted to the Conservatives, and the working class who favour Labour. Nevertheless, the argument that Labour is essentially a working class party is evidently open to question. That said, Labour members who subjectively perceive themselves as belonging to a social class are more likely to claim that they are working class (Table 7.5). Thus, while 'objective' measures indicate a more middle class party, subjectively the party's largest group is working class.

Table 7.5 **Self-perceived class.**

% saying they belonged to social class	Voters	Con	Lab	Greens
Yes	46	62	73	60
No	54	38	28	40
if yes				
Upper class	0	5	0	1
Middle class	36	56	28	83
Working class	63	40	70	17
Other	2	1	3	—

Sources: see p.142.

Table 7.6 **Tenure.**

(%)	Voters	Con	Labour
Own property	75	91	75
Rented from council	21	3	18
Other rented	5	5	6

Sources: see p.142.

In contrast, in terms of subjective class figures, the Conservatives appear to be less class dominated; indeed, the Greens appear to be more middle class. That said, what is noticeable about all parties is that a significant minority in each do not consider themselves to be part of any social class grouping, and while that minority is smallest in the Labour Party it still constitutes more than a quarter of the party's membership. Nevertheless, since the majority in each party do classify themselves (unlike voters), it does indicate that party competition is still viewed partly, at least, in terms of social class by many members.

In terms of housing tenure the Labour Party membership is a fairly accurate reflection of the electorate, around three-quarters being home owners. Conservatives, in contrast, are more likely to be property owners and much less likely to rent in the public sector. Conservative members, then, reflect well their party's long-term emphasis upon private property (Table 7.6).

Regarding education, party members tend to be more qualified than the electorate although this occurs in the Labour Party to a greater extent than the Conservatives. While both main parties recruit most of their members from those that left school at 16 or younger, Labour members are more likely to have entered into higher education than Conservatives. The reason for this, however, is likely to be a reflection of the Conservative's relatively elderly

Table 7.7 **Age at end of full-time education.**

(%)	Voters	Con	Labour
0–16	70	55	58
17–18	16	25	12
19+	14	19	30

Sources: see p.142.

Table 7.8   **Household income.**

(%)	Voters	Con	Labour
Under £10,000	35	26	38
£10,000–£15,000	16	19	18
£15,000–£20,000	15	15	15
£20,000 and over	33	42	32

Sources: see p.142.

membership who would have had fewer opportunities to enter higher education, rather than any general trend (Table 7.7).

Finally, just as the objective class data showed Labour members to be from a wider social range than the Conservatives, so it is the case with household income (Table 7.8). The income profile of Labour members is remarkably similar to that of voters. Moreover, while the Conservatives have the highest paid members, it is not the case that the most wealthy totally dominate the party. Although the largest group of Conservative members do come from the highest income quartile, there are still significant minorities in the lower quartiles, especially among the least wealthy group with a household income of under £10,000.

As with voters, a newspaper is often selected as a reflection of a person's views rather than as a means of dictating them. So, with

Table 7.9   **Newspaper readership.**

%	Voters	Con	Labour
None	33	11	13
The Times	2	6	1
Independent	3	2	7
Daily Telegraph	6	2	2
Guardian	3	<1	35
Financial Times	<1	1	1
Daily Mail	9	17	1
Daily Express	7	14	1
Today*	2	1	1
Daily Mirror	17	1	29
Sun	12	3	1
Daily Star	2	<1	1
Other	5	8	4

Sources: see p.142.
* Now defunct.

party members, we see an element of such selection (Table 7.9). Due no doubt to a greater than average interest in politics, party members are more likely to read a newspaper regularly than typical voters. Whereas around a third of voters do not read a newspaper, this applies only to between 11 per cent and 13 per cent of members of the two main parties. As far as Labour members are concerned, their choice of newspaper is unsurprising. Most read the leftward leaning *Guardian* or *Daily Mirror*. The only other paper with a significant readership among this group is the *Independent*. Conservatives, however, are less predictable. Despite the long tradition of Conservative support by the *Daily Telegraph*, only 2 per cent of Conservative members read it; the same proportion as of Labour members. More popular are the rightward leaning tabloids, the *Daily Mail* and *Daily Express*. *The Times* is the only other newspaper read by a significant proportion of the Conservative membership. Of course, one might argue that the reason the distribution of Conservative members' reading habits is so broad is that there is much greater choice for the right-wing reader. Labour members, by contrast, have to content themselves with a rather narrower choice of traditionally left-wing newspapers.

Armed with these data we can draw some further conclusions about the representativeness of political parties, at least in terms of resemblance. While we might consider that elite representatives will be unlikely to reflect the broader population, there could be some suggestion that the membership of parties would be a more accurate reflection. What we find is that certain groups are clearly underrepresented among the party memberships, at least in comparison with voters. Women, the young and the working class (measured 'objectively') seem to find least representation overall. That said, there are few areas of gross underrepresentation and thus we might argue that in aggregate terms, parties do serve to represent most groups within society (but some parties represent some groups better than others).

The views of party members on political issues

In this section we examine and compare a number of key attitudes of Conservative and Labour Party members. First we look at series of opinions on key political issues; then we examine party members' views on what we may describe as constitutional issues. Obviously, not all the questions from the party membership surveys are detailed here. A number of key issues have simply been selected where there are comparable data from each survey. More detail (and data) can be found in the original texts on the party membership surveys.

In the first set of statements, party members were asked to give their views on whether the government should take intervening action in a number of areas. In the first, which asks whether more money should be spent on reducing poverty, there is broad agreement between Conservative and Labour members upon the desire for governments to take action. Labour members are, however, slightly more keen than their Conservative counterparts. Regarding healthcare, we see both similarities and differences between party members. Broadly speaking Conservatives are in favour both of private and public health provision, while Labour

Table 7.10 **Political attitudes.**

% saying government should/should not	Conservative members		Labour members	
	Should	Should not	Should	Should not
Spend more money to get rid of poverty	81	11	99	1
Encourage the growth of private medicine	52	32	4	92
Put more money into the NHS	80	13	99	1
Encourage private education*	65	15	25	61
Spend less on defence	44	51	86	12
Reduce government spending generally	60	31	21	72
Give workers more say in the places where they work	64	23	94	3
Introduce stricter laws to regulate trade unions	66	21	12	78

Note: percentages will not add up to 100% as 'Don't knows' not shown.
* Derived from non-identical question on Labour Party Survey.
Sources: see p.142.

members support the NHS alone. Significantly, it is worth noting that although a majority of Conservatives support private health care, a notable minority (32 per cent) feel that the government should not encourage it. A majority of Conservatives also support the growth of private education. More significantly, perhaps, a substantial minority of Labour members also approve. Regarding other areas of public expenditure, Conservative members are fairly evenly divided on the subject of defence spending. A slim majority think that spending should not be cut, despite the fact that most think that governments should reduce public spending in general. However, it is worth noting that a large proportion of Conservative members do oppose general public spending cuts. Conversely, Labour members are broadly in favour of defence cuts, although oppose cuts in government spending generally. However, a notable proportion favour general cuts (Table 7.10).

Finally, most Conservative members are in favour of greater employee participation in the workplace, although a similar proportion wish to see an aspect of worker participation (through trade unions) regulated further. Labour members are overwhelmingly in favour of worker participation and most oppose further restrictions on unions, although a significant minority support further curbs.

Overall, it is clear from Table 7.10 that some issues divide party members more than others. To be sure, there are clear divisions on issues such as private medicine, private education, trade unions and overall government spending. However, some issues bring about broad agreement, such as poverty, the NHS and worker participation, while defence spending offers no clear partisan pattern. In short, party members are often as ideologically similar in single-issue terms as they are different.

The second table detailing political attitudes illustrates the responses where members were asked to state their agreement or disagreement with a pre-set statement (Table 7.11). The question of taxation is one that has dominated political discussion in recent elections. Conservatives are quite united in their views upon high income tax, seeing it as a disincentive in the workplace. As we have seen, however, the tax burden is in fact much broader than simple income tax and there is apparently little difference between the taxes paid under any post-war government in the United Kingdom. Nevertheless, Conservative members still see high income

Table 7.11　**Political attitudes.**

Statement	Conservative members		Labour members	
	Agree	Disagree	Agree	Disagree
High income tax makes people less willing to work	82	13	35	54
The next Conservative/ Labour government should establish a prices and incomes policy as means of controlling inflation	43	46	64	20
Restrictions on immigration into Britain are too loose and should be tightened*	91	4	41	42

Note: Percentages will not add up to 100% as 'Don't knows' not shown.
* Derived from non-identical question on Labour Party Survey.
Sources: see p.142.

tax as a disincentive. Significantly, Labour members are less opposed to the statement than we might imagine. While a majority reject the high income tax/low work incentive theory, a significant minority support it. Conservative and Labour members are more alike on another aspect of economic management, prices and incomes policies. Indeed, the Conservatives are evenly split on this issue which is surprising, given the opposition to such policies from the Thatcher and Major administrations. While both have attempted to peg public sector pay at least, no attempt has been made to fix prices as a means of controlling inflation. Also surprising is the level of support from Labour members, particularly given the collapse of such policies in the 'Winter of Discontent' under the last Labour government. That said, a significant proportion of Labour members oppose prices and incomes policies.

Finally the last figures, referring to immigration, reveal that Conservative members are more united on this issue, and display particular concern that immigration controls should be tightened.

Labour members on the other hand are divided, with similar proportions wishing to see a tightening of regulations or a relaxation.

Again, Table 7.11 reveals that members of the Conservative and Labour Parties often share similar positions. The subject of immigration controls clearly shows this and suggests that this is not an issue that will generate partisan support. Importantly, however, tax and inflation are issues which are seen to divide the two main parties. The evidence here is that while we can detect some partisan differences, they are not as clear-cut among the members as we might assume, particularly in the fields of the means by which to control inflation.

As far as constitutional issues are concerned, however, party members differ quite substantially. Conservative members are by and large opposed to the idea of a change in the electoral system to a form of proportional representation and reject, in similar proportions

Table 7.12   **Constitutional issues.**

Statement	Conservative members		Labour members	
	Agree	Disagree	Agree	Disagree
Britain's present electoral system should be replaced by a system of proportional representation	10	89	58	31
Coalition governments are the best form of government for Britain	10	80	7	81
A future Conservative/ Labour government should introduce a directly elected Scottish assembly with taxing powers	23	51	58	20
There is no need for a Bill of Rights in this country	40	34	12	78
Conservatives/Labour should resist further moves to integrate the European Community	54	30	16	72

Note: Percentages will not add up to 100% as 'Don't knows' not shown.
Sources: see p.142.

the possible outcome of electoral system change, coalition govern-ments. Labour members, on the other hand, are more keen on a change in the electoral system although, like Conservatives, reject the notion that coalition governments are beneficial. This reason-ing may, of course, be a product of the fact that Labour has not won a General Election under the current arrangements since 1974 (Table 7.12).

Regarding the devolution of powers (to Scotland at least) La-bour members are more supportive, although a significant minor-ity opposes the idea. For Conservatives, while most oppose the idea of a Scottish Assembly there are a number that support it, which may seem at odds with the traditionally unionist perspective of the party. As far as a Bill of Rights is concerned Conservatives are split, with a slight majority opposing the idea while Labour members are far more in favour, despite the oft-quoted reserva-tions of Labour politicians that such an idea would give too much power to unelected judges. Finally, on the issue of Europe, it is clear that Labour members overall are more supportive of further integration. Conservatives, while supporting further integration overall, include a significant minority that oppose it.

If any issues consistently divide party members, then, it is consti-tutional ones. By and large Conservatives are more committed to the status quo (as we might expect) than their Labour counter-parts. That said, there is evidently some wavering among Conser-vatives on the subject of a Bill of Rights. Ironically, it seems that the issues that appear to divide party members so much are those pursued by the Liberal Democrats and yet they are not pursued to the same extent electorally as issues where party members, at least, appear to be in some agreement. What is also clear is that many party members are evidently not the extremists that have been commonly portrayed.

The views of party members on their own parties

We now turn to members' views about their own parties. First, we examine the perceived importance of electoral success. Interest-ingly, Conservatives are far more inclined than Labour members to argue that the party should stick to its principles even if doing so would lose the party an election. This is surprising since, as we

Table 7.13 **Views about the party.**

Statement	Conservative members		Labour members	
	Agree	Disagree	Agree	Disagree
The Conservative/Labour Party should always stick by its principles even if this should lose it an election	82	10	61	27
The Conservative/Labour Party should adjust its policies to capture the middle ground of politics	70	17	57	20
The party leadership doesn't pay a lot of attention to the views of ordinary party members	43	33	39	44
People like me can have a real influence on politics if they are prepared to get involved	57	24	74	14

Note: Percentages will not add up to 100% as 'Don't knows' not shown.
Sources: see p.142.

have seen, the Labour Party has traditionally laid greater emphasis upon ideology while one of the secrets of the Conservative Party's success has been its ability to adapt its principles to prevailing circumstances. Moreover, Conservatism has sometimes defined itself rather as a state of mind than a principled ideology. Nevertheless, we may be witnessing a variety of interpretations of political principles since it is clear that Conservative members are happy to shift their policies to the middle ground of politics. Similarly, while most Labour members thought the party should stick by its principles even if this meant electoral defeat, a majority feel Labour should move towards the centre ground (Table 7.13).

Regarding their own party experiences a significant proportion of both groups of members feel that the party leadership is remote, although in the Conservative Party this is a majority. This is perhaps reflected in the fact that Conservative members clearly feel that they can have less influence as members than do Labour members. This, of course, may not be a criticism from Conservative members since it is clear that many would not want members to be more involved. Nonetheless, it is clear that the whole structure of the Conservative Party almost certainly contributes to this view. For Labour, while most members believe they can make a difference (should they so wish), it is worth noting that despite ongoing reforms, a significant minority feel that they cannot make a significant contribution.

Overall, there is further evidence here that party members are not the extremists that have often been portrayed. There is a general willingness to try and reflect public opinion rather than dictate it, although stronger commitment remains to general party principles. It would appear as though there are some grounds for discontent among party members. Significant proportions of both parties would evidently question the idea that political communication between the leadership and membership is a two-way process and this is particularly reflected among Conservatives.

Party activism

The popular image of the party member is (or was) a highly committed individual. However, party membership surveys reveal that, in fact, many party members are largely inactive. When asked about party activities frequently undertaken by members over the preceding 5 years, only two-thirds at most had even displayed an election poster, perhaps the mode of party participation that requires the least effort. Not surprisingly as the cost of party activity rises, defined in terms of time required, as well as effort and finance involved, so the participation rate declines, as is the case for participation outside political parties (Parry, Moyser and Day, 1992). Nevertheless, it is still apparent that less than half the members of all three main parties actually attend party meetings. Of course, the role of the local party varies from party to party which may explain different rates of participation to an extent. As we have seen, for example, Conservative members have traditionally concerned themselves more with mobilising support and social activities than policy debates. Nevertheless, the activities that all

Table 7.14   **Party activity.**

% who had done the following frequently in the last 5 years	Con	Labour	Lib Dem
Displayed election poster	19	65	64
Delivered election leaflets	22	57	63
Donated money to party funds	30	33	38
Attended party meeting	17	42	31
Canvassed voters	10	36	23
Stood in an election	3	9	16

Sources: see p.142.

parties partake in at election time are seemingly only undertaken be a minority of party members (Table 7.14).

What is most apparent is the significant lack of activity among Conservative members. Across each category of participation, Conservative members are least active of the three main parties. Only 10 per cent had canvassed voters as opposed to 36 per cent of Labour members. On the other hand, the fact that the membership of the Conservative party is at least three times that of Labour and probably around six or seven times that of the Liberal Democrats may in part explain these facts. In simple terms, if there are many more fellow members to undertake an activity the imperative to become personally involved lessens. Nevertheless, overall it is still clear that many members are sleeping members in that they only awake at elections and even then, for some the slumber remains unbroken.

Of course, this lack of political activity may be confirmation of McKenzie's prediction that the role of party members in elections would become increasingly peripheral. In a sense, we may simply be observing the manifestation of the view that local campaigning is pointless and has little bearing upon the actual result of an election. Certainly, anyone who has canvassed on a cold, dark evening and experienced a seemingly unresponsive electorate might be tempted to draw a similar conclusion. However, there is some evidence to suggest that local party campaigning does matter and that this lack of activity among members may in fact be a source of lost electoral opportunities for both parties. Johnston and Pattie, for example, show that the level of campaign expenditure can have an impact on results. In short, for all parties there is a positive relationship between local spending and the local share of the vote (Johnston and Pattie, 1995:269).

Campaign expenditure, however, is only one aspect of party activity and does not necessarily suggest that party members are being politically active, but that parties are good at spending money on areas that will increase its vote. Whiteley *et al.* (1994) have taken investigations a stage further and calculated that levels of activity among local party members, alongside local expenditure, can have an influence on electoral success. They found that for both Labour and Conservative Parties, the level of activism had a positive impact on their party's share of the constituency vote. They then estimated the effects of increasing both spending and activity, concluding that if between 1983 and 1987 Labour had recruited 100 more members who displayed typical levels of activism per constituency, it would have increased its vote in 1987 by 4.85 per cent (Seyd and Whiteley, 1992:197). Conducting a similar experiment for the Conservative Party, they estimated that if the Conservatives had canvassed and spent 25 per cent more than they did they would have gained a further 16 seats in 1987 (Whiteley *et al.*, 1994:214).[2] Their conclusion was therefore that although local campaigning could not be said to be a major influence on national campaigns, it can under certain circumstances be crucial, especially if majorities are slim and should therefore not be ignored.

Predictably, while Seyd and Whiteley (1992) and Whiteley *et al.* (1994) have made a convincing case for suggesting that local activity is important to electoral results many still support McKenzie's (untested) thesis. Nevertheless, they and others (for example, Denver and Hands, 1993) who examine local effects have managed to reopen debate about the electoral importance of party members and certainly have shown that the often time-consuming efforts of members may not have been in vain.

Conclusions

A number of conclusions can be drawn from this examination of the party members. First, we can argue that there is further

[2] The estimations of the effect on the Conservative vote were undertaken in a rather different manner than was the case for the Labour vote – see original text for details.

evidence to suggest the health and importance of parties. Although memberships are relatively small, there is clearly a wide distribution of social characteristics within the parties which results in most social groups receiving reasonable levels of representation in terms of resemblance to wider society. Secondly, we might also argue that the internal health of parties is shown by the wide variety of views held within them. In only a minority of areas do we see almost universal opinion on an issue. Party members, then, are not the unrepresentative extremists commonly portrayed. Thus party members may be said to be fulfilling their roles in terms of reflecting political views 'on the ground'. On the other hand, there is evidently some doubt as to whether they are able to perform the role of communicating the messages from the ground to the leadership.

However, there appears to have been a decline in party activism. This may be a reflection of the perceived importance of national politics and relative unimportance of local politics as well as a lack of political efficacy. However, other factors may account for the decline. For members of the Labour Party, the failure to win a General Election for more than 20 years might be expected to have had a demotivating effect upon members. Just as football crowds decline when a club experiences a constant lack of success, so Labour Party members may be increasingly fatalistic. On the other hand, success can also bring about its own problems. Consistent success can breed complacency, thus Conservatives may feel that success will be assured, regardless of their own efforts. Whatever the reasons, it is nevertheless striking how few members become involved in political activity, despite the fact that local campaigning appears to have the potential to make an electoral difference. In that sense, party members may not be wholly fulfilling their roles of communicating messages to the wider public, nor mobilising the vote. It is clear that party members are certainly worthy of examination and are crucial to the general health and legitimacy of political parties in Britain. Their role has been understated and it is clear that they are of fundamental importance to the survival of political parties.

8

VOTING AND ELECTIONS

Introduction

It is at elections that political parties are perhaps most visible. Here is an opportunity for parties not only to compete, but also to arrive at a result of that competition. Parties of course compete in all sorts of ways, but elections, with the accompanying result which decides the shape of the appropriate representative chamber, are the area where we can clearly ascertain winners and losers. As we have already seen, different party ideologies claim to put different emphases on election victory. Seventy per cent of Conservative members, for example, feel that their party should adjust its policies to capture the middle ground as opposed to 57 per cent of Labour members (Whiteley, Seyd and Richardson, 1994:252; Seyd and Whiteley, 1992:230).

Many might also argue that what is at stake is long-term ideological triumph rather than mere electoral success. From this perspective, we might argue that although the Green Party has never won a parliamentary seat in Britain, it has succeeded in placing environmental issues onto the political agenda in recent years. One might also argue that despite the Labour Party's electoral defeats in the 1950s, it succeeded in establishing a political consensus during the 1945–51 period which was by and large maintained until the 1970s. Similarly, many have argued that the experience of Conservative government since

1979 will create its own new consensus, and thus its success will be assured.[1]

Nevertheless, in this chapter we will be considering first some trends in General Election results and then examining why people vote for the parties that they do.

Trends in election results

An examination of General Election results over the last fifty years demonstrates that there are some clear trends to be observed (see Appendix I). To begin with, the Conservative and Labour parties both experienced a fall in their support after 1970. Between 1945 and 1970, the Conservatives averaged 45.3 per cent of the vote, whilst Labour averaged 46.1 per cent.[2] However, from 1974 to 1992 the Conservatives averaged only 40.7 per cent and Labour 34.6 per cent. Moreover, neither party has received a vote share greater than their average for 1945–70 in any subsequent General Election.

Secondly, the Liberal Party and its electoral successors have experienced a considerable increase in national vote share, with an especially large increase in the first election of 1974. Since then, its vote share declined before recovering during the electoral pact with the SDP and whilst the Liberal Democrats in 1992 did not secure the same level of support enjoyed by the Liberals in the mid-1970s, it was still a creditable result given the circumstances analysed in Chapter 5.

Thirdly, votes for 'Others' have also grown to some extent since 1970. Notwithstanding the fact that votes for Unionist candidates were classified as others after 1970 rather than for the Conservative Party, there has also been a general if erratic growth in nationalist voting together with a growth in votes for smaller parties, like the Greens. This has in part often been an artifact of

[1] In fact, opinion polls and surveys seem to indicate that the public has not become Thatcherite and still favours much of the so-called post-war consensus. However, many government institutions are likely to be permanently changed.
[2] Until 1970, the votes for Ulster Unionist candidates were added to the Conservative total since Ulster Unionist MPs took the Conservative Party whip in the House of Commons. After 1970, however, Unionist MPs no longer took the Conservative whip and thus in subsequent elections, votes for Unionist candidates were placed in the 'Others' category.

greater numbers of such minor party candidates standing for election as much as anything else.

However, these changes in vote share have not been reflected to any great extent in the composition of the House of Commons. Between 1945 and 1970, the Conservative and Labour parties won 97.9 per cent of the seats, whilst between 1970 and 1992, the figure was 93.9 per cent. By contrast, whilst the Liberals and their successors have averaged a vote share of 19.6 per cent since 1974, they have only won an average of 2.7 per cent of the seats.

Notwithstanding this final point, such figures have suggested a growth in electoral volatility, particularly after 1970. Yet, a key question to consider here is how to measure volatility. A commonly used measure is the so-called Pederson Index which measures net electoral change. This index is calculated by adding together the percentage point change in all parties' share of the vote between two elections and dividing the result by two (Denver, 1994:151). The Pederson scores for 1950 to 1992 are shown in Table 8.1. The average score for elections up to 1970 is 4.7, whilst for elections after 1970, it is 7.6. Moreover, during the latter period, there have been two particularly high scores (1970 and 1983). On this basis then, it would seem that the period after 1970 has been more volatile in electoral terms. Moreover, Crewe shows that changes in voting intention as measured by monthly opinion

Table 8.1 **Pederson Index scores 1950–92.**

General Election	Pederson Index
1950	3.7
1951	7.2
1955	2.4
1959	3.2
1964	6.0
1966	4.2
1970	5.9
1974 (February)	14.5
1974 (October)	3.0
1979	8.1
1983	11.6
1987	3.2
1992	5.2

Table 8.2 **Trends in overall volatility.**

	Switched parties (%)	Switched parties or abstained in either election (%)
1959–1964	18	35
1966–1970	16	34
1970–1974 (February)	24	42
1974 (October)–1979	22	37
1979–1983	23	40
1983–1987	19	37
1987–1992	19	34

Sources: Heath *et al*. (1991:20); Denver (1994:75).

polls also point to increased volatility from the mid-1970s onwards (Crewe, 1993:100–101).

Yet these analyses do not tell the whole story. The Pederson Index only tells us the aggregate difference between one election and another. It does not tell us if voters on an individual level actually behaved any differently from the previous election. Similarly, aggregate analyses of opinion polls do not tell us whether voters intend to switch party support. A possible alternative to these indicators is overall or gross volatility. This is calculated using survey data and measures not only how respondents voted not in one election, but also how they voted previously. This allows a measurement of what proportion of voters have switched parties or abstained in one election but voted in another. Table 8.2 illustrates overall volatility since 1959. It shows that in the first General Election of 1974, there was indeed a increase in volatility. Yet that rise was relatively modest and has receded to the extent that overall volatility between 1987 and 1992 was much as it had been between 1959 and 1964.

An examination of overall volatility adds a different perspective to the examination of electoral trends over time. To be sure, since 1970 the main parties, in particular Labour, have experienced significant changes in their vote share. Yet this does not necessarily mean that individual voters have become more volatile. It is against this backdrop then that we should consider the reasons for people voting as they do.

Studies of voting behaviour

In the rest of this chapter what we want to do is establish why people vote for particular parties. Of course, there is no definitive answer to this question; that perhaps is the Holy Grail of politics! Indeed, there are many competing arguments which attempt to explain voter choice. We cannot cover them all in depth here.[3] Whole volumes are devoted not just to discussions of various models of voting, but to individual types of model. However, we can summarise the main points before examining various influences on party choice in the 1992 General Election. For simplicity, I have divided models of British voter choice into three areas: social–psychological models; issue voting models and economic voting models.

Social–psychological models

Social–psychological models of voting behaviour are perhaps most familiar to many students. They refer to voting upon the basis of social characteristics and long-term party affiliation. The models are not identical but there is considerable room for overlap. We will examine social bases of the vote first. In this model, vote is primarily determined by sociodemographic characteristics, including class, religion and sex. Social class has been regarded as the principal social cleavage around which voting behaviour can be predicted. As we have seen, this is quite consistent with the development of the party system in Britain. Indeed, perhaps the most famous (and probably overused) phrase written about British electoral behaviour is Pulzer's quotation:

> Class is the basis of British politics; all else is embellishment and detail. (quoted in Denver, 1994: 34)

Essentially, voting studies in the 1960s concluded that British electoral behaviour was based upon class. In short, one could expect the majority of middle class (defined as non-manual workers) people to vote Conservative and the majority of working class

---

[3] Perhaps the best summary is Denver (1994). For more depth see Denver and Hands (1992).

(defined as manual workers) people to vote Labour. This period in British politics has been referred to as 'the age of alignment'. Essentially, it was one where political behaviour was seen to be fairly predictable and stable. This view of the stability of the period has been questioned, yet the commonly held view was that class voting held until the 1970s, when a period of class and partisan dealignment occurred.

Of course, class is not the only sociodemographic factor that can affect party choice. Others have been suggested. Age, for example, is commonly held to be a conservative force. That is, in simple terms, the older one is, the more likely one is to vote Conservative and vice versa. There are two possible explanations for this. First there are the factors of lifestyle and stake in society. Younger people have less stake in society and fewer responsibilities. This makes them more amenable to ideologies which seek to change the status quo. By contrast, increasing age and the responsibilities and lifestyle that tend to accompany the ageing process (such as buying property and having children) tend to make voters less amenable to any rapid social change. Thus they take a more conservative approach. The second view challenges this universal assumption about age, and argues instead that what is critical is the political awakening of age cohorts. Different generations experience different political events, such as wars, social change or periods of markedly unpopular government. Thus, it is argued that a collectivist experience such as the Second World War will be reflected in that age cohort of remaining Labour voters, while a cohort whose political awakening was in the late 1970s, when groups such as the trade unions were unpopular and the Labour government was in disarray, might take a different view.

Sex is also advanced on occasions to help explain the vote. Certainly in the past, women have tended to lean more towards the Conservative Party and men to Labour. However, many have argued that this has little to do with any inherent factors and more to do with other, more powerful, explanatory variables. Women, for example, tend to live longer than men, so the conserving dynamic of age is one possible explanation. Secondly, when women have been in employment they have tended to be in non-manual occupations (Norris, 1993:135). As we have seen, non-manual occupations have tended to be associated with voting Conservative. Nevertheless, women in non-manual occupations have still been found to be a little more Conservative in their voting. Finally, the phenomenon may also be partially explained by non-working women.[4] In short, those women that remain in the home are isolated and not exposed to collective work identity and industrial disputes; factors seen as essential for class identity and therefore class voting.

All these factors have had some influence on the vote. However, to simply assume that voting takes a resolutely deterministic line would be a questionable approach. To be sure, all the variables play a role, but we have to examine how voters come to identify with parties and largely, it is argued, stick with them. The term to describe this process is 'partisan alignment' or 'partisan identification'. Like the social determinism factors described above, this model of voter choice is seen as a long-term issue, rather than one of voters constantly changing affiliation. Partisan affiliation may and probably does draw upon social factors such as class, sex and religion, but it also draws upon lifetime experiences such as the political outlook of one's parents and friends. Essentially, this model of party choice is one whereby a voter develops an attachment to a party which is likely to remain over time. This does not preclude voting for another party on occasions, but the expectation is that the voter will generally 'return to the fold'. This is referred to as the homing tendency. Perhaps a good parallel is the support of a football team. Most football fans will agree that once a person begins supporting a team, they do so for life! Thus, one may be a Brentford fan or a Scunthorpe fan. If you are a Brentford fan, you probably are so for a variety of reasons: locality, family, friends, and so on. You will probably follow them for many seasons. In despair, you may begin watching another side in the hope of seeing some consistent success, but the likelihood is that you will return to Brentford in the long run (believe me!).

The model of partisan alignment uses one's partisan identification to predict a vote by the individual. In the 1950s and 1960s partisan alignment, like class, was a good predictor of the vote. The parties had loyal supporters. Partisan identification, then, is a psychological model which develops from a voter's experiences. These often include social factors and the identification is long term. It is, however, different from voting itself. Partisan identification is

---

[4] By non-working, I mean non-working within the labour force.

psychological, whereas voting is behavioural. Partisan alignment is 'cost-free' as opposed to voting which is not. Secondly, partisan alignment occurs over a long period of time as opposed to voting, which occurs only at elections. Finally, partisan identification can vary in intensity, whereas voting cannot. By that we mean that one can vary the level of commitment to party, just as people are committed to football teams to differing degrees. The outcome is that weak partisans are more susceptible to voting shift.

In the 1950s and 1960s Britain was apparently fairly stable electorally, brought about largely by strong partisan alignment and class voting. However, in the 1970s many political scientists began to argue that voters' anchorages were becoming less secure and that Britain was experiencing class and partisan dealignment. The 1970s saw a decline in the strength of partisan identification. Voters were classifying themselves as partisan, but the intensity had declined. Why had this occurred? A variety of theses have been advanced. First, the expansion of educational provision had led to increased political awareness. Thus, voters were less inclined towards 'blind' partisanship. Education led not only to increased political awareness, but also to increased employment opportunities which could complicate the original partisan affiliation though increased cross-group pressures. Secondly, the growth of television led to increased political awareness. It was only in the 1960s that television ownership became widespread. Moreover, rules and conventions for news coverage of politics tended to lead to minimal and uncritical coverage. The growth of televisual coverage of elections arguably led to a greater understanding of the issues thus, alongside the growth in education, providing the potential at least for a loosening of party ties.

The performance of the parties also led to dealignment. Fuelled no doubt by education and television there has been increasing dissatisfaction with party performances. The Wilson governments of the 1960s were very unpopular at times, and under Edward Heath in the early 1970s Britain experienced a 3-day working week and frequent power cuts resulting in families all around Britain having no television and conversing by candlelight! It goes without saying that government is an extraordinarily complex task, yet voters grew impatient and probably had unrealistically high expectations for 'their' party in power. These problems were no doubt compounded by external factors such as the oil shock over which

Britain or indeed other Western countries had little or no control. Finally, it has been argued that the voters outgrew the old politics of Labour and the Conservatives, and questioned whether the political system was working and whether the policies offered by parties in the 1970s reflected voters' views or indeed offered any real choice. This final point is certainly open to question and the enduring electoral strength of the main parties is testament to the fact that most 'new' expressions of politics have fizzled away (in electoral terms at least) just as quickly as they have emerged.

All these factors were compounded (and indeed were interlinked) with an *alleged* parallel decline in class alignment. I stress alleged because there has been furious debate about this topic. Suffice to say, many studies of voting behaviour have pointed to class dealignment but there is one distinct school of thought which has challenged this orthodoxy. Let us first examine the majority view.

In simple terms, class voting was seen as manual workers being far more likely to vote Labour than Conservative and non-manual workers being more likely to vote Conservative rather than Labour. Liberals were excluded from the equation as their vote share in the 1960s was very small. Psephologists discovered that class voting was in decline. Their evidence, essentially, was as follows. The existence of class voting could be examined in two ways, first, by using a score known as the Alford Index, named after the political scientist that created it. This index is calculated by subtracting the percentage of non-manual workers that voted Labour from the percentage of manual workers voting Labour. The index can also be calculated on the Conservative vote by reversing the process. The index then runs from 0 to 100, with 100 meaning total class voting and 0 meaning none. The second technique was the measure of absolute class voting, calculated by adding the number of non-manual workers voting Conservative to the number of manual workers voting Labour and calculating this total as a percentage of all voters. It is a measure which tells us the percentage of those voting along class lines. All indices point to a significant decline in class voting since 1964,[5] and especially during the 1970s (Table 8.3).

[5] 1964 is used as this was the first General Election in Britain when a full national survey of voters was taken.

Table 8.3   **Measures of class voting 1964–92.**

	1964	1966	1970	(Feb.) 1974	(Oct.) 1974	1979	1983	1987	1992
Alford Index (Labour)	42	43	33	35	32	27	25	25	27
Alford Index (Conservative)	34	35	31	29	27	25	20	19	20
Absolute class voting	63	66	60	55	54	55	47	49	54

Source: **Denver (1994).**

The projected reasons for apparent class dealignment are inter-linked with partisan dealignment. There are, however, some additional reasons advanced. First the process of *embourgoisement*, whereby the working class were becoming more affluent during the 1960s and thus adopted more middle class values and aspirations. Secondly, technological change brought about significant change in the workplace. In simple terms, the broad shift from manufacturing to service industries led to there being significantly fewer manual occupations. This has had two principal effects. First, the shift to non-manual work has not been accompanied by large-scale unionisation in the non-manual sector. Thus the combination of this and the decline of large manual labour communities has led to a loosening of ties with the Labour Party.

Secondly, there is little reason to suggest that all those who moved to non-manual occupations from manual backgrounds would vote Conservative. Frequently old class loyalties have been maintained. This has also led to more people being in what are known as 'cross-class locations'. This has partly been a consequence of the increase of women in the workforce, which has created more households with cross-class sympathies. Thirdly, it may even be that class as it defined here is no longer as relevant as it was. Dunleavy, for example, has advanced the thesis that it is people's relation to the public and private sectors which determines their vote (Dunleavy, 1980; Dunleavy and Husbands, 1985). This cleavage manifests itself both in occupation: working for the public or private sector and consumption: consuming services in either, for example, housing, transport or health. Thus, those that work and/or consume predominantely in the private sector might be expected to favour a party committed to cuts in public spending and taxes. Conversely, those working and/or consuming predominantely in the public sector might be expected to favour a party committed to the maintenance or growth of the public sector. Finally, Crewe has argued that it is no longer sensible to consider the working class as one group, but rather to distinguish between the traditional working class in the North who are council tenants and heavily unionised with the new working class, who live in the South, are owner-occupiers and who are less unionised or not at all (Crewe, 1992a).

This broad view of class dealignment was fiercely challenged by Heath, Jowell and Curtice in the 1980s. They argued that far from there having been class dealignment, there had been nothing more than 'trendless fluctuation' (Heath, Jowell and Curtice, 1985). Their arguments ran as follows. First, the measure of class on the manual/non-manual dichotomy was wholly inadequate. They argued that this two-category definition did not, in any way, reflect an accurate picture of the British class system. Instead, they proposed a five-point class schema, originally devised by Goldthorpe and Heath for a study of social mobility in the 1970s. There was much to commend this criticism. There are countless ways to define class and while the manual/non-manual dichotomy had an attractive simplicity, it created many problems in categorising people accurately in terms of class interests. In short, the manual/non-manual schema may well have been appropriate half a century ago, but society and industry had moved on. Heath *et al.*'s class schema, while not the only alternative, did at least allow for a more accurate reflection of status and economic interests of the workforce without creating an unmanageable number of categories.[6]

Their second criticism was a rejection of absolute class voting. They argued that this measure would be distorted if Labour polled badly in an election, since if Labour did badly then logically fewer

---

[6] Of course, there is no reason why class must be defined in terms of occupation. In fact, in many ways such a basis can present its own problems. Occupational class, for example, tends to overlook domestic situations such as child-rearing and also tends to downgrade occupations traditionally undertaken by women. Nevertheless, most conventional class schema tend to have their basis in occupation. An alternative, of course, is self-perceived class: a schema based upon self-classification.

Table 8.4   **Odds ratios of class voting 1964–92.**

	1964	1966	1970	1974 (Feb.)	1974 (Oct.)	1979	1983	1987	1992
Odds ratio	9.3	7.3	3.9	6.1	6.4	4.9	6.3	5.8	5.0

working class people would vote for them. What absolute class voting was measuring, then, was not whether class was still a principal factor but how well Labour was perform electorally. They concluded, therefore, that what needed to be measured was the likelihood of cross-class voting: relative rather than absolute class voting. The measure they devised was the odds ratio. This was calculated by comparing the percentage of the top category in their class schema (the salariat) voting Conservative rather than Labour, divided by the percentage of the bottom group (the working class) voting Conservative rather than Labour. Thus in 1992 the ratio would be as follows:

$(54/19)/(31/54) = 5.0$

The larger the odds ratio, the stronger the relative class voting. Their results are shown in Table 8.4.

The conclusion drawn by Heath *et al.* was that there had been no regular pattern of class dealignment, rather that relative class voting simply fluctuated with no discernible trend. Given that Heath *et al.* had rejected the thesis of class dealignment and its relationship to the declining electoral fortunes of the Labour Party, some alternative explanation was required. Their conclusion was that it was the sizes of the social classes that had changed; in short the manual working class was shrinking in size and the salariat and routine non-manual groups were expanding. This could account for the Labour Party's decline.

Heath *et al.*'s challenge to the orthodox opinion on the subject has itself been challenged. Criticism was largely levelled at the use of the odds ratio as a technique for measuring the existence or not or class dealignment. It was argued that, first, absolute measures of class voting should not be rejected; it was undeniable that fewer people were voting for their 'natural' class party. Secondly, it was argued that the odds ratio itself was very sensitive to small percentage changes in the calculation. Thus, the ratio should not be used as a precise index as Heath *et al.* had done. Thirdly, the odds ratio ignored votes for other parties. Given that in 1983, Labour was almost pushed into third place in terms of share of the vote by the Alliance, this was a curious omission. Fourthly, while Heath *et al.* had rightly criticised the use of the manual/non-manual class schema, they themselves resorted to a dichotomous measure of salariat and working class for their odds ratio. Given that the two groups combined accounted for only 60 per cent of the electorate, this seemed odd. Moreover, it was argued that if dealignment was occurring, it would be more likely to occur in the 'intermediate' class groups where old divisions were more blurred (Crewe, 1992b; Dunleavy, 1992).

While both Heath *et al.* and their critics have revised their positions to an extent, the debate continues to this day. Nevertheless, most analysts argue that at least some dealignment has occurred which helps explain the apparent electoral volatility which has emerged, whereby it is arguably far more difficult to predict voters' behaviour than was the case previously. If we accept for a moment that partisan and class dealignment has occurred, then other explanations of the vote must be advanced. Two main schools of thought emerge: issue voting and economic voting.

Issue voting

An ideal type of voter in democratic theory would be one that considered each election on its merits. That is, they would consider each party programme and vote for that party whose programme evoked most sympathy. However, many previous studies almost ignored the issues in elections, preferring to concentrate on class or partisan identification. Given that voters apparently freed themselves from the shackles of habitual voting by the 1970s, we must consider under what circumstances issue voting can occur. Butler and Stokes (1969) identified four conditions to be satisfied. Most are quite obvious, but are often overlooked in analyses.

1. The voter must be aware of the issue concerned.
2. The voter must have some attitude towards an issue.
3. The voter must perceive that different parties have different policies towards the issue.

4. The voter must cast his vote for that party which the voter perceives to be closest to his position.

In addition to this, we should note that some issues do not divide parties or electors. Few if any want an increase in crime any more than few if any seek economic recession. The issues that concern this model of voting behaviour are 'position' issues rather than 'valence' issues, where there is widespread agreement about a desired outcome.

During the 1960s little evidence was found that voters cast their votes in this way. For example, Butler and Stokes took the issue of nationalisation (a particularly salient issue of the post war period) and asked voters to indicate their positions over four separate interviews. Less than half were consistent in their positions on this issue. Secondly, voter's issue positions were not consistent over a series of related variables. For example, voters did not tend to be consistently left or right wing on issues, although that may, of course, be a reflection of political scientists' preconceptions. Generally speaking we might expect individuals to be likely to hold opinions that are mutually consistent, such as liberal or authoritarian views. Nevertheless individuals often hold some apparently contradictory views, for example being very liberal on one social issue, such as premarital sex, and very authoritarian on another, such as views on homosexuality. Of course, such contradictions may be a result of ignorance or misinformation. Where opinion is translated into action the possibility of inconsistency is bound to increase, since salience will emerge. Choosing between particular political parties or candidates in an election may entail making a choice between general support for a party or candidate and the range of policies for which a candidate stands. Not all policies presented will necessarily be acceptable to the voter. In the 1980s, for example, not all Conservative voters were committed to a strong nuclear defence policy any more than all Labour voters were committed to unilateralism.

Thirdly, Butler and Stokes found that while voters were able to distinguish between parties' policy stances on some big issues, it was not the case on others, even when there were key differences between the parties' positions. Moreover, voters were particularly vague on where the Liberals stood on most issues. Finally, many voters who were aware of the issues, had a view on them and recognised the parties' different policy positions on them, still voted for the 'wrong' party. Many Labour voters were opposed to nationalisation, for example, yet continued to vote for the party that promoted that policy.

The theory of issue voting has also presented two methodological problems. First the problem of causation, which also relates to economic voting. For example, let us suppose that there was a positive relationship between voters' views on defence and voting for a particular party. We can interpret this result in (at least) two ways. We might say that the issue of defence had been a deciding factor in determining voter choice. On the other hand, we might argue that the voter adopted his position on defence as a result of his existing partisan identification. That is to say, a Conservative identifier would support whatever Conservative defence policy was at any given time. This reflects the quotation we saw in Chapter 4 that claimed 'Socialism is what a Labour government does'.

Secondly, there is the problem of issue trade-offs. For example, different voters give different issues differing levels of salience. Just as some people feel strongly about particular issues, so they will also feel more strongly about one issue compared with another. The relative importance of issues, moreover, is likely to vary. Thus, whereas strikes and unions were considered very important in 1979, they are clearly no longer considered to be a major electoral issue, although propaganda from all political sides might indicate otherwise. Just as the intensity of opinion can affect levels of political behaviour, so can the salience of an issue for a voter. The difficulty for the researcher is that there is no reliable way of assessing which issues have been most salient in determining the vote.

Nevertheless, despite these problems with issue voting there have been studies that have suggested that issue voting has come increasingly to the fore. Sarlvick and Crewe, for example, suggested that one could test salience by assessing what percentage of voters mentioned an issue as one of importance in their voter choice. Secondly, one could measure the party that is preferred in the issue, and finally the credibility of the parties' claims that they would achieve policy goals on the issue in question. Additionally, Sarlvick and Crewe developed a sophisticated technique for analysing the impact of position and valence issues on voter choice. Although not without its critics, Sarlvick and Crewe were able to

Table 8.5   Issue opinions and party choice in the 1979 General Election.

	% who have position	% who locate Con and Lab differently	Corre-lation opinion/ party (a)	Corre-lation opinion/ party (b)	Corre-lation opinion/ party (c)
Tax cuts v. govt services	87	80	0.25	0.33	0.44
How to tackle unemployment	85	82	0.35	0.42	0.46
Incomes policy	87	73	0.00	0.32	0.42
Laws to regulate trade unions	87	83	0.41	0.47	0.62
EC economic policies	80	66	0.11	0.24	0.47
Improving race relations	87	70	0.07	0.19	0.36
Social services	98	83	0.28	0.39	0.51
Nationalisation	94	88	0.45	0.48	0.60

Notes: (a) Correlation with vote.
      (b) Correlation with closest party.
      (c) Correlation with party choice for those who considered the issue 'Extremely important'.
      Correlation measures the strength of relationship between two variables on a scale between 0 and 1, where 1 means perfect association and 0 means no association.
Source: Denver (1994).

demonstrate that issue voting was of some importance. They ana-lysed opinion on eight issues and asked respondents to choose between policy alternatives in each case. At each stage of their research they considered the four conditions of issue voting (Sarlvick and Crewe, 1983). Their results from 1979 are shown in Table 8.5.

Here, we see that Butler and Stokes's conditions are satisfied. Voters are aware of and have a position on the issue (column 1); they perceive different parties as having different policies on the issue (column 2) and voters tend to vote for the party closest to their view or for the party 'believe' to be closest to their view (columns 3 and 4), at least on certain issues. In the final column, the voter choice of those voters that consider an issue to be 'Ex-tremely important' is examined. This column attempts to test sali-ence. The correlations indicate that on some issues the relationship is very strong.

Table 8.6   Valence issues and party choice in the 1979 General Election.

	Average % assessing Lab and Con	Correlation assessment/party (a)	Correlation assessment/party (b)
Strikes	96	0.52	0.53
Rising prices	97	0.52	0.60
Unemployment	95	0.51	0.56
Law and order	96	0.39	0.44

Notes: Correlation (a) with party choice; correlation (b) for those that considered
       issue 'Extremely important'.
Source: Denver (1994).

Sarlvick and Crewe also tested voter choice in valence issues, attempting to test whether assessments of the parties' abilities were translated into votes. The results are shown in Table 8.6. As we can see, there is a good relationship between voter assessment and party choice which increases with the importance the voter places on the issue.

Sarlvick and Crewe's analysis, together with their demonstrations of partisan and class dealignment, were powerful and formed the basis of a new orthodoxy. Indeed, it is testament to the enduring resilience of their work that students today continue to quote the ideas as received wisdom; yet, as with any model of voter choice, there have been criticisms.

Heath *et al.*, with Rose and McAllister to an extent, challenged the view that voters considered specific party policies. Rather, they argued that voter judgements on issues were themselves a product of party preference (Heath *et al.*, 1985; Rose and McAllister, 1986, 1990). Thus a voter's judgements were not based upon which party they considered to have the best policy on an issue. Rather, voters preferred the Labour Party's policy on unemployment, for instance, because they were Labour supporters. Indeed, Heath *et al.* showed that if voters in the 1983 General Election had voted along the lines of the closest party to the issue they considered to be the most important, the result would have been a close run between the Conservatives and Labour. What in fact happened was that Labour performed very badly.

Heath *et al.* did not wholly reject issue voting, however. They devised a new model based upon general values or principles acting as influences on voter choice rather than specific issues. Both Heath *et al.* and Rose and McAllister argued that what was important was the overall picture of the party as a collectivist one or an individualist one, for example. Short-term issues which might become relevant in a particular election were not seen as having much impact. These principles could develop through socialisation, either in childhood or through a 'lifetime of learning' as Rose and McAllister put it. In short, critics of issue voting rejected the idea of the free-thinking voter, arguing instead that voters developed their own set of values (no doubt shaped, to an extent, by the parties' offerings) and voted accordingly. Moreover, changes in values were themselves likely to be linked to a voter's social context. Thus, social mobility might be expected to produce changes in values.

Economic voting

The notion that voter choice is linked to the economy is not a new one, but it is only in recent years that it has become the dominant area in studies of voting behaviour. In some senses, the role of the economy has been the best-kept open secret in politics. By that I mean that politicians and pundits have long assumed that voters choose based upon a punishment–reward model: they punish governments with a poor economic record by voting against them, and reward governments with good economic records by voting for them. Moreover, it has also been assumed that voters have relatively short memories and will reward a government that produces an economic boom in the period before an election. Thus governments have been accused of attempting to 'buy' the electorate by manufacturing a period of economic growth through government intervention just prior to an election.

In fact, while there may be some substance in these claims, studying economic voting is a more complex matter. Essentially, there are four ways to examine the impact of the economy on voter choice (see Figure 8.1). Retrospective judgements refer to voter assessments of a party's past record. Prospective judgements are those which the voter makes if he or she expects certain outcomes should that party be elected. Sociotropic voting is utilitarian in outlook in that it refers to voting on the basis of the good of the community, be that community local, regional or

Figure 8.1 Dimensions of economic voting.

	Retrospective	Prospective
Sociotropic	1	2
Egocentric	3	4

more commonly, national in character. Egocentric voting refers to behaviour designed only to consider the outcome of the individual concerned and perhaps his immediate family. Thus, using these techniques we can consider the role of the economy in four ways.

First, retrospective sociotropic voting (1) would refer to a voter that made his choice for the good of the country or community, based upon the past economic performance of parties (usually, the incumbent party). By contrast, a prospective sociotropic voter would vote for the party most likely to benefit the country or community in the future (2). A retrospective egocentric voter (3) would vote in the interests of himself based upon the government's record in improving or worsening his economic circumstances. Finally, the prospective egocentric voter (4) votes for the party most likely to improve his economic circumstances in the future. Of course, egocentric and sociotropic voting may not be mutually exclusive. A successful sociotropic vote could also improve an individual's economic circumstances and vice versa. What is important, however, is which judgement is most important to the voter in making his or her choice. A classic pundit's view might be that most voters will fit into category 4, the prospective egocentric voter, but survey evidence has often found such individuals notoriously hard to find. Moreover, survey evidence has also suggested that retrospective considerations tend to be more influential than prospective ones and that voters are more ready to punish an incumbent government than reward it.

Another major consideration, as with issues, is how voters perceive the economy and its relative health or malaise. In simple terms, what is important in a factor influencing a voter is how the voter perceives that factor, regardless of whether the perception is accurate. Or, to put it another way, the economy may be technically in excellent shape, but this will be of little relevance unless voters perceive it as such. Just as issues demand interest and comprehension from voters, so it is with the economy. It is fair to say that certain economic indicators, such as the balance of trade or the strength of the pound, neither interest voters nor, in the short term at least, affect their lives. Clearly, then, some objective measures of the economy are more important than others in terms of influencing votes. Measures such as interest rates, unemployment and the value of properties are likely to have more direct impact on voters' perceptions.

Moreover, there may also be a degree of difference between voters' egocentric or sociotropic judgements and the 'actual' state of economic affairs. This may be generated by a number of factors. Frustratingly for governments, voters often stubbornly refuse to be cheerful even when there is apparently economic good news. For this reason, studies of voter choice have increasingly turned to perceptions of the economy, rather than relying on voters to respond to the 'facts'. To be sure, positive or negative evaluations of the economy may actually display a consistent lag behind objective measures. After all, economic optimism or pessimism is not simply plucked from the air, but for the purposes of voter choice it is more important to know how voters feel rather than attempt to estimate how they are going to feel.[7]

The most consistently successful attempt to tie economic evaluations to voting behaviour has been by David Sanders and various colleagues. In 1987 they presented remarkable evidence which challenged one of the widely held truths of the 1980s: namely that Mrs Thatcher won the 1983 Election largely because of the 'Falklands Factor'. The early years of Mrs Thatcher's government were very turbulent and both she and her government were, at the time, the most unpopular government in living memory, yet they recovered and trounced the opposition in 1983. Many ascribe this to Britain's successful military involvement in the Falkland Islands in 1982. Sanders *et al.* argued, however, that this was misleading; arguing that in fact the resurgence of the government's fortunes could more accurately be explained by a revival and continuing rise in personal economic expectations. Using opinion poll data

[7] That said, David Sanders was remarkably successful in predicting the outcome of the 1992 General Election, suggesting that what drove personal economic expectations could be predicted largely by levels of inflation and interest rates (Sanders, 1991).

they argued that Mrs Thatcher's victory in 1983 could be explained by prospective egocentric voting. In short, the government's revival in popularity in early to mid-1982 could be explained by a revival in voters' perception of their economic future rather than rewarding the government for defeating the Argentinians (Sanders, Ward and Marsh, 1987).

Sanders has continued to refine and update his model, and continues to provide very convincing arguments. Nevertheless, there have been criticisms which suggest that the appealing logic of Sanders' and other economic models may be flawed. First, there is the question of voter perception. While Sanders *et al.* anticipate that personal economic evaluations may be at odds with reality, they do not deal with the role of other factors which themselves may colour these perceptions. The way in which voters receive their economic information becomes important. In this way a newspaper's interpretation of economic news can be influential. After all, the Conservatives won the 1992 Election during an economic recession which one might expect to affect personal economic expectations. If, however, voters become convinced that their economic expectations will improve or worsen, one may place greater emphasis on the messenger for determining that view and the subsequent vote. Secondly, partisan identification may affect economic evaluations. While the strength of partisanship has declined, the number of voters who are partisans has not. Thus one's partisanship can provide a lens for economic evaluations. In simple terms, a Conservative is more likely to perceive and expect economic improvements under a Conservative government than is a Labour supporter and vice versa. In short, partisan identification may still provide an excellent clue to voting and the real task is perhaps to explain what determines partisan identification. Perhaps we have not come so far at all in the study of voting behaviour!

Conclusions

The most obvious conclusion to make about the study of voting behaviour is that there is evidently no single correct answer. Certainly, new techniques and models emerge with regularity which appear very convincing, yet the problem of causation remains. It is exceptionally difficult at times to see which variable is being changed by the effects of another; which are the dependent and independent variables. Indeed, as we have seen, even the very sophisticated models of issue voting and economic voting can return to the question of partisan identification. If they do then the question must be what causes partisan identification! This is obviously a big topic and one that will continue for many years. In the meantime, we can examine data from the 1992 *British Election Survey* to try to make some limited assessment ourselves.

Evidence from the 1992 General Election

In order to assess these various approaches, albeit at a very basic statistical level, we can examine some evidence from the 1992 *British Election Survey*. There are three groups of tables reflecting the three broad schools of thought outlined in this chapter. The tables are illustrative and do not attempt to challenge findings made with much more sophisticated techniques. They do, however, allow us to examine voting behaviour in some very general terms.

In this first group of tables we examine the social characteristics of voters. Each table tells us first the opinions of all voters and then breaks answers down by party vote. The percentages in these and the following tables tell us the proportion of each group of people that voted for the main three parties in the 1992 Election. Those that voted for other parties are not shown, but are included in the overall calculations. The tables, then, allow us to compare both the relative support for parties among groups as well as which parties were the greatest recipients of votes from each group. Finally, to give us some idea of the overall size of each group, the percentage that each formed of the voting population is shown in the first column.

How groups voted in 1992

Taking the first set of sociodemographic variables, we can make a series of observations (Table 8.7). First, there were more women voters than men. Secondly, there were barely any differences

Table 8.7   **Voting behaviour of sex, age and ethnic groups in 1992.**

(%)	All	Con	Lab	Lib Dem
Male	46	44	36	17
Female	54	47	33	18
18–24	9	41	37	18
25–34	20	44	35	18
35–44	19	43	32	21
45–54	17	50	31	16
55–59	7	46	35	18
60–64	8	44	37	16
65+	20	49	36	14
White	97	46	33	18
Non-white	3	35	61	4

Note 1: all non-voters excluded.
Note 2: tables will not add up to 100% as votes for 'Others' not shown here but
included in calculations.
Sources: *British Election Survey 1992.*

between the voting behaviour of men and women. If there is any
pattern, it is that women were slightly more inclined to vote Conservative and slightly less inclined to vote Labour. Regarding age,
the Conservatives 'won' in every group. However, we can note that
the gap between the Conservatives and Labour was smallest (4 per
cent) in the youngest group and largest in the group aged 45–54 (19
per cent). Indeed, the gap between the two main parties rose
steadily in this group before slipping away again. It reasserted
itself in the 65 years and over group. The Liberal Democrat vote
was fairly similar, although fell away in this oldest group. In general there was some small trend of increasing Conservatism with
age, confirming the commonly held view.

Finally, an examination of ethnic background illustrates a strong
tendency for non-white voters to favour the Labour Party and
reject the Liberal Democrats. Whites favoured the Conservatives
over Labour by 13 per cent whereas non-whites did the reverse by
26 per cent. However, we should exercise some caution. The survey reveals that in fact only 3 per cent of voters were non-white,
thus we should be cautious when ascribing firm patterns. Survey
data often have difficulties measuring ethnic minorities as, taking
Britain as a whole, there are comparatively few non-white citizens

Table 8.8   **Class voting in 1992.**

	All	Con	Lab	Lib Dem
Salariat	29	54	19	24
Routine non-manual	24	52	29	17
Petty bourgeoisie	7	64	16	18
Manual foreman	5	39	44	15
Working class	35	31	54	12
Non-manual	60	54	23	20
Manual	40	32	52	12
Self-perceived middle class	17	57	20	21
Self-perceived working class	28	24	59	13
Self-perceived no class	54	54	26	18
Prompted self-perceived middle class	38	61	17	20
Prompted self-perceived working class	62	35	46	15

Note 1: all non-voters excluded.
Note 2: tables will not add up to 100% as votes for 'Others' not shown here but included in calculations.
Source: *British Election Survey 1992.*

(about 6 per cent). Given that surveys such as this are generally of the order of 3000 respondents, it is often the case that only a small number of respondents are classified as non-white, even accounting for this broad categorisation. Thus, although this is a randomly collected sample, we should at least be cautious in assigning any firm indication of ethnic minority political behaviour.

In Table 8.8 we examine voting by three different models of class: the Goldthorpe–Heath model, the manual/non-manual occupation model and the self-designated model. For this final model two versions are shown. First, there are results taken when respondents were simply asked whether they would assign themselves to a social class. This reveals a significant proportion that did not assign themselves. Those that did not assign themselves were then asked to choose again and were urged to place themselves in a class category. Those that subsequently categorised themselves were then added to the previous group.

Taking the Goldthorpe–Heath model we can see that in some class groups there were significant differences in voting behaviour. Both the petty bourgeoisie and the salariat displayed a strong tendency to vote Conservative rather than Labour. Conversely, the working class favoured Labour significantly more than the Conservatives, although only by the same margin as the third most Conservative group, the routine non-manual. Manual foremen were fairly evenly distributed between the two main parties. There were also class effects for the Liberal Democrat vote, with the salariat being clearly the group most likely to have voted for them.

Using the manual/non-manual dichotomy, more than 50 per cent in both classes voted for their 'natural party'. However, there was a greater difference among non-manual voters and this appears to have been explained by a higher vote for the Liberal Democrats by this group. Using the first model of self-perceived class, similar patterns emerged for those who assigned themselves to a class. Additionally, among those that initially saw themselves as 'classless' (which accounted for more than 50 per cent of voters), voting behaviour was consistent with middle class and non-manual voters. The second self-designated model revealed strong pro-Conservative middle class voting but far weaker pro-Labour voting among the working class. The Liberal Democrat vote remained unaffected.

These tables tell us first, that 'objective' measures of class can still serve as reasonable predictors of the vote. However, it is also clear that many voters do not perceive themselves as belonging to a class group, which raises some questions about the usefulness of class as a variable. That said, where people are prompted to make a choice between class identities their chosen class location, despite being largely working class, does not benefit Labour.

The partisan identification model emphasises a voter's home background. In the first set of figures here, we examine the effects of the voting choice of a voter's parents (Table 8.9). What is apparent is that there is remarkably similarity between the effects of the mother and father. This would suggest that neither parent is more influential than the other. It is also a result of the strong similarities in voting behaviour between marriage partners.[8] From these tables we can see that Labour was a more popular choice among parents. However, whereas around 70 per cent of Conservative parents produced Conservative voting children, for Labour the figure was only around 50 per cent. Moreover, there has been a far more

---

[8] In this survey nearly 90 per cent of mothers and fathers voted for the same party as each other.

significant shift from Labour to Conservative than vice versa. Interestingly, Liberal Democrat voters were more likely to have come from Conservative than Liberal stock.

Housing tenure also illustrates certain voting patterns, and these were strongest among those renting in the public sector. The difference was smaller among the private ownership sector but still significant. Moreover, this group has greater potential impact as it constitutes 75 per cent of voters. The Liberal Democrat vote was largely unaffected by housing tenure. Regarding education, the Conservatives 'won' at every level except that of 'no qualifications' where Labour dominated. However, it is significant that the next smallest group to vote Conservative were those with degrees. The Labour vote decreased as qualifications increased. The opposite was true for the Liberal Democrats.

Table 8.9   Voting and family politics, tenure, education and income in 1992.

	All	*Con*	*Lab*	*Lib Dem*
Father voted Conservative	35	71	12	15
Father voted Labour	57	30	50	17
Father voted Liberal	6	48	19	30
Mother voted Conservative	37	70	11	16
Mother voted Labour	53	27	54	16
Mother voted Liberal	8	49	18	31
Own/buying property	75	54	27	18
Rent (council/trust, etc.)	21	20	63	14
Rent (private sector)	5	44	37	15
Degree	8	42	22	34
Higher education below degree	15	54	20	23
A level or equivalent	11	51	27	17
O level or equivalent	31	48	31	17
No qualifications	35	38	49	10
Less than £5,999	21	32	52	14
£6,000–11,999	22	34	47	16
£12,000–19,999	24	45	32	19
£20,000 +	33	60	19	19
Trade union/staff association member	25	33	43	20
Non-member	75	50	32	16

Note 1: all non-voters excluded.
Note 2: tables will not add up to 100% as votes for 'Others' not shown here but included in calculations.
Sources: *British Election Survey 1992.*

Household income appears to have been strongly associated with votes for the two main parties, at least, although the effect of incomes over £20,000 was twice that of the lowest incomes. The Liberal Democrat vote remained relatively similar across income groups. In short, the chances of voting Conservative increased with income and vice versa for Labour. Finally, collective employment activity in the form of trade unions and staff associations had some effect, but perhaps less than one might expect. While union or association membership indicated a greater willingness to vote Labour and among non-members the reverse, non-membership led to a greater difference in vote share between the two main parties.

These tables illustrate that Conservatives are better able to retain voters than Labour, since children of Conservative backgrounds are more likely to vote as their parents than children of Labour ones. Further, the view that consumers of the public sector (in this case, housing) tend to favour Labour is supported. It should be pointed out that the electorate is heavily skewed towards property ownership, which will lessen the impact of any housing sector effect (Table 8.9).

Table 8.10   **Voting and newspaper readership 1992.**

	All	*Con*	*Lab*	*Lib Dem*
Sun	18	47	36	15
Daily Mirror/Daily Record	25	15	68	11
Daily Star	3	36	50	13
Daily Express	10	76	13	9
Daily Mail	13	77	10	12
*Today**	3	40	24	36
Guardian	4	11	50	35
Independent	4	39	26	34
Daily Telegraph	9	79	9	12
The Times	3	77	12	6
Financial Times	<1	86	0	0
Other	7	50	18	20

Note 1: all non-voters excluded.
Note 2: tables will not add up to 100% as votes for 'Others' not shown here but included in calculations.
* Now defunct.
Sources: *British Election Survey 1992.*

Much is made in Britain about the power and partisanship of the press and the implication is that there is some socialisation effect upon voters. Indeed, the *Sun* even claimed after the 1992 Election that it was 'The Sun wot won it'. The data here cast a little doubt on this. Notwithstanding the arguments that newspaper readership may be an expression of a reader's partisanship rather than the reverse, the Table 8.10 shows that there were only 11 per cent more Conservative voters than Labour voters among *Sun* readers. Conversely, the lead for Labour among readers of the more left-ward leaning *Daily Mirror* was 53 per cent. Moreover, there were 7 per cent more voters among this readership than that of the *Sun*. However, examining the other large readership newspapers we see a strong Conservative lead. For both the *Daily Express* and *Daily Mail*, the lead was 63–67 per cent. Furthermore, the biggest selling broadsheet, the *Daily Telegraph*, provided a 70 per cent lead for the Conservatives over Labour.

Key political attitudes

In this section we examine voters' views on key political issues. While this in itself does not provide a clear case for or against issue voting, it does at least allow us to see whether certain issues divided voters more than others. In each question, voters were asked to indicate their agreement or disagreement with a statement. Each table tells us first the opinions of all voters and then breaks answers down by party vote (Tables 8.11–8.14).

Most voters were satisfied with the public and private sector mix of the economy and favoured no change. Those that disagreed

Table 8.11   **Vote and nationalisation/privatisation 1992.**

	All	*Con*	*Lab*	*Lib Dem*
More nationalisation	23	7	45	23
Left as they are	49	49	43	59
More privatisation	24	41	6	13

Note 1: non-voters excluded.
Note 2: tables will not add up to 100% as votes for 'Others' and responses 'Don't
    know' not shown here but included in calculations.
Source: *British Election Survey 1992.*

Table 8.12   **Vote and job creation 1992.**
The government should spend more money to create jobs

	All	*Con*	*Lab*	*Lib Dem*
Agree	83	72	96	86
Neither agree nor disagree	8	13	2	8
Disagree	8	14	1	6

Note 1: non-voters excluded.
Note 2: tables will not add up to 100% as votes for 'Others' and responses 'Don't
     know' not shown here but included in calculations.
Source: *British Election Survey 1992.*

Table 8.13   **Vote and wealth redistribution 1992.**
Income and wealth should be redistributed

	All	*Con*	*Lab*	*Lib Dem*
Agree	47	27	71	48
Neither agree nor disagree	20	22	17	21
Disagree	31	49	10	28

Note 1: non-voters excluded.
Note 2: tables will not add up to 100% as votes for 'Others' and responses 'Don't
     know' not shown here but included in calculations.
Source: *British Election Survey 1992.*

Table 8.14   **Vote and poverty 1992.**
The government should spend more money to get rid of poverty

	All	*Con*	*Lab*	*Lib Dem*
Should	92	87	97	94
Doesn't matter	3	3	1	3
Should not	5	8	2	3

Note 1: non-voters excluded.
Note 2: tables will not add up to 100% as votes for 'Others' and responses 'Don't
     know' not shown here but included in calculations.
Source: *British Election Survey 1992.*

were evenly spread. Not surprisingly, a substantial proportion of
Conservative and Labour voters favoured more privatisation and
nationalisation, respectively. Importantly, however, a substantial
minority of both favoured the status quo. In the case of Liberal
Democrat voters, there was most sympathy for the retention of

current circumstances. Regarding government investment to stimulate employment there was broad consensus, a majority of all voters across all parties favouring such a move. However, Labour voters were far more committed to the notion than Conservatives. Thirdly, voters' opinions were quite spread on wealth redistribution. While the largest group favoured the practice, there was a substantial minority that opposed it. Not surprisingly, Conservative voters were most likely to oppose the notion although a large minority agreed with the idea. Labour and, to a lesser extent, Liberal Democrat voters were more committed to the notion. Finally, as with job creation, there was overwhelming support for government measures to address poverty, with little difference between party voters. Overall, then, it is clear that certain questions about the economy did not divide the electorate along partisan lines, but the idea of wealth redistribution was a more pivotal issue.

Table 8.15   **Vote and trade union law 1992.**
The government should introduce stricter laws on trade unions

	All	*Con*	*Lab*	*Lib Dem*
Should	36	50	25	27
Doesn't matter	19	22	15	20
Should not	38	24	51	49

Note 1: non-voters excluded.
Note 2: tables will not add up to 100% as votes for 'Others' and responses 'Don't know' not shown here but included in calculations.
Source: *British Election Survey 1992.*

Table 8.16   **Vote and law and order 1992.**
Lawbreakers should get stiffer sentences

	All	*Con*	*Lab*	*Lib Dem*
Agree	81	84	81	75
Not sure either way	11	10	10	12
Disagree	7	5	9	12

Note 1: non-voters excluded.
Note 2: tables will not add up to 100% as votes for 'Others' and responses 'Don't know' not shown here but included in calculations.
Source: *British Election Survey 1992.*

Table 8.17   **Vote and the death penalty 1992.**
Britain should bring back the death penalty

	All	*Con*	*Lab*	*Lib Dem*
Agree	45	48	44	39
Not sure either way	15	16	15	13
Disagree	39	34	40	47

Note 1: non-voters excluded.
Note 2: tables will not add up to 100% as votes for 'Others' and responses 'Don't
           know' not shown here but included in calculations.
Source: *British Election Survey 1992.*

Table 8.18   **Vote and welfare 1992.**
Too many people like to rely on government handouts

	All	*Con*	*Lab*	*Lib Dem*
Agree	60	75	47	50
Not sure either way	12	11	13	13
Disagree	27	13	39	37

Note 1: non-voters excluded.
Note 2: tables will not add up to 100% as votes for 'Others' and responses 'Don't
           know' not shown here but included in calculations.
Source: *British Election Survey 1992.*

Opinion was very evenly spread on the issue of trade union laws. Conservative and Labour voters were almost a mirror image of each other and Liberal Democrat voters were almost identical to Labour. What is worth noting, however, are the substantial minority of Labour and Conservative voters who felt that there should or should not be stricter laws for trade unions, respectively (Table 8.15). Evidently, attitudes towards trade unions still divide the electorate to some extent.

Turning to what we might call measures of liberal/authoritarian values (Tables 8.16–8.18), we see that there was widespread agreement with the view that criminal punishments should be more severe, with little difference between voters. Similarly, there was broad agreement between voters for different parties on the subject of the death penalty, although Liberal Democrat voters were slightly less enthusiastic than other voters. Overall, however,

Table 8.19   **Vote and the EC 1992.**
Should Britain stay a member of the EC?

	All	Con	Lab	Lib Dem
Continue	73	76	69	77
Withdraw	22	21	24	20

Note 1: non-voters excluded.
Note 2: tables will not add up to 100% as votes for 'Others' and responses 'Don't know' not shown here but included in calculations.
Source: *British Election Survey 1992.*

Table 8.20   **Vote and the electoral system 1992.**
Should Britain change its voting system?

	All	Con	Lab	Lib Dem
Change voting system	33	15	38	67
Keep it as it is	60	79	54	28

Note 1: non-voters excluded.
Note 2: tables will not add up to 100% as votes for 'Others' and responses 'Don't know' not shown here but included in calculations.
Source: *British Election Survey 1992.*

opinion was strongly divided. Finally, while there was significant agreement with the view that too many rely on government 'handouts', the issue clearly divided Conservative voters from others. Labour and Liberal Democrat voters were far less likely to agree with the statement although for both parties, the largest groups agreed with the statement. In short, questions of crime and punishment may not be partisan issues, but attitudes towards welfare seem to display a partisan effect.

If we examine finally what we might refer to as constitutional issues (Tables 8.19 and 8.20), we see that most voters favoured retaining membership of the European Community, although Labour voters were slightly less enthusiastic. Significantly, Liberal Democrats were no more likely to favour Europe than Conservatives. The issue of the electoral system did divide some voters along party lines, however. Overall most voters favoured retention of the current system, yet, while most Conservatives reflected this view, Labour voters were more divided while Liberal Democrats were strongly in favour. Importantly however, there was a large minority of Liberal Democrats who favoured retention of the system, which runs counter to a central plank of Liberal Democrat policy.

Overall, it is clear that only certain issues divided the electorate, as do those that might not be seen as pivotal issues at an election. Rather, as Heath *et al.* and Rose and McAllister suggested, the differences seem to be ones of general political values.

Subjective economic indicators

We turn finally to voters' perception of the economy. Voters were asked to give an evaluation of a variety of economic issues, indicating for each whether they considered that circumstances had improved or deteriorated. There is a combination, then, of retrospective egocentric and sociotropic judgements (Tables 8.21–8.27). Again, each table tells us first the opinions of all voters and then breaks answers down by party vote. We begin with retrospective sociotropic judgements.

Table 8.21   **Prices since the last General Election.**

	All	*Con*	*Lab*	*Lib Dem*
Increased	96	95	97	96
Stayed the same	2	2	1	1
Fallen	2	2	1	2

Note 1: non-voters excluded.
Note 2: tables will not add up to 100% as votes for 'Others' and responses 'Don't know' not shown here but included in calculations.
Source: *British Election Survey 1992.*

Table 8.22   **Unemployment since the last General Election.**

	All	*Con*	*Lab*	*Lib Dem*
Increased	92	88	95	96
Stayed the same	4	5	2	2
Fallen	4	5	3	2

Note 1: non-voters excluded.
Note 2: tables will not add up to 100% as votes for 'Others' and responses 'Don't know' not shown here but included in calculations.
Source: *British Election Survey 1992.*

Table 8.23   Taxes since the last General Election.

	All	Con	Lab	Lib Dem
Increased	53	42	63	57
Stayed the same	16	20	12	17
Fallen	23	31	14	20

Note 1: non-voters excluded.
Note 2: tables will not add up to 100% as votes for 'Others' and responses 'Don't know' not shown here but included in calculations.
Source: *British Election Survey 1992.*

Table 8.24   The British economy in the last 10 years.

	All	Con	Lab	Lib Dem
Got stronger	32	49	14	28
Stayed the same	42	25	59	50
Got weaker	19	19	20	17

Note 1: non-voters excluded.
Note 2: tables will not add up to 100% as votes for 'Others' and responses 'Don't know' not shown here but included in calculations.
Source: *British Election Survey 1992.*

Table 8.25   General standard of living since the last General Election.

	All	Con	Lab	Lib Dem
Increased	31	46	15	21
Stayed the same	24	27	21	22
Fallen	43	25	61	54

Note 1: non-voters excluded.
Note 2: tables will not add up to 100% as votes for 'Others' and responses 'Don't know' not shown here but included in calculations.
Source: *British Election Survey 1992.*

There was almost universal agreement that prices had increased with no party variation. Regarding unemployment, there was broad agreement that it had gone up, although Conservative voters were slightly less inclined to think that this was the case. Thirdly, the largest group of voters across all parties agreed that taxes had increased, but Conservatives were much more likely to

Table 8.26   **Household income has kept up with prices.**

	All	Con	Lab	Lib Dem
Fallen behind	45	33	58	51
Kept up with	40	50	31	34
Up more than prices	12	15	9	13

Note 1: non-voters excluded.
Note 2: tables will not add up to 100% as votes for 'Others' and responses 'Don't
        know' not shown here but included in calculations.
Source: *British Election Survey 1992.*

Table 8.27   **Own standard of living since the last General Election.**

	All	Con	Lab	Lib Dem
Increased	34	45	22	35
Stayed the same	37	40	35	33
Fallen	29	15	42	31

Note 1: non-voters excluded.
Note 2: tables will not add up to 100% as votes for 'Others' and responses 'Don't
        know' not shown here but included in calculations.
Source: *British Election Survey 1992.*

perceive that they had fallen. Fourthly, most voters felt that the
economy had remained the same. However, Conservative voters
were much more likely to detect an improvement than other
voters. Around 50 per cent of them thought that this was the case
as opposed to only 14 per cent of Labour voters. Among those that
thought the economy had become weaker, there was no party
variation. In contrast with views on the economy, most voters felt
that the general standard of living had fallen. However, there was a
clear difference between Conservative and non-Conservative
voters. While around a quarter of Conservatives felt that the
standard had fallen, nearly a half thought that it had improved.
This contrasts with 61 per cent and 54 per cent of Labour and
Liberal Democrat voters, respectively, who felt that the standard
of living had fallen.

    In terms of egocentric judgements, few voters thought that their
own household income had overtaken the level of prices. However, Conservatives were more likely than other voters to argue

that their income relative to prices had at least been maintained. Nevertheless, a substantial minority of Conservatives concur with the majority of Labour and Liberal Democrat voters who claimed that their income had fallen behind. Opinion on individual standards of living was evenly spread. However, Conservatives were again more likely to perceive conditions to have improved. Labour voters, on the other hand, felt the reverse, while Liberal Democrat voters were very evenly distributed across all shades of opinion. Most of these questions point to favourable judgements on the economy favouring the incumbent party, the Conservatives. However, as we argued earlier we may be observing a partisan identification effect, whereby Conservative or Labour voters are allowing their partisanship to influence their judgement.

Conclusions

While this case study of the 1992 General Election is very basic in terms of electoral analysis, it has nevertheless allowed us to examine a variety of factors that hitherto we might have imagined would all divide voters. Clearly, not all the variables examined here had any great effect on the vote. Again we see that there is no definitive answer to why people vote as they do, although in this analysis we should note that questions on the economy did provide at least some consistency in the outcome of partisan action.

9

CONCLUSION

Parties and their functions

Throughout this book I have argued that British political parties are not only an entrenched feature of British democracy, but that they perform important functions. Moreover, I have argued that without political parties, Britain's democratic life would require immense upheaval and would be poorer for the experience. In order to assess this view, we should perhaps return initially to the opening section of the book which itemised the role of parties in Britain. By re-examining these roles, we can begin to assess whether parties are performing their functions adequately and whether they are as necessary to representative democracy as I have suggested.

Beginning with provision of *electoral choice*, I have argued that one could examine the concept in two ways: first through choice of alternative political programmes, and secondly through providing alternative choice should the incumbent party be rejected. The latter is easier to show. Parties do offer electoral choice because no seats are uncontested at constituency level elections. Thus, in every parliamentary seat in the United Kingdom, electors are offered a choice of party candidates. Indeed, in Britain (England, Scotland and Wales), voters are offered the choice of candidates from at least all the main three parties in every constituency. Moreover, in Wales and Scotland there is the extra choice of at least the Scottish National Party or Plaid Cymru. In Northern Ireland, while from the mainland only the Conservatives field

Table 9.1   **Perceptions of difference between Labour and Conservative Parties.**

	(%)
Great difference	56
Some difference	32
Not much difference	12

Note: 'Don't knows' excluded.
Source: *British Election Survey 1992.*

candidates, voters are still provided with an electoral choice between the parties that operate there.

In terms of offering a choice of alternative party programmes, however, the case requires a little more investigation. We can look at the choice in two ways, 'objectively' and 'subjectively'. In objective terms we can state that parties do offer a choice. Notwithstanding the element of non-partisan pledges highlighted in Chapter 2, Topf's analysis of the main three parties' manifestos demonstrates not only that the parties differ on occasions in the policies they seek to emphasise, but also that they stress different ideological positions. That said, some important areas of policy (such as Europe and education) have not figured strongly in party manifestos since 1979. Moreover, the analysis points to an overall rightward drift in terms of ideological balance. Nevertheless, parties appear to be offering a choice of programmes (Topf, 1994). What is also significant is whether the electorate themselves see the parties as offering such a choice; whether there is a choice in subjective terms. Table 9.1 shows us that in 1992 most voters perceived the Conservatives and Labour, at least, to be different in their policy offerings, although Table 9.2 shows us that a significant minority saw the differences as having lessened. In short, then, political parties do offer an electoral choice, both in terms of simple alternatives and in terms of programme choice. Importantly, this is shown both in terms of an examination of manifestos and in terms of citizen's perceptions.

As far as *representation* is concerned, we need to examine the various meanings of the term. Generally, parties seem to offer representation of the main segments of opinion within Britain. In broad terms, many of the voters' views are reflected in party

Table 9.2   Perceptions of difference between Labour and Conservative
Parties since last General Election.

	(%)
More now	26
Same	38
Less now	36

Note: 'Don't knows' excluded.
Source: *British Election Survey 1992.*

programmes. There are exceptions, however. We highlighted earlier the fact that in 1992, for example, there was no mainstream party representation of the anti-European stance of some voters. Moreover, in the *British Election Survey* of 1992, of those who expressed an opinion 24 per cent were in favour of withdrawal from the European Community (*British Election Survey*, 1992: v27). Similarly, the question of the resurrection of death penalty, which has long been used as an indicator of non-representation of public opinion by parties, was supported by 46 per cent in 1992 (*British Election Survey*, 1992: v47d). Nevertheless, in most policy areas parties represent the main strands of public opinion.

The second way of examining representation is through assessing the level of resemblance of parties' elected representatives. As we have seen, this is one area where parties clearly fail since the proportions of candidates from various social groups is not an accurate reflection of society at large, especially in the case of women.

However, if we consider the other models of representation as outlined earlier, we can assess the views of the electorate. Table 9.3 considers the various roles of an MP and the degree to which these roles are considered important by electors. Importantly, all roles outlined here are considered to be important. However, what is noticeable is that the constituency model of representation is seen by electors, at least, as being the most important type of role. In this sense parties may be seen to partially compromise the level of representation that the electorate desire, since MPs only spend around a third of their time on constituency matters (Norris and Lovenduski, 1995:229) and around half consider their primary role to be in Parliament rather than helping constituents (Norris and Lovenduski, 1995:261). This is no doubt a reflection of the fact that

Table 9.3   Importance of the roles of an MP.

(%)	Important	Not important
Hold regular constituency meetings	94	6
Help with individual problems	93	7
Speak in Parliament	85	15
Defend party policy	85	15
Support the party leader	86	14

Note: 'Don't knows' excluded.
Source: *British Election Survey 1992.*

95 per cent of MPs consider that electors vote primarily for the party rather than the candidate (Norris and Lovenduski, 1995:261). That said, most MPs claim to find constituency work very rewarding (Norris and Lovenduski, 1995:261).

Regarding the function of *policy making*, parties do have a role. Moreover, if we view policy making as having a number of component parts, then we can argue that policy initiation at least occurs at a variety of levels in most parties. Notwithstanding external factors which can drive or restrict policy options, it is apparent that the leaderships of the parties do become involved both in policy initiation and formation. Thus parties formulate policies to pursue when in power or in a position to influence another party in power. Below the elite level we can, in most parties, see at least some policy initiation. Through both formal and informal means, there are avenues by which party members can 'fly policy kites'. Moreover, forums exist for policy ideas to be debated and formed into more coherent ideas. Nevertheless, it is apparent that in the parties examined, the main role in both policy initiation and formation is played by the central elite of the party.

Political parties certainly provide the bulk of *parliamentary candidates* and have a virtual monopoly upon MPs. Only at very exceptional times in recent history have there been MPs independent of political parties. Some MPs have been denied the party whip on occasions and there have been some that resigned from their party. However, 'whipless' MPs have not remained so for long periods of time, and those that have resigned from their party have generally joined another one. Thus it is fair to say that in parliamentary terms, at least, political parties play an essential role of recruiting and selecting candidates, and especially MPs. Of course, candidate selection techniques vary but a common pattern is that while grassroots members clearly play an important role in selection, party elites also have both overt and covert influence. Elites can (and do) intervene on occasions, but are not overtly involved at every stage of selection. However, there is a case to argue that elites display more subtle influence in that grass-roots members may select candidates mindful of the possible reaction of the elite.

As far as the function of *political education and communication* is concerned parties do play a role, although there may be reason to suggest that the role is at least shared by other actors. On one hand, parties help to set political agendas which can provide for political education. In a broad sense, one might argue that one of the Thatcher governments' main achievements was to provide a genuine political alternative for voters to consider and evaluate, thus improving their political education. That said, repeated evidence has disputed the extent to which voters 'became Thatcherite' in any real sense (Crewe:1992a,b). In a more narrow sense, however, parties can initiate greater political knowledge by forcing electors to make a choice at elections.

However, there is evidence to suggest that political parties may not be said to fulfil wholly their function of political education. First, parties are only able to devote very small proportions to political research (Home Affairs Committee, 1994:xxiii; Fisher, 1996). Thus, if political research is downplayed by parties (through financial necessity or otherwise) it is difficult for parties to provide a reasonable level of political education. In the second sense, it is reasonable to argue that a significant proportion of political education and communication is performed by the mass media. To be sure, parties collaborate in some sense here through agenda-setting and so on, but it is clear that parties are not in total control of the processes. The media are able to raise items on the agenda and provide political education upon them virtually independently of party concerns. This, of course, is a very wide area and cannot be discussed at any length here. Suffice to say that the role of political education and communication is not wholly or even largely performed by parties, and the lack of resources made available to producing political research can only exacerbate this position.

Finally, in the role of *political participation*, parties play a role. They recruit party members and provide participation opportunities for non-members. However, the level of participation by members is remarkably low. As we saw earlier, this is particularly the case with Conservative members. Moreover, party membership overall is low; yet political participation among the general population as a whole is not especially high. Beyond voting, individuals in Britain tend largely only to sign petitions or make contact with local government. Indeed, beyond the relatively 'cost free' acts of voting and petition signing, fully 46 per cent claim not to embark on any other modes of participation and 22 per cent only one further act (Parry, Moyser and Day, 1992:44–9). Placed in that context, political participation facilitated by parties becomes relatively more important, although by no means impressive.

In general political parties still fulfil their roles. There are areas where we might detect under-performance, although in the case of political education, at least, we might argue that a diffusion of sources is a welcome development. In a sense, society is more pluralist for parties not having a monopoly on political education or communication. Many still have misgivings about the alternative forms of communication and education, particularly since sections of the mass media seem to favour particular parties. Moreover, the values and objectives of parties may be said to be rather different from those of the mass media. While parties clearly want to win power, they also wish to create a society which in their view is as desirable, just and efficient as possible. Of course, some sections of the media may well wish to do this to an extent themselves. However, the mass media also has the motivation of market share. That is not to suggest that political education is necessarily inferior for that fact; simply that we should bear it in mind before regarding political communication from such quarters as being above partisan commitment. Whatever our view on this point is, however, it is clear that parties are unable to devote sufficient resources to new political research and this is likely to inhibit their roles in democratic life.

British political parties and the future

The situation for British parties, then, is arguably quite healthy. As we have seen, the thesis that they are in terminal decline is difficult to sustain. Moreover, they are evidently an essential component in current democratic procedures. Parties have displayed considerable resilience as well as an acceptance that they must respond to political circumstances. Thus in virtually all of the parties discussed in this book, internal ideological and organisational change has occurred in order to maintain the party's strength. The message is apparently clear: that parties that resist change or refuse to accept changed circumstances are unlikely to survive.

Nevertheless, for all these qualities there are two particular areas which parties should address. They are underfunded. Running a political party is an expensive business and it is clear that none of the parties can maintain organisations at an acceptable level. It is quite remarkable that the most successful product in the political marketplace (the Conservative Party) is in such deep financial debt. While the parties are not wholly reliant on voluntary support, the assistance given by the state is not sufficient. Beyond the payment of MPs, parties do receive other limited forms of state funding, especially at elections: free mailing, free use of public halls and, for the larger parties, free broadcasting. Opposition parties additionally receive 'short' money for their work in Parliament. One might also add state security at Party Conferences, which has increased significantly since the bomb at the 1984 Conservative Party Conference in Brighton.[1] These subsidies are modest compared with many other Western countries (Nassmacher, 1993) and, crucially, are largely directed at elections. The fact that party activity needs to be maintained beyond any electoral cycle suggests that these subsidies are insufficient.

Given that parties play such an essential role in political life, the case for additional funding is compelling. Moreover, arguments for a relatively even electoral contest also suggest that an extension of state funding of political parties is desirable (Ewing, 1992; Linton, 1994); but many oppose state funding on the grounds that first, it is not the role of the state to support voluntary organisations with public funds and secondly, that parties would be less inclined to respond to the grass-roots if they received a steady income from the state.

These arguments are, however, misleading. Since political parties play such an important role in democratic life, it seems

---

[1] This might seem a contentious point, but it is worth pointing out that at football matches the costs of policing are borne by the football clubs.

sensible that the state should act to help preserve such an important facet of British democracy, as they evidently struggle to maintain themselves adequately. The question of alienation from the grass-roots is also problematic. In the first instance one should point out that existing arrangements of party finance have not themselves produced mass membership parties and it is clear that significant proportions of party members already consider their leaderships to be remote. Secondly, critics have shown little imagination in terms of the basis of state funded allocations. Most have suggested that it would be based upon electoral support. However, there is no reason why parties could not be awarded funds on the basis of other criteria such as 'matching' other forms of fundraising (as in the United States) or more significantly, on the basis of their party memberships. If this was adopted, parties would have the incentive not only to recruit members but also to keep them, since this would generate income. Moreover, in order to retain members parties would need to provide sufficient incentives to renew membership. Thus, state funding on this basis could potentially increase political participation rather than decrease it, as critics have suggested (Fisher, 1995:193–5).

As a footnote to this, one might also add that the cost of supporting parties would not be excessive. However, for all these arguments the most recent enquiry into party finance in Britain did not endorse increased state funding nor any substantive change in the current arrangements (Home Affairs Select Committee, 1994). Since state funding is both Labour and Liberal Democrat policy, any change in government may put the results of this enquiry under review.

The second main problem for political parties in Britain (which is related to the first) is the level of party membership and activity within the parties. While the individual membership of the Labour Party (350 000) is rising at present, it is still considerably lower than it was in the 1970s (1970: 680 191; 1979: 666 091) when serious questions about the political system and its successful operation were increasingly being asked. Similarly, the Conservatives' membership has declined considerably from a figure of 1 500 000 in 1974 to 1 200 00 in 1982 and to a maximum of 750 000 today. For the Liberal Democrats the picture is slightly more encouraging (103 000), although for comparison, the Liberals and the SDP had combined memberships of 150 000 in 1984 (Webb, 1992a:847).

Thus, the question might reasonably be raised as to how representative parties can continue to exist if their level of mass membership
support is so low. This is further exacerbated by the fact that much
party activity is undertaken by a minority in the parties.

From this perspective, one might question the validity of the
thesis that parties are essential to representative democracy.
Certainly, parties need to address the levels of internal activity and
offer attractive incentives for membership, and certainly, some
might argue that the oligarchic tendencies that are apparent in all
of the political party studies here may act as a barrier to renewal.
On the other hand, parties have thrived in the past with arguably
more oligarchic structures. Moreover, people join parties for a
number of reasons, only some of them overtly political. Parties,
then, must offer more to build a genuine mass membership and as
a result, develop the potential to be more responsive to grass-roots
ideas.

Political parties in Britain are not without their problems and
these require action for their own health and that of representative
democracy in general; yet, for all these problems, parties remain an
important and essential component of British democracy. They
continue, by and large, to perform useful functions successfully
and because they are responsive both to grass-roots and external
pressures they will survive in the future of British politics.

Of course, their resilience in their current form may be said to
be partly a result of electoral arrangements. The existence of the
Single Member Simple Plurality (SMSP) electoral system, as well
as the absence of separate assemblies in Scotland, Wales and perhaps the English regions, has a clear impact upon party successes
as well as electoral strategies. Thus, any change in the current
arrangements would be likely to impact upon party organisations
and structures. The establishment of assemblies, particularly in
Scotland and Wales, would be likely to lead to a refocusing of
nationalist party activity, both in terms of their probable change in
status from minority to mainstream parties and in their relation-
ships with other parties. Similarly, any change in the electoral
system nationally would also be likely to force parties to re-
examine their own position and approaches.

Arguably we can say, then, that parties respond to four distinct
external pressures. First, the social composition of the electorate:
we have seen that all parties' strategies have been influenced by

various changes in the social and demographic make-up of the population. Secondly, parties respond to political change as expressed through the changing values of the electorate. Thirdly, parties respond to institutional conditions. The electoral system, for example, arguably has a strong impact on party strategies. Finally, parties respond to circumstances outside the nation state. International political co-operation and economic globalisation have clearly had an effect on party strategies and have highlighted their ability (and sometimes inability) to respond to developments. Overall, however, parties have been responsive and mindful of these pressures, which is why they have survived and will undoubtedly continue to do so.

APPENDICES

Appendix I General Election results 1945–92

General Election	1945	1950	1951	1955	1959	1964	1966	1970	1974 (Feb.)	1974 (Oct.)	1979	1983	1987	1992
Government	Lab	Lab	Con	Con	Con	Lab	Lab	Con	Lab	Lab	Con	Con	Con	Con
No. of MPs elected	640	625	625	630	630	630	630	630	635	635	635	650	650	651
Conservative														
Share of vote %	39.8	43.5	48.0	49.7	49.4	43.4	41.9	46.4	37.8	35.8	43.9	42.4	42.3	41.9
Seats	213	298	321	344	365	304	253	330	297	277	339	397	376	336
Share of seats %	33.3	47.7	51.4	54.6	57.9	48.3	40.2	52.4	46.8	43.6	53.4	61.1	57.8	51.6
Labour														
Share of vote %	48.3	46.1	48.8	46.4	43.8	44.1	47.9	43.0	37.1	39.2	37.0	27.6	30.8	34.4
Seats	393	315	295	277	258	317	363	287	301	319	269	209	229	271
Share of seats %	61.4	50.4	47.2	44.0	41.0	50.3	57.6	45.6	47.4	50.2	42.4	32.2	35.2	41.6
Liberal/SDP–Liberal Alliance/Liberal Democrats														
Share of vote %	9.1	9.1	2.5	2.7	5.9	11.2	8.5	7.5	19.3	18.3	13.8	25.4	22.6	17.8
Seats	12	9	6	6	6	9	12	6	14	13	11	23	22	20
Share of seats %	1.9	1.4	1.0	1.0	1.0	1.4	1.9	1.0	2.2	2.0	1.7	3.5	3.4	3.1
Others														
Share of vote %	2.8	1.3	0.7	1.2	0.9	1.3	1.7	3.1	5.8	6.7	5.3	4.6	4.3	5.8
Seats	22	3	3	3	1	0	2	7	23	26	16	21	23	24
Share of seats %	3.4	0.5	0.5	0.5	0.2	0.0	0.3	1.1	3.6	4.1	2.5	3.2	3.5	3.7

Sources: Butler and Butler (1994:216–19); King et al., (1992:249).

Appendix II **European Election results in Britain 1979–94.**

European Election	1979	1984	1989	1994
No. of MEPs elected	78	78	78	84
Conservative				
Share of vote %	50.6	40.8	34.7	27.9
Seats	60	45	32	18
Share of seats %	76.9	57.7	41.0	21.4
Labour				
Share of vote %	33.1	36.5	40.1	44.2
Seats	17	32	45	62
Share of seats %	21.8	41.0	57.7	73.8
Liberal/SDP–Liberal Alliance/Liberal Democrat				
Share of vote %	13.1	19.5	6.2	16.7
Seats	0	0	0	2
Share of seats %	0.0	0.0	0.0	2.4
Others				
Share of vote %	3.2	3.3	19.0	11.2
Seats	4	4	4	5
Share of seats %	1.3	1.3	1.3	2.4

Note: Northern Ireland not included. European Elections for the three seats in
Northern Ireland are conducted by Single Transferable Vote, making direct
comparisons problematic.
Source: Butler and Butler (1994:220–1); Wilder (1994:82).

REFERENCES AND BIBLIOGRAPHY

Alderman, K. and Carter N. (1994) 'The Labour Party and the Trade Unions: Loosening the Ties?' *Parliamentary Affairs* 47 pp.321–37.

Allen, M. (1993) 'The Union Link: The Case For Continuity' *Renewal* 1 pp.36–44.

Aughey, A. (1994) 'The political parties of Northern Ireland' in *Britain's Changing Party System* Robins, L., Blackmore, H. and Pyper, R. (eds) London: Leicester University Press.

Baker, D., Fountain, I., Gamble, A. and Ludlam, S. (1995) 'Conservative Backbencher Attitudes to European Integration' *Political Quarterly* 66 pp.221–33.

Baker, D., Ludlam, S. and Gamble, A. (1993) '1846 . . . 1906 . . . 1996? Conservative Splits and European Integration' *Political Quarterly* 64 pp.420–34.

Baldwin, N.D.J. (1990) *The Conservative Party,* Barnstable: Wroxton Papers in Politics.

Ball, A.R. (1987) *British Political Parties*, London: Macmillan.

Ball, S. (1994) 'The National and Regional Party Structure,' in *Conservative Century* Seldon, A. and Ball, S. (eds) Oxford: Oxford University Press.

Balsom, D. (1979) 'Plaid Cymru: the Welsh National Party' in *Multi-Party Britain* Drucker, H.M. (ed.) London: Macmillan.

Barnes, J. (1994) 'Ideology and factions' in *Conservative Century* Seldon, A. and Ball, S. (eds) Oxford: Oxford University Press.

Beer, S. (1982) *Modern British Politics*, London: Faber and Faber.

Behrens, R. (1989) 'The Centre: Social Democracy and Liberalism' in *Party Ideology in Britain* Tivey, L. and Wright, A. (eds) London: Routledge.

Bellamy, R. (1993) 'Liberalism' in *Contemporary Political Ideologies* Eatwell, R. and Wright, A. (eds) London: Pinter.

Bennie, L., Curtice, J. and Rüdig, W. (1995) 'Liberal, Social Democrat or Liberal Democrat? Political Identity and British Centre Party Politics' in *British Elections & Parties Yearbook 1994* Broughton, D., Farrell, D.M., Denver, D. and Rallings, C. (eds) London: Frank Cass.

Blackburn, R. (1990) *Constitutional Studies*, London: Mansell.

Blackburn, R. (1995) *The Electoral System in Britain*, London: Macmillan.

Blackwell, R. and Terry, M. (1987) 'Analysing the Political Fund Ballots: a Remarkable Victory or the Triumph of the Status Quo?' *Political Studies* 35 pp.623–42.

Blair, T. (1994) *Socialism*, London: Fabian Tract, p.565.

Blake, R. (1985) *The Conservative Party From Peel to Thatcher*, London: Fontana.

Bogdanor, V. (1982) 'Reflections on British Political Finance' *Parliamentary Affairs* 35 pp.367–80.

Bogdanor, V. (1994) 'The Selection of the Party Leader' in *Conservative Century* Seldon, A. and Ball, S. (eds) Oxford: Oxford University Press.

Brand, J. (1992) 'SNP members: the way of the faithful' in *British Elections and Parties Yearbook 1992* Norris, P., Crewe, I., Denver, D. and Broughton, D. (eds) Hemel Hempstead: Harvester Wheatsheaf.

Brand, J., Mitchell, J. and Surridge, P. (1994) 'Will Scotland come to the aid of the party?' in *Labour's Last Chance?* Heath, A., Jowell, R. and Curtice, J. (eds) Aldershot: Dartmouth.

British Election Survey 1992, Essex: ESRC Data Archive.

Broughton, D. (1995) 'Plaid Cymru and Welsh Nationalism' paper presented at The American Political Science Association Annual Conference, Chicago.

Broughton, D., Farrell, D.M., Denver, D. and Rallings, C. (eds) (1995) *British Elections and Parties Yearbook 1994*, London: Frank Cass.

Bulmer-Thomas, I. (1965) *The Growth of the British Party System. Vol. 1, 1640–1923*, London: John Baker.

Bulpitt, J. (1991) 'The Conservative Party in Britain: A Preliminary Portrait' paper presented to the Political Studies Association Annual Conference, University of Lancaster.

Butler, D. and Butler, G. (1994) *British Political Facts 1900–1994*, London: Macmillan.

Butler D. and Kavanagh, D. (1984) *The British General Election of 1983*, London: Macmillan.

Butler, D. and Kavanagh, D. (1988) *The British General Election of 1987*, London: Macmillan.

Butler, D. and Kavanagh, D. (1992) *The British General Election of 1992*, London: Macmillan.

Butler, D. and Ranney, A. (eds) (1992) *Electioneering*, Oxford: Clarendon Press.

Butler, D. and Stokes, D. (1969) *Political Change in Britain*, London: Macmillan.

Callaghan, J. (1988) *Time and Chance*, London: Fontana.

Callaghan, J. (1989) 'The Left: The Ideology of the Labour Party' in *Party Ideology in Britain* Tivey, L. and Wright, A. (eds) London: Routledge.

Clarke, H. and Whiteley, P. (1990) 'Perceptions of Macroeconomic Performance, Government Support and Conservative Party Strategy in Britain 1983–1987' *European Journal of Political Research* 18 pp.97–120.

Coates, D. (1989) *The Crisis of Labour*, Oxford: Philip Allen.

Coates, K. and Topham, T. (1980) *Trade Unions in Britain*, Nottingham: Spokesman.

Coates, K. and Topham, T. (1986) *Trade Unions and Politics*, Oxford: Basil Blackwell.

Conley, F. (1994) *General Elections Today*, Manchester: Manchester University Press.

Connolly, M. (1990) *Politics and Policy-making in Northern Ireland*, Hemel Hempstead: Philip Allan.

Conservative Party (1989–1995) *Income and Expenditure Accounts*, London: Conservative Central Office.

Conservative Party (1993) *The Funding of Political Parties: Memorandum of Evidence to the Select Committee on Home Affairs*, London: Conservative Central Office.

Constitutional Reform Centre (1985) *Company Donations to Political Parties*, London: Constitutional Reform Centre.

Crewe, I. (1992a) 'The 1987 General Election' in *Issues and Controversies in British Electoral Behaviour* Denver, D. and Hands, G. (eds) Hemel Hempstead: Harvester Wheatsheaf.

Crewe, I. (1992b) 'On the death and resurrection of class voting: some comments on *How Britain Votes* in *Issues and Controversies in British Electoral Behaviour* Denver, D. and Hands, G. (eds) Hemel Hempstead: Harvester Wheatsheaf.

Crewe, I. (1993) 'Parties and Electors' in *The Developing British Political System in the 1990s* Budge, I. and McKay D. (eds) London: Longman.

Crewe, I., Fox, T. and Alt, J. (1992) 'Non-voting in British general elections, 1966–October 1974' in *Issues and Controversies in British Electoral Behaviour* Denver, D. and Hands, G. (eds) Hemel Hempstead: Harvester Wheatsheaf.

Crewe, I. and Harrop, M. (eds) (1986) *Political Communications: The General Election of 1983*, Cambridge: Cambridge University Press.

Crewe, I. and Harrop, M. (eds) (1989) *Political Communications: The General Election Campaign of 1987*, Cambridge: Cambridge University Press.

Crewe, I. and King, A. (1994) 'Did Major Win? Did Kinnock Lose? Leadership effects in the 1992 election' in *Labour's Last Chance?* Heath, A., Jowell, R. and Curtice, J. (eds) Aldershot: Dartmouth.

Crewe, I., Norris, P., Denver, D. and Broughton, D. (eds) (1992) *British Elections and Parties Yearbook 1991*, Hemel Hempstead: Harvester Wheatsheaf.

Crosland, A. (1956) *The Future of Socialism*. London: Jonathan Cope.

Curtice, J., Rüdig, W. and Bennie, L. (1993) *Liberal Democrats Reveal All*, Strathclyde: University of Strathclyde Papers on Government and Politics No.96.

Denver, D. (1994) *Elections and Voting Behaviour in Britain*, Hemel Hempstead: Harvester Wheatsheaf.

Denver, D. and Hands, G. (eds) (1992) *Issues and Controversies in British Electoral Behaviour*, Hemel Hempstead: Harvester Wheatsheaf.

Denver, D. and Hands, G. (1993) 'Measuring the intensity and effectiveness of constituency campaigning in the 1992 general election' in *British Elections and Parties Yearbook 1993* Denver, D., Norris, P., Broughton, D. and Rallings, C. (eds) Hemel Hempstead: Harvester Wheatsheaf.

Denver D., Norris, P., Broughton, D. and Rallings, C. (eds) (1993) *British Elections and Parties Yearbook 1993*, Hemel Hempstead: Harvester Wheatsheaf.

Dewdney, K. (1992) 'Who does run Labour?' *Fabian Review* 104 (4) 4.

Drucker, H.M. (1979a) *Doctrine and Ethos in the Labour Party*, London: George Allen and Unwin.

Drucker, H.M. (ed) (1979b) *Multi-Party Britain*, London: Macmillan.

Drucker, H.M. (1981) 'Changes in the Labour Party Leadership' *Parliamentary Affairs* 34 pp.369–91.

Drucker, H.M. (1982) 'The Influence of the Trade Unions on the Ethos of the Labour Party' in *Trade Unions in British Politics* Pimlott, B. and Cook, C. (eds) London: Longman.

Dunleavy, P. (1980) 'The political implications of sectoral cleavages and the growth of state employment' *Political Studies*, 28 pp.364–83, 527–49.

Dunleavy, P. (1992) 'Class dealignment in Britain revisited' in *Issues & Controversies in British Electoral Behaviour* Denver, D. and Hands, G. (eds) Hemel Hempstead: Harvester Wheatsheaf.

Dunleavy P. and Husbands, C. (1985) *British Democracy at the Crossroads*, London: Allen & Unwin.

Dunleavy, P., Margretts, H. and Weir, S. (1992) 'Replaying the Election' *Parliamentary Affairs* 45 pp.640–55.

Durham, M. (1989) 'The Right: The Conservative Party and Conservatism' in *Party Ideology in Britain* Tivey, L. and Wright, A. (eds) London: Routledge.

Eatwell, R. and Wright, A. (eds) (1993) *Contemporary Political Ideologies*, London: Pinter.

Eccleshall, R. (1984) 'Conservatism' in *Political Ideologies* Eccleshall, R., Geoghegan, V., Jay, R. and Wilford, R. (eds) London: Unwin Hyman.

Eccleshall, R., Geoghegan, V., Jay, R. and Wilford, R. (1984) *Political Ideologies*, London: Unwin Hyman.

Ewing, K.D. (1982) *Trade Unions, The Labour Party and The Law*, Edinburgh: Edinburgh University Press.

Ewing, K. (1987) *The Funding of Political Parties in Britain*, Cambridge: Cambridge University Press.

Ewing, K. (1992) *Money, Politics and Law*, Oxford: Clarendon Press.

Fatchett, D. (1987) *Trade Unions and Politics in the 1980s*, London: Croom Helm.

Fisher, J. (1992) 'Trade union political funds and the Labour Party' in *British Elections & Parties Yearbook 1992* Norris, P., Crewe, I., Denver, D. and Broughton, D. (eds) Hemel Hempstead: Harvester Wheatsheaf.

Fisher, J. (1994a) Political Donations to the Conservative Party' *Parliamentary Affairs* 47 pp.61–72.

Fisher, J. (1994b) 'Why Do Companies Make Donations To Political Parties?' *Political Studies* 42 pp.690–9.

Fisher, J. (1995) 'The Institutional Funding of British Political Parties' in *British Elections & Parties Yearbook 1994* Broughton, D., Farrell, D.M., Denver, D. and Rallings, C. (eds) London: Frank Cass.

Fisher, J. (1996) 'Party Finance' in *The Conservative Party* Norton P. (ed) Hemel Hempstead: Harvester Wheatsheaf.

Gallagher, T. (ed) (1991) *Nationalism in the Nineties*, Edinburgh: Polygon.

Gamble, A. (1992) 'The Labour Party and economic management' in *The Changing Labour Party* Smith, M.J. and Spear, J. (eds) London: Routledge.

Garner, R.W. (1989) *The Ideological Impact of the Trade Unions on the Labour Party 1918–1931*, Manchester: Manchester Papers in Politics.

Garner, R. and Kelly, R. (1993) *British Political Parties Today*, Manchester: Manchester University Press.

Goodwin, B. (1987) *Using Political Ideas*, Chichester: Wiley.

Grant, D. (1987) 'Mrs Thatcher's Own Goal: Unions and the Political Fund Ballots' *Parliamentary Affairs* 40 pp.57–72.

Grant, W. (1980) 'Business Interests and the British Conservative Party' *Government and Opposition* 15 pp.143–61.

Grant, W. (1993) *Business and Politics in Britain*, London: Macmillan.

Guiver, C. (1992) 'The Labour Party, small businesses and enterprise' in *The Changing Labour Party* Smith, M.J. and Spear, J. (eds) London: Routledge.

Gunlicks A.B. (ed.) (1993) *Campaign and Party Finance in North America and Western Europe*, Boulder: Westview.

Gwyn, W.B. (1962) *Democracy and the Cost of Politics*, London: Athlone.

Ham, C. and Hill, M. (1994) *The Policy Process in the Modern Capitalist State*, Hemel Hempstead: Harvester Wheatsheaf.

Hanham, H.J. (1978) *Elections and Party Management*, Hemel Hempstead: Harvester Wheatsheaf.

Hansard Society (1981) *Paying For Politics*, London: Hansard Society.

Harrison, M. (1960) *Trade Unions and the Labour Party Since 1945*, London: Allen & Unwin.

Harrop, M. and Miller, W. (1987) *Elections and Voters*, London: Macmillan.

Healey, D. (1989) *The Time of My Life*, London: Michael Joseph.

Heath, A., Curtice, J., Jowell, R., Evans, G., Field, J. and Witherspoon, S. (1991) *Understanding Political Change*, Oxford: Pergamon.

Heath, A., Evans, G. and Martin, J. (1993) 'The Measurement of Core Beliefs and Values: The Development of Balanced Socialist/*Laissez-Faire* and Libertarian/Authoritarian Scales' *British Journal of Political Science* 24 pp.115–58.

Heath, A., Jowell, R. and Curtice, J. (1985) *How Britain Votes*, Oxford: Pergamon.

Heath, A., Jowell, R. and Curtice, J. (1992) 'Partisan dealignment revisited' in *Issues and Controversies in British Electoral Behaviour* Denver, D. and Hands, G. (eds) Hemel Hempstead: Harvester Wheatsheaf.

Heath, A., Jowell, R. and Curtice, J. (eds) (1994) *Labour's Last Chance?*, Aldershot: Dartmouth.

Hogwood, B. (1992) *Trends in British Public Policy*, Buckingham: Open University Press.

Holmes, M. (1985) *The Labour Government 1974–79*, Basingstoke: Macmillan.

Home Affairs Select Committee (1994) *Funding of Political Parties*, London: HMSO.

Hughes, C. and Wintour, P. (1990) *Labour Rebuilt*, London: Fourth Estate.

Ingle, S. (1987) *The British Party System*, Oxford: Basil Blackwell.

Johnston, R.J. (1986) 'A Further Look at British Political Finance' *Political Studies* 34 pp.466–73.

Johnston, R. and Pattie, C. (1995) 'The Impact of Spending on Party Constituency Campaigns in Recent British General Elections' *Party Politics* 1 pp.261–73.

Johnston, R., Pattie, C. and Fieldhouse, E. (1994) 'The geography of voting and representation: Regions and the declining importance of the cube law' in *Labour's Last Chance?* Heath, A., Jowell, R. and Curtice, J. (eds) Aldershot: Dartmouth.

Jones, B. and Kavanagh, D. (1994) 'Political Parties' in *Politics UK* Jones, B., Gray, A., Kavanagh, D., Moran, M., Norton, P. and Seldon, A. Hemel Hempstead: Harvester Wheatsheaf.

Kavanagh, D. (ed.) (1982) *The Politics of The Labour Party*, London: Allen and Unwin.

Kellas, J.G. (1990) 'Scottish and Welsh Nationalist Parties Since 1945' in *UK Political Parties Since 1945* Seldon, A. (ed) Hemel Hempstead: Philip Allan.

Kelly, R. (1989) *Conservative Party Conferences*, Manchester: Manchester University Press.

King, A., Crewe, I., Denver, D., Newton, K., Norton, P., Sanders, D. and Seyd, P. (1992) *Britain at the Polls 1992*, Chatham: Chatham House.

Klingemann, H., Hofferbert, R.I. and Budge, I. (1994) *Parties, Policies and Democracy*, Oxford: Westview.

Labour Party (1988–94) *Income and Expenditure Accounts*, London: Labour Party.

Lawson, N. (1993) 'The Union Link' *Renewal* 1 pp.24–7.

Leonard, D. (1982) *Paying for Party Politics*, London: PEP.

Levy, R. (1994) 'Nationalist Parties in Scotland and Wales' in *Britain's Changing Party System* Robins, L., Blackmore, H. and Pyper, R. (eds) London: Leicester University Press.

Liberal Democrats (1988–94) *Income and Expenditure Accounts*, London: Liberal Democrats.

Linton, M. (1994) *Money and Votes*, London: IPPR.

Lynch, P. (1995) 'Professionalization, new technology and change in a small party: the case of the Scottish National Party,' paper presented to the Annual Conference of the Political Studies Association Specialist Group on Election, Parties and Public Opinion, London Guildhall University.

Marsh, D. (ed.) (1983) *Pressure Politics*, London: Junction Books.

Maynard, G. (1988) *The Economy Under Mrs. Thatcher*, Oxford: Basil Blackwell.

McAllister, I. (1979) *Party Organisation and Minority Nationalism: A Comparative Study in the United Kingdom*, Strathclyde: Centre for the Study of Public Policy.

McBride, S. (1986) 'Mrs Thatcher and the Post-War Consensus: The Case of Trade Union Policy' *Parliamentary Affairs* 39 pp.330–40.

McKee, V. (1994) 'The Politics of the Liberal Democrats' in *Contemporary Political Studies 1994* Dunleavy, P. and Stanyer, J. (eds) Exeter: Political Studies Association.

McKenzie, R.T. (1955) *British Political Parties*, London: Heinemann.

McKibbon, R. (1974) *The Evolution of the Labour Party*, Oxford: Oxford University Press.

Minkin, L. (1980) *The Labour Party Conference*, Manchester: Manchester University Press.

Minkin, L. (1991) *The Contentious Alliance*, Edinburgh: Edinburgh University Press.

Mitchell, A. (1990) *The Labour Party*, Barnstable: Wroxton Papers in Politics.

Morgan, K.O. (1989) *Labour People*, Oxford: Oxford University Press.

Muller, W.D. (1977) *The Kept Men?* Atlantic Highlands: Humanities Press.

Müller-Rommel, F. and Pridham, G. (eds) (1991) *Small Parties in Western Europe*, London: Sage.

Mullin, W.A.R. (1979) 'The Scottish National Party' in *Multi-Party Britain* Drucker, H.M. (ed.) London: Macmillan.

Nassmacher, K.H. (1993) 'Comparing Party and Campaign Finance in Western Democracies' in *Campaign and Party Finance in North America and Western Europe* Gunlicks, A.B. (ed.) Boulder: Westview Press.

Norris, P. (1993) 'The gender–generation gap in British elections' in *British Elections & Parties Yearbook 1993* Denver, D., Norris, P., Broughton, D. and Rallings, C. (eds) Hemel Hempstead: Harvester Wheatsheaf.

Norris, P., Crewe, I., Denver, D. and Broughton, D. (eds) (1992) *British Elections and Parties Yearbook 1992*, Hemel Hempstead: Harvester Wheatsheaf.

Norris, P. and Lovenduski, J. (1995) *Political Recruitment*, Cambridge: Cambridge University Press.

Norton, P. (1990) 'The Lady's Not For Turning, But What About the Rest? Margaret Thatcher and the Conservative Party 1979–89' *Parliamentary Affairs*, 43 pp.41–58.

O'Sullivan, N. (1993) 'Conservatism' in *Contemporary Political Ideologies* Eatwell, R. and Wright, A. (eds) London: Pinter.

Park, T., Lewis, M. and Lewis, P. (1986) 'Trade Unions and the Labour Party: Changes in the Group of Sponsored MPs' *Political Studies* 34 pp.306–12.

Parry, G., Moyser, G. and Day, N. (1992) *Political Participation and Democracy in Britain*, Cambridge: Cambridge University Press.

Pattie, C. and Johnston, R. (1995) 'Paying their way: Constituency organisations and Conservative Party finance,' paper presented to the Political Studies Association Annual Conference, University of York.

Peden, G.C. (1991) *British Economic and Social Policy*, Hemel Hempstead: Philip Allan.

Pimlott, B. and Cook, C. (eds) (1982, 1991) *Trade Unions in British Politics*, London: Longman.

Pinto-Duschinsky, M. (1972) 'Central Office and "Power" in the Conservative Party' *Political Studies* 20 pp.1–16.

Pinto-Duschinsky, M. (1981) *British Political Finance 1830–1980*, London: American Enterprise Institute.

Pinto-Duschinsky, M. (1985) 'Trends in British Political Funding 1979–1983' *Parliamentary Affairs* 38 pp.329–47.

Pinto-Duschinsky, M. (1989a) 'Trends in British Party Funding 1983–1987' *Parliamentary Affairs* 42 pp.197–212.

Pinto-Duschinsky, M. (1989b) 'Financing the British General Election Campaign of 1987' in *Political Communications: The General Election Campaign of 1987* Crewe, I. and Harrop, M. (eds) Cambridge: Cambridge University Press.

Pugh, M. (1982) *The Making of Modern British Politics 1867–1939*, Oxford: Basil Blackwell.

Robbins, K. (1994) *The Eclipse of a Great Power*, London: Longman.

Robins, L., Blackmore, H. and Pyper, R. (eds) (1994) *Britain's Changing Party System*, London: Leicester University Press.

Rosamond, B. (1992) 'The Labour Party, trade unions and industrial relations' in *The Changing Labour Party* Smith, M.J. and Spear, J. (eds) London: Routledge.

Rose, R. (1967) *Influencing Voters*, London: Faber and Faber.

Rose, R. (1974) *The Problem of Party Government*, London: Macmillan.

Rose, R. (1984) *Do Parties Make a Difference?*, London: Macmillan.

Rose, R. and McAllister, I. (1986) *Voters Begin to Choose*, London: Sage.

Rose, R. and McAllister, I. (1990) *The Loyalties of Voters*, London: Sage.

Rüdig, W., Bennie, L. and Franklin, M. (1991) *Green Party Members: A Profile*, Glasgow: Delta.

Rüdig, W., Curtice, J. and Bennie, L. (1995) 'The Membership Dynamics of British Centre Parties: From Liberals and Social Democrats to Liberal Democrats' in *Contemporary Political Studies 1995* Lovenduski, J. and Stanyer, J. (eds) Exeter: Political Studies Association.

Rüdig, W., Franklin, M. and Bennie, L. (1993) *Green Blues*, Strathclyde: University of Strathclyde Papers on Government and Politics No.95.

Rush, M. (1992) *Politics and Society*, Hemel Hempstead: Harvester Wheatsheaf.

Sanders, D. (1991) 'Government popularity and the next general election' *Political Quarterly*, 62 pp.235–61.

Sanders, D. (1992) 'Why the Conservative Party Won – Again' in *Britain at the Polls 1992* King, A., Crewe, I., Denver, D., Newton, K., Norton, P., Sanders, D. and Seyd, P. Chatham: Chatham House.

Sanders, D., Ward, H. and Marsh, D. (1987) 'Government popularity and the Falklands war: A reassessment' *British Journal of Political Science* 17 pp.281–313.

Sarlvick, B. and Crewe, I. (1983) *Decade of Dealignment*, Cambridge: Cambridge University Press.

Sassoon, D. (1993) 'The Union Link: The Case For a Friendly Divorce' *Renewal* 1 pp.28–35.

Seldon, A. (ed.) (1990) *UK Political Parties Since 1945*, Hemel Hempstead: Philip Allan.

Seldon, A. and Ball, S. (eds) (1994) *Conservative Century*, Oxford: Oxford University Press.

Seyd, P. and Whiteley, P. (1992) *Labour's Grassroots*, Oxford: Clarendon Press.

Shaw, E. (1994) *The Labour Party Since 1979*, London: Routledge.

Sked, A. and Cook, C. (1984) *Post-War Britain*, Harmondsworth: Penguin.

Smith, G. (1991) 'In Search of Small Parties: Problems of Definition, Classification and Significance' in *Small Parties in Western Europe* Müller-Rommel, F. and Pridham, G. (eds) London: Sage.

Smith, M.J. (1992) 'A return to revisionism? The Labour Party's Policy Review' in *The Changing Labour Party* Smith, M.J. and Spear, J. (eds) London: Routledge.

Smith, M.J. and Spear, J. (eds) (1992) *The Changing Labour Party*, London: Routledge.

Swaddle, K. and Heath, A. (1992) 'Official and reported turnout in the British general election of 1987' in *Issues and Controversies in British Electoral Behaviour* Denver, D. and Hands, G. (eds) Hemel Hempstead: Harvester Wheatsheaf.

Taylor, A.J. (1987a) 'The Politics of Non-Partisan Trade Unions: The British Case' *Politics* 7 pp.8–13.

Taylor, A.J. (1987b) *The Trade Unions and the Labour Party*, London: Croom Helm.

Taylor, A.J. (1989) *Trade Unions and Politics*, London: Macmillan.

Taylor, A.J. (1990) 'Non-partisan Trade Union Political Action: An Anglo-American Comparison' *Political Studies* 38 pp.137–43.

Taylor, R. (1987) 'Trade Unions and the Labour Party: Time for an Open Marriage' *Political Quarterly*, 58 pp.424–32.

Tivey, L. and Wright, A. (eds) (1989) *Party Ideology in Britain*, London: Routledge.

Topf, R. (1994) 'Party Manifestos' in *Labour's Last Chance?* Heath, A., Jowell, R. and Curtice, J. (eds) Aldershot: Dartmouth.

Walsh, T. and Tindale, S. (1992) 'Time for Divorce' *Fabian Review* 104 (4) 9–11.

Ware, A. (1995) *Political Parties and Party Systems*, Oxford: Oxford University Press.

Webb, P. (1992a) 'The United Kingdom' in *Party Organisations* Katz, R.S. and Mair, P. (eds) London: Sage.

Webb, P. (1992b) *Trade Unions and the British Electorate*, Aldershot: Dartmouth.

Webb, P. (1995a) 'Are British Political Parties in Decline?' *Party Politics* 1 pp.299–322.

Webb, P. (1995b) 'Reforming the Labour Party-Trade Union Link: An Assessment' in *British Elections & Parties Yearbook 1994* Broughton, D., Farrell, D.M., Denver, D. and Rallings, C. (eds) London: Frank Cass.

Whitehead, P. (1985) *The Writing on the Wall*, London: Michael Joseph.

Whiteley, P., Seyd, P. and Richardson, J. (1994) *True Blues*, Oxford: Clarendon.

Wilder, P. (1994) 'The British Elections to the European Parliament June 1994' *Representation* 32 pp.81–4.

Wright, A. (1993) 'Social Democracy and Democratic Socialism' in *Contemporary Political Ideologies* Eatwell, R. and Wright, A. (eds) London: Pinter.

Young, H. (1990) *One of Us*, London: Pan Books.

INDEX

absolute class voting, 166, 167, 168–9
Adams, G., 136
Alford Index, 166, 167
Alliance Party, 133–4
Alt, J., 27
Alternative Economic Strategy, 88, 89
Anglo-Irish Agreement 1985, 132, 133, 135
anti-party parties, 31
Ashdown, P., 99, 113, 115
Association of Liberal Democrat Councillors (ALDC), 98
Atlee, C., 11
Aughey, A., 135

Baker, D., 59n
Ballot Act 1872, 6
Balsom, D., 125, 127, 129, 130
Barnes, J., 57
Beer, S., 3
Behrens, R., 107
Beith, A., 99
Bellamy, R., 105
Benn, T., 67, 71, 82, 90
Bennie, L., 111, 142
Bevan, A., 88
Beveridge Report, 11
Beveridge Society, 113
Bevin, E., 11

Bidwell, S., 25
Blackburn, R., 45
Blair, T., 39, 73, 85, 89, 91, 92
Bogdanor, V., 38n, 44
Bow Group, 58
Brand, J., 121n, 122
Bretton Woods, 13
British Election Survey, 21, 142, 179–93, 195–6, 197
Broughton, D., 127, 128, 130
Browne, J., 25
Bulmer-Thomas, I., 4
Butler, D., 10n, 46, 72, 75, 76, 77, 78, 100, 101, 102, 119, 125, 170, 171, 173, 204, 205
Butler, G., 10n, 72, 119, 125, 204, 205
Butler, R.A.B., 12

Callaghan, John, 82, 83
Callaghan, James, 15, 82
Campaign for Labour Party Democracy (CLPD), 88–9
Campaign Group, 90
candidates at elections, 22, 24–5, 197–8
Chard Group, 113–14
Charter Movement, 58
Churchill, W., 11
citizenship, 106
class dealignment, 166–70

class, measurement of, 168
cleavages, class, 8–9, 10, 16–17
cleavages, imperialism, 9
cleavages, religious, 9
Coates, D., 83
Coates, K., 68
Connolly, M., 131, 132, 134
Conservative Party
  1922 Committee, 36, 38, 42
  and authoritarianism, 54
  and capitalism, 53–4
  and Europe, 37–8, 59–61, 62–3
  and hierarchy, 33–5, 36–8
  and ideology, 51–2
  and ideology of governing, 55
  and organicism, 52
  and political scepticism, 52–3
  and tradition, 52
  area organisation, 34, 35
  back-benchers, 37–8
  Central Office, 7, 35
  commercial activities, 51
  conference, 36–7
  constituency quota income, 51
  donations, 48–51
  leadership election 1965, 39–40
  leadership election 1975, 40
  leadership election 1989, 40–1
  leadership election 1990, 41–2
  leadership election 1995, 43
  leadership election procedures,
    38–9, 40, 42–3
  local organisation, 34, 35
  manifestos, 35, 56–7
  members and ideology, 54–5
  MPs and candidates, age, 46
  MPs and candidates, educational
    background, 46, 47
  MPs and candidates, ethnic
    background, 46
  MPs and candidates,
    occupational background,
    47–8
  MPs and candidates, sex, 46
  national organisation, 34, 35–6
  National Union of Conservative
    and Unionist Organisations,
    35–6

content analysis, 55–6
Corrupt and Illegal Practices
  (Prevention) Act 1883, 1, 5
Crewe, I., 15, 31, 44n, 160, 161,
  168, 170, 172, 173, 174, 198
Crosland, A., 84, 108, 109
Crouch, C., 68n
Curtice, J., 28, 111, 142, 168

Day, N., 26, 154, 199
Democratic Unionist Party (DUP),
  132, 133
Denver, D., 29, 30, 141, 156, 160,
  161, 162, 167, 173
Disraeli, B., 7,19, 53
Douglas-Home, A., 39
Drucker, H., 82
Dunleavy, P., 16, 167, 170

Eccelshall, R., 51, 52
economic voting
  dimensions of, 175–6
  methodological issues, 178
  punishment reward model, 175
  voter perception, 176–8
Eden, A., 39
electoral choice, 19–20, 194–5
electoral system, 15–16, 202
electoral turnout, 29–31
electoral volatility, 28, 160–1
Engels, F., 80, 81
European Monetary Union
  (EMU), 60–1
Ewing, K., 200
Exchange Rate Mechanism
  (ERM), 60
extra-parliamentary party
  organisation, development
  of, 2–3

Fabian Society, 9, 80, 81, 87, 89,
  107
Fieldhouse, E., 16, 115, 116
Fisher, J., 49, 51, 68, 198, 201
Fitt, G., 136
Foot, M., 71, 90
Fourier, C., 81
Fowler, Sir N., 49

Fox, T., 27
franchise, 2, 15
Franklin, M., 142
Fraser, H., 40

Gaelic language and Scotland, 120
Gaitskell, H., 12, 85
Gamble, A., 59n
Garner, R., 53
Gladstone Club, 113
Gladstone, W., 3, 5
Goodwin, B., 52

Ham, C., 23
Hands, G., 141, 156, 162
Hansard Society, 19
Hardie, K., 83n
Harrison, M., 82
Harrop, M., 20, 22, 26
Hastings Agreement, 74
Hattersley, R., 73
Healey, D., 15, 71, 73
Heath, A., 15, 28, 31, 161, 168, 169, 170, 174, 175
Heath, E., 14, 37, 38, 53, 59, 165
Heseltine, M., 41, 42, 43
Hill, M., 23
Hogwood, B., 84
Home Affairs Committee, 198, 201
Howe, G., 41
Hume, J., 135
Hurd, D., 41, 42
Husbands, C., 167

In Place of Strife, 75
Independent Labour Party (ILP), 9, 87
industrial relations, 13
Industrial Relations Act 1971, 14, 75
Ingle, S., 2, 10, 20
International Monetary Fund (IMF), 13
Irish Home Rule, 3, 9, 119, 125, 132
Irish Republican Army (IRA), 134, 135

issue voting
    conditions of, 170–1
    methodological issues, 172
    position issues, 171, 172–3
    salience, 172–3
    valence issues, 171, 174
    values and principles, 174–5

Jenkins, R., 108
Johnston, R., 16, 115, 116, 141, 155
Jones, B., 34
Joseph, K., 53
Jowell, R., 28, 168

Kavanagh, D., 34, 46, 68n, 72, 75, 76, 77, 78, 100, 101, 102
Keep Left Group, 89
Kellas, J., 119, 125
Kelly, R., 36, 37, 53
King, A., 44n, 204
Kinnock, N., 39, 67, 71, 73, 85, 88, 89, 90, 91, 92

Labour Party
    and internal democracy, 65, 89
    and parliamentary democracy, 83
    and public ownership, 83–4
    and socialism, 82–3
    and the welfare state, 83, 84
    block vote, 68–9
    Business Plan, 78–80
    Clause IV, 70, 83–4, 85, 88, 92
    conference, 65, 67, 68–9
    deputy leadership contests, 71–3
    fundamentalists, 88, 89–90
    leadership contests, 71, 72
    leadership election procedures, 71, 88
    local organisation, 65, 66
    manifestos, 67, 86–7, 88
    members and ideology, 85–6
    MPs and candidates, age, 76, 77
    MPs and candidates, educational background, 77
    MPs and candidates, ethnic background, 76, 77

Labour Party (*continued*)
  MPs and candidates,
    occupational background,
    77, 78
  MPs and candidates, sex,
    76–7
  National Executive Committee
    (NEC), 67, 69, 74, 92
  national organisation, 65–7
  pact with Liberal Party, 14
  Policy Review, 70, 86, 91
  power of the leadership, 91–2
  regional organisation, 65, 66
  revisionists, 84, 88, 89
  trade union funding of, 78
  trade union sponsorship of
    candidates, 74–6
Labour Representation
  Committee (LRC), 9–10
labourism, 82–3
Lawson, N., 40, 41, 60
Levy, R., 127, 130
Liberal Democrats
  and citizenship, 110
  and ideological identity, 110, 115
  and international co-operation,
    110
  and liberal groups, 113
  and social democratic groups,
    113–14
  and social policy, 110
  and the economy, 109–10
  and the electoral system, 115
  Associated Organisations, 98
  Federal Executive, 97
  Federal Policy Committee, 97
  ideology, 109–11
  leadership election procedures,
    99
  local organisation, 96, 97
  manifestos
    (Liberal/Alliance/Liberal
    Democrat), 111–12
  members and ideology, 111
  merger and launch, 94–5
  MPs and candidates, age, 100–1
  MPs and candidates, educational
    background, 101

MPs and candidates, ethnic
  background, 100–1
MPs and candidates,
  occupational background,
  101–2
MPs and candidates, sex, 100–1
name, 94–5
national conference, 97–8
national organisation, 96, 97–8
sources of funding, 102
Specified Ancillary
  Organisations, 98
state organisation, 96, 97
Liberal Information Network
  (LINK), 113
Liberal Philosophy Group, 113
liberalism, 104–7
  community, 106–7
Linton, M., 200
Lovenduski, J., 22, 24, 45, 99, 100,
  123, 129, 196, 197
Ludlam, S., 59n
Lynch, P., 121, 123, 124

Maastrict Treaty, 20, 37, 42, 62–3
MacDonald, R., 10
Macmillan, H., 39, 53
Major, J., 25, 41, 42, 59, 61, 62,
  137
Margretts, H., 16
Marsh, D., 178
Marx, K., 80, 81
McAllister, I., 117, 118, 119, 125,
  126, 134, 174, 175
McKee, V., 98, 110, 113, 114
McKenzie, R., 65, 139, 140, 141,
  155, 156
Meadowcroft, M., 95, 113
Meyer, Sir A., 41, 43
Michels, R. and *iron law of
  oligarchy*, 139
Militant, 13, 74
Mill, J.S., 105, 106
Miller, W., 20, 22, 26
Minkin, L., 70, 74, 75, 76
Mitchell, J., 122
Monday Club, 58
Morrison, H., 82

Moyser, G., 26, 154, 199
Mullin, W.A.R., 119, 120, 121

Nassmacher, K.-H., 200
national campaigns, growth of, 4
National Liberal Foundation
    (NLF), 5–6
National Union of Conservative
    and Constitutional
    Associations (NUCCA), 7
nationalisation, 83–4, 85, 108, 171,
    172
Nationalism, 134
nationalist or small parties, reasons
    for formation, 117–18
No Turning Back Group, 59
Nonconformity and the Liberal
    Party, 5, 105
Norris, P., 22, 24, 45, 69, 99, 100,
    123, 129, 163, 196, 197
Northern Ireland, political
    identities in, 131–2
Nozick, R., 105

odds ratio, 169–70
oil shocks, 13
one member-one vote (OMOV),
    70, 73
Ostrogorski, M., 139
overall volatility, 161
Owen, D., 108, 109, 112
Owen, R., 81

Paisley, Rev. I., 133
Parliamentary Labour Party
    (PLP), 67
Parry, G., 26, 154, 199
participation and party members,
    26, 154–5, 198–9
participation and non-party
    members, 27, 198–9
partisan dealignment, 165–6
partisan identification, 28–9, 164–5
party discipline, growth of, 3
party finance, 17
party leaders, 25
party manifestos, 4, 20, 55

party members
    and activism, 154–5
    and fund-raising, 140–1
    and ideological principles, 152–3
    and mobilising the vote, 141,
        155–6
    and newspaper readership,
        146–7
    and political communication,
        141
    and political views, 149–52
    and representatives of party, 141
    and resemblance, 147
    and selecting candidates, 140
    and views on influence of
        members, 153–4
    social background, 142–6
party membership levels, 26, 201–2
party membership surveys, 140
party organisation decline, 27–8
Party Reform Steering Committee,
    58
party system 1945–1970, 11–13
party system 1970–1979, 13–15
Pattie, C., 16, 115, 116, 141,
    155
Pederson Index, 160
Peel, R., 4, 5, 53
Phillips, M., 82
Pinto-Duschinsky, M., 1, 3, 6, 8, 48,
    49, 51, 69
Plaid Cymru (PC)
    alliances with other parties, 128
    and cultural objectives, 125–6,
        127
    and factionalism, 125–6, 127, 128
    and the Labour Party, 130
    formation and development,
        124–6
    ideology, 127–9
    membership, 127
    organisation, 126–7
policy-making, 23, 197
political education, 25–6, 198
Poll Tax (Community Charge), 41,
    121
Portillo, M., 43
Powell, E., 53

Prescott, J., 73
Primrose League, 7–8, 58, 142
Pugh, M., 2, 3, 4, 5, 7, 9
Pulzer, P., 162

Rüdig, W., 111, 142
Redwood, J., 43, 59
replacement of Liberal Party by
    Labour Party, 10
representation
    and demands, 21–2
    and resemblance, 22, 196
    of groups, 20–21
    models of, 22–3, 196–7
Representation of the People Acts,
    2, 4, 5, 10, 74
Richardson, J., 7, 26, 37, 44n, 140,
    156, 158
Robbins, K., 13n
Rogers, W., 108
Rosamund, B., 70
Rose, R., 20, 30, 174, 175
Rush, M., 27

Saint-Simon, C.-H., 81
Sanders, D., 42, 77, 178
Sands, B., 136
Sarlvick, B., 172, 173, 174
Scottish National Party (SNP)
    formation and development,
        118–20
    factionalism, 121–2
    ideology, 122–3
    membership, 120–1
    organisation, 120–1
Scottish Referendum 1979, 121
Selsdon Group, 59
Seyd, P., 7, 26, 37, 44n, 85, 86, 91,
    140, 141, 142, 156, 158
Shadow Communications Agency,
    67
share of seats in the House of
    Commons, 160
Single European Act 1987, 59, 62
single issue groups, 5, 21–2, 32
Sinn Fein, 135–6
Skinner, D., 67
small parties, importance of, 137–8

trends amongst, 137–8
Smith, A., 104
Smith, G., 137
Smith, J., 39, 71, 85, 89, 91, 92
Social and Democratic Labour
    Party (SDLP), 134–5
Social Contract, 14–15
social democracy, 107–8
    and the SDP, 108–9
Social Democratic Foundation
    (SDF), 9, 87
Social Democratic Voice, 113
socialism, 80–1
sovereignty, 59–60
Spencer, H., 105
state funding of political parties,
    200–1
Steel, D., 106, 115
Stokes, D., 170, 171, 173
Surridge, P., 122
Swaddle, K., 31

Taverne, D., 25
Taylor, A., 70
Thatcher, M., 25, 37, 40, 41, 42, 53,
    54, 55, 58, 59, 60, 61–2, 132,
    177, 178
Tindale, S., 70
Topf, R., 4, 56, 57n, 86, 112, 195
Topham, T., 68
Tory Reform Group, 58
Trade Union Group (TUG), 75–6
trade unions and the Labour Party,
    67–70, 74–6, 78, 91
Trades Union Congress, 9
Tribune Group, 89, 90

Ulster Unionist Party (UUP),
    132–3
Unionism, 131–2
Unity Group, 89

Value Added Tax (VAT),
    37
Victory for Socialism, 89
voter hesitancy, 29
voting and social background,
    162–4

voting in 1992
  and issues, 185–90
  and newspaper readership,
    184–5
  and social background,
    179–84
  and the economy, 190–3

Walsh, T., 70
Ward, H., 178
Webb, P., 26n, 27, 28, 31, 34, 69,
    74, 82, 201
Weir, S., 16

Welsh identity, 129–130
Welsh language and Wales, 124,
    126, 130
Whitelaw, W., 40
Whiteley, P., 7, 26, 37, 44n, 45n, 51,
    54, 58, 61, 85, 86, 91, 140,
    141, 142, 156, 158
Wilder, P., 205
Williams, S., 108
Wilson, H., 13, 39, 88
Winter of Discontent, 15
Worker's Party, 131
Wright, A., 80, 81